STUDY GUIDE

STEINBERG/MEYER:
CHILDHOOD

WENDY DUNN
Coe College

McGraw-Hill, Inc.
New York St. Louis San Francisco Auckland Bogotá Caracas Lisbon London Madrid
Mexico City Milan Montreal New Delhi San Juan Singapore Sydney Tokyo Toronto

Study Guide to Accompany
STEINBERG/MEYER: CHILDHOOD

Copyright © 1995 by McGraw-Hill, Inc. All rights reserved. Printed in the United States of America. Except as permitted under the United States Copyright Act of 1976, no part of this publication may be reproduced or distributed in any form or by any means, or stored in a data base or retrieval system, without the prior written permission of the publisher.

2 3 4 5 6 7 8 9 0 SEM SEM 9 0 9 8 7 6

ISBN 0-07-061235-8

The editor was Beth Kaufman;
the production supervisor was Kathryn Porzio.
Semline, Inc., was printer and binder.

Contents

Introduction for the Instructor iv

Introduction for the Student v

Chapter

1. The Study of Human Development 1

2. Conception, Heredity, and Prenatal Development 15

3. Birth and the Newborn 31

4. Physical Development in Infancy 45

5. Cognitive and Language Development in Infancy 57

6. Social and Emotional Development in Infancy 71

7. The Social Context of Infancy 85

8. Physical, Cognitive, and Language Development in Early Childhood 97

9. Social and Emotional Development in Early Childhood 111

10. The Social Context of Early Childhood 125

11. Physical and Cognitive Development in Middle Childhood 139

12. Social and Emotional Development in Middle Childhood 153

13. The Social Context of Middle Childhood 167

14. The Transition into Adolescence 181

Answer Key 197

Introduction for the Instructor

One of the most successful features of Steinberg and Meyer's *Childhood* is its purposeful integration of research and theory, of explanation and practical examples into a textbook that is both complete and readable. This *Study Guide* has also been carefully prepared to provide high-quality activities to accomplish three purposes: to guide the student's study, to provide feedback to the student regarding the effectiveness of that study, and to encourage the development of the student's ability to organize information from the text into clear, concise conceptual units which can be expressed effectively in written form. Toward this end, the *Study Guide* provides a set of activities for each of the text's chapters which includes a Preview of the Chapter; a set of about ten Learning Objectives; a detailed, but concise, Chapter Summary; and a series of Self-Test items including Matching Questions, a set of twenty Multiple-Choice questions in the same form but not identical to those written for the *Test File* which accompanies the text, and two Essay Questions along with their Scoring Schemes and Model Answers. The Introduction written for students on the following pages outlines each of these features in more detail and offers suggestions to students about how each learning aid might be used effectively.

This *Study Guide* is written in such a way that instructors need not be involved in its use: Students can work with it on their own since correct answers are provided for all of the objective items and instructions are given for the scoring of the essay questions. I invite you, however, to look through the materials presented herein and consider how some or all of these materials could be adapted for purposeful use in your classes. Undoubtedly, instructors, if they wish, can find several ways in which to incorporate various features in this *Study Guide* into their individual approaches to teaching, and I encourage you to use these materials however they might prove useful to you.

Finally, I wish to acknowledge the work and ideas of several people who contributed to this project. Jane Vaicunas and Beth Kaufman, editors at McGraw-Hill, were helpful in planning the *Study Guide* and in improving its quality throughout the editorial process. Peggy Knott at Coe College designed the format for the *Study Guide* and through her thoughtful and careful work has improved the accessibility to students of the ideas herein. She also edited the manuscript, and I appreciate her help very much. Finally, I'd like to thank Coe College and Greg Dunn for their support during the time I worked on this project.

Wendy Dunn

Introduction for the Student

This *Student Study Guide* has been written to aid your learning in three ways: to help you study effectively and learn the basic content presented in each chapter of *Childhood*, to give you practice in taking tests and provide feedback to you about how effective your study has been, and to guide your thinking as you organize the content of each chapter into meaningful conceptual units. To help you achieve these purposes, this *Study Guide* includes a set of six different learning aids for each chapter in the text: Preview of the Chapter, Learning Objectives, Chapter Summary, Matching Questions, Multiple-Choice Questions, and Essay Questions. In this introduction, we will describe what information is provided in each of these learning aid sections, and will give you suggestions about how you can best make use of the features of this *Study Guide*.

Preview of the Chapter

If you turn to any chapter in this *Study Guide*, the first thing you will see is a relatively brief outline of the chapter. This outline includes the major headings from the text, and, if you look at it briefly before you begin your study, you may find that it helps you organize the information on which you will be concentrating into an integrated unit. Also, when reviewing for an exam, a look through the topics in the outline can help remind you about what information is included in the text.

Learning Objectives

The Learning Objectives are statements about what a student should be able to do to demonstrate that he or she has mastered the content of a chapter. We list about ten or so Learning Objectives which summarize the important concepts presented in each chapter in *Childhood*. These objectives can be useful to you in two ways. First, before you read the chapter in the text, reading through the Learning Objectives along with the Preview of the Chapter will tell you what is in the text, how it is organized, and what information is most important. Second, after reading the text chapter, you can turn back to the Learning Objectives and test yourself to see if you can do what the objectives ask. If you can, you will have a good grasp of the chapter material. If you can't, you can review the text sections on which you need more work. You will probably find it helpful to write out your answers to the Learning Objectives. This activity serves as an excellent means of learning the material, and your notes will be useful when you are preparing for a test.

Chapter Summaries

There are two summaries for each text chapter, one in the text at the end of each chapter and one in this *Study Guide*. The summaries in the text are relatively short, focus primarily on basic terminology, and provide a good review of basic chapter content. The Chapter Summaries in the *Study Guide* are longer and more detailed and, while they, too, include definitions of basic terms, they also focus on the major ideas in a chapter. They highlight the relationships among the various topics, they review important research findings, they outline basic theoretical explanations, and they are aimed at briefly explaining the most important points in each chapter. Rereading these Chapter Summaries from time to time will serve as a good review and will help you keep the ideas of the chapter fresh in your mind. You may find them especially useful as you review material for an examination. However, they are *not* intended as a substitute for reading the text, since they do not provide the detailed information given in the text.

Self-Tests

For several reasons, you may find the Self-Tests to be the most useful sections of the *Study Guide*. Students come from a variety of educational backgrounds, and some students may be unfamiliar with testing methods used in college courses. Furthermore, many students suffer from test anxiety to an extent that it adversely affects their grades. The questions in the *Study Guide* give you the opportunity to practice taking psychology tests, which should help you reduce your anxiety and prepare you for actual testing. This alone warrants the inclusion of sample exam questions in the *Study Guide*. Undoubtedly, however, for most students the major advantage of Self-Tests is the feedback they provide about the effectiveness of your study. Three types of self-test questions are included in this *Study Guide*: matching questions, multiple-choice questions, and essay questions.

Matching Questions

Each chapter in this *Study Guide* includes some matching questions designed primarily to test your grasp and comprehension of vocabulary and other factual information presented in the chapter. In some questions, there are more responses available than there are question stems, so not all answer choices will be used. In other questions, some responses may be used more than once. As you answer these matching questions, try to remember the information they contain. You may find it helpful to record your answers on a blank sheet of paper so you can answer the matching questions more than once without seeing the responses you have made previously. You should not stop practicing the matching questions until you have achieved one-hundred-percent accuracy. Also, you should review them regularly throughout the duration of your course to help keep the information they cue fresh in your memory. The correct answers to these questions are included in the scoring keys printed at the end of the *Study Guide*.

Multiple-Choice Questions

This *Study Guide* includes in each chapter a set of twenty multiple-choice questions, each referenced to the domain of learning it measures, to a Learning Objective for the chapter, and to its estimated degree of difficulty. If you look at any of the multiple-choice questions in the chapter, you will see these references printed to the right of each question.

On the top line of the reference, you will find that each question is labeled either "factual," "conceptual," or "application." Factual questions are intended to measure your ability to recall factual information presented in the text. Essentially, they measure your ability to comprehend and understand the content of the text. Conceptual questions are more complex: They require that you draw, from the facts presented in the chapter, conclusions about how those facts are related to each other. They may also prompt you to analyze or synthesize textual information and may measure your ability to evaluate the truth or falseness of a particular set of statements. Many students find these "conceptual" questions to be more difficult than the "factual" questions, since they tap more complex domains of learning. Finally, some of the questions in the multiple-choice portion of the self-test are labeled as "application" questions. These questions require that you apply a principle, a theoretical idea, or a research finding to a new situation. Thus, they require that you understand the information in the text and that you generalize from it to other novel settings. Students often find these application items, like those testing conceptual abilities, more difficult than those items which measure factual recall.

On the next line of the reference for each multiple-choice question is printed the objective number for that question. This number simply refers to the Learning Objective that the question is designed to measure. One useful way to use this information about learning objectives is to target your review: If you answer a question incorrectly, you can review that portion of the text from which the question is drawn, using the Learning Objective to focus your study.

The last line of the reference refers to the difficulty level of the question. Generally, most students will find those questions labeled "basic" to be the easiest to answer, and those labeled "advanced" to be the most difficult. Of course, each instructor emphasizes different ideas in class, and each student learns information differently from every other. Thus, you should not be surprised if you sometimes can answer more difficult questions correctly but make errors on "basic" or "moderate" questions. These labels are provided only to give you a general approximation of the level of difficulty of each question.

We recommend that you use the multiple-choice items as a practice quiz and prepare for it the same way you would get ready for a chapter quiz given in class. Read and study the text carefully before you look at these questions. Then put your text and your notes away, and answer the twenty questions as best you can, giving yourself about fifteen minutes to complete them. When you have finished your self-quiz, correct your answers using the answer key printed at the end of the *Study Guide*, which includes both the correct answers and cross references to the page or pages in the text on which the correct answers can be found. If you did not achieve a perfect score, look up in the text the answers to the questions you missed and focus your attention not only on why the keyed answer is correct, but also on why the answer you chose is incorrect. This sort of study-test-review is one of the most successful of all study strategies, and one which you are likely to find especially useful as you work to master the content of each chapter in the text.

Essay Questions

Two essay questions, along with the schemes by which their answers can be scored and model answers which are sample responses to the questions, are included for each chapter of the text. Many students have little opportunity to practice the skills required to respond effectively to essay questions, and these essay question exercises are intended to help you improve your skill at organizing information and presenting it in a clear, concise format. We recommend you try the following approach in your work on the essay questions.

Of course, as for the other self-test items, you should not attempt the essay items until you have read and thoroughly studied the corresponding material in the text. When you believe you are prepared for the test, read the essay questions carefully, one at a time, and think for a few minutes about what exactly the question is asking. When you believe you understand the question asked, try jotting down a very brief outline of your ideas about how you can express your answer. Many students find that this outline helps them organize their ideas and flesh them out fully so that when they begin to write, the answer they produce is well-organized and as complete as they can offer. After you feel you know what you will say and the order in which you will make your points, you should write your answer to the question in the space provided or, if you wish, on a separate sheet of paper. When you have finished your answers to the two questions in each chapter, be sure to reread them to check for omissions, misspellings, and other grammatical errors. Then turn to the Scoring Schemes presented on the pages following each question.

These Scoring Schemes provide a method of grading your answers similar to that used by many instructors. For each question, a specified number of points is to be awarded for particular ideas or facts which should be included in a thorough, correct answer. Use these scoring schemes to grade your answers as if you were the instructor evaluating these responses. Or, if you are studying the material with a friend, an ideal approach is to have your friend grade your answers, thus giving you a more objective appraisal as to the number of points your answer has earned. As you or your friend "grades" your answers, note in some way the particular points you earned and those you lost. For example, if a question asked for three advantages of a certain method, each worth two points, you may wish to mark "+2" on the answer form following each correctly stated advantage you describe.

Of course, the evaluation of essay responses is always somewhat subjective and based on the grader's judgment. You will need to evaluate in some cases how close your answer is to that specified in the Scoring Scheme. My advice here is to reread carefully the sections of the text which supply the information required for the answer, to be as honest as you can in evaluating your work, but not to worry about the exact number of points you award. Remember, the purpose of the exercise is to teach you to critically evaluate your own work. Only you will see the score you earn.

After you have evaluated your answers to the questions or, if your friend has graded your responses, examined the way your answer was rated, turn your attention to the Model Answers provided with each question. These answers portray a correct response which might be offered by a student who understood the material well. These answers are not perfect, nor are they necessarily the best way a question could be answered. They do, however, represent the kind of answer the author of this *Study Guide* would consider to be worth all the points offered for the question. Read through the Model Answers and consider how your answers differed from them. Are there ideas or facts expressed in the Model Answers which could have been included in your responses? Does the organization of information make sense and pertain to the question in a way different from your approach to the question? In what way is the Model Answer better than the one you wrote? In what way is it weaker? A useful exercise here is to apply the Scoring Scheme to the Model Answer the same way you used it to grade your own responses. In each case, you should be able to award the maximum number of points possible to the Model Answer.

If you take the work you do on each chapter's Essay Questions seriously and work hard to understand the mechanics of scoring, your effort should lead you to both a deeper, more complete understanding of the chapter content and a more effective style of responding to essay questions on tests in this class as well as in other classes you will undertake in your academic career.

Wendy Dunn

Chapter 1

∎

The Study of Human Development

Preview of the Chapter

I. **Themes in the Study of Human Development**
   A. Biology and the Environment: Interacting Forces
   B. Development Is Dynamic
   C. Development Occurs in a Social Context
   D. Development Is Flexible

II. **Theories: How We Think About Development**
   A. Psychoanalytic Theories
      1. Freud's theory of psychosexual stages
      2. Freud's view of personality structure
      3. Erikson's theory of psychosocial development
   B. Learning Theories
      1. The behaviorist view
      2. Social learning theory
   C. Cognitive Theories
      1. Piaget's theory
      2. Contemporary cognitive views
   D. Biological Theories
      1. Sociobiology
      2. Behavioral genetics

III. **Research Methods: How We Study Development**
   A. Using the Scientific Method
   B. Choosing a Research Design
      1. The experiment
      2. The correlational study
      3. The case study
      4. Approaches to studying change over time
   C. Gathering Data
      1. Structured observation
      2. Naturalistic observation
      3. Questionnaires
      4. Interviews
      5. Standardized tests
   D. Ethics and Research

2   *The Study of Human Development*

Learning Objectives

1. Distinguish between nature and nurture and describe how these factors interact.

2. Identify the major distinctions between psychoanalytic, behavioral learning, and cognitive theories of development.

3. Describe Freud's theory of personality, paying particular attention to his stages of psychosexual development and his concept of the structure of personality.

4. Outline Erik Erikson's theory of development and compare it to that proposed by Freud.

5. Describe the behaviorist view of development and comment on the significance of classical and operant conditioning.

6. Compare social learning theory to the behaviorist view and describe its basic tenets.

7. Describe and critique the cognitive theories of development, focusing particularly on the theory proposed by Jean Piaget.

8. Define the focus of biological theories of development and describe the central ideas of sociobiology and behavioral genetics.

9. Define and describe the scientific method.

10. Describe and compare the various research designs used by developmentalists.

11. Describe and compare the various methods by which developmentalists gather their data.

12. Define and explain the value of the ethical principles that govern developmental research.

Chapter Summary

I. Biology and Environment: Interacting Forces
1. The three emphases of this text are: (1) the context in which development occurs matters, (2) there is tremendous diversity in normal development, and (3) there are important universals in patterns of development.
2. In the nature-nurture debate, **nature** refers to those traits which are genetically based and **nurture** refers to those traits which are learned. Research confirms that nature and nurture work together and both influence the course of development.
3. Development is **dynamic**, meaning that the environment influences behavior and that behavior also influences the kind of environment experienced by the person. Development occurs in a **social context** meaning that the particular setting in which we live influences our behavior. Development is **flexible**, meaning that disadvantages at one stage in development can be compensated for at other stages.

II. Theories: How We Think About Development
1. The major theories about human development fall into four categories, the **psychoanalytic**, which focuses on emotions, the **learning** or **behavioristic**, which focuses on behavior, the **cognitive**, which focuses on thought, and the **biological**, which are drive by biology.

2. Sigmund Freud (1856-1939) proposed that many nervous disorders resulted from unconscious drives and conflicts. He believed that sexual energy focuses on different parts of the body at different developmental or, as he called them, **psychosexual** stages.
3. In the **oral** stage (age 0-1), erotic pleasure comes from sucking, chewing and biting. The **anal** stage (age 1-3) centers around toilet training. In the **phallic** stage (age 3-5) the sexual energy, called libido, shifts to the genital region, and boys experience the **Oedipus complex**, in which they come to realize they cannot possess their mothers and they come to **identify** with their fathers. Girls experience a parallel process, the **Electra complex**, which results in identification with their mothers. The internalization of moral values through identification gives rise to the **superego**, which serves as a conscience. After the Oedipus and Electra complexes are resolved, children enter a **latency** stage (age 5-12) in which the libido becomes less influential and during which their attention focuses on finding appropriate outlets for their desires. The final stage of development, the **genital** stage (age 12 on) is characterized by mature interest in peers as sexual partners.
4. Freud viewed personality development as the struggle between the **id**, the pool of psychic energy present from birth, and the **superego**, which represents moral considerations. These conflicts are mediated by the **ego**, which develops early in life and which often uses **defense mechanisms** to repress or redirect the demands of the id.
5. Erik Erikson, another psychoanalytic theorist, believed that Freud's work focused too much on the pleasure-demanding id and not enough on the problem-solving ego. He proposed a sequence of eight **psychosocial** stages of development through which we move, each focusing on a different kind of developmental challenge.
6. **Behaviorists** argue that we need not focus on internal concepts like thoughts or feelings to explain behavior. Instead, explanations are made by observing the environmental stimuli that produce behavior and the specific responses these stimuli elicit, with the aim of revealing a set of universal laws.
7. **Classical conditioning**, first demonstrated by Ivan Pavlov, involves the learning of an association between a previously neutral stimulus, like the sound of a bell, and some stimulus-response reflex, like salivation when food is placed in the mouth. **Operant conditioning**, advocated by B.F. Skinner, explains present behavior as the result of the consequences that have been associated with the behavior in the past. If a behavior is followed by **positive reinforcement**, or reward, that behavior will be strengthened and more likely to occur again. **Negative reinforcement**, the removal of an unpleasant consequence, also strengthens the behavior it follows. **Punishment**, the application of an unpleasant consequence, differs from both types of reinforcement because it decreases the frequency of the response it follows.
8. **Social learning theorists**, like Albert Bandura, focus on how people learn from each other, oftentimes through **observational learning** in which we see what happens to others and learn from their behaviors. Social learning theorists differ from behaviorists in that they acknowledge the role played by expectations and motives and they also focus on abilities unique to humans.
9. As compared to social learning theorists, **cognitive theorists** tend to focus less on perceptions and more on the development of thinking itself. Jean Piaget (1896-1980), an influential cognitive theorist, believed that human thought is organized into mental categories called **schemes**. Throughout development, these schemes become elaborated through **assimilation**, the process by which people incorporate new information into an existing scheme, and **accommodation**, in which people alter their schemes to include new information that doesn't fit with old ways of thinking. Assimilation and accommodation balance each other through the process called **equilibration** so that learning is usually a mix of fitting in new information with old (assimilation) and adjusting one's thoughts to fit the new circumstances (accommodation).
10. Neo-Piagetians have elaborated Piaget's views and suggest that cognitive development is more gradual and uneven than Piaget thought. Information-processing theorists focus less on the idea

of stages of development and compare human thought to the operation of complex computer programs.
11. Although **biological theorists** don't ignore the environment, they place special emphasis on innate, inborn influences and how they play out in development. **Sociobiology** is based in Charles Darwin's theory of evolution in which **natural selection**, through which adaptive traits are passed on to future generations, plays a major role in explaining human behavior. **Behavior genetics** focuses on the interplay between biological and environmental influences.

III. Research Methods: How We Study Development

1. The **scientific method** is a procedure to collect reliable, objective information that can be used to support or refute a theory. The steps in the scientific method include: defining the question to be studied, reviewing the scientific literature on the topic, formulating a **hypothesis**—an educated guess about how the factors being studied are related to each other, choosing a research method for gathering data, and analyzing the data and drawing conclusions.
2. One frequently used research design is the **experiment**, which is designed to investigate the cause-effect relationship. In an experiment, the researcher controls all the factors that might influence an outcome except the one being studied. Subjects in the experiment experience the factor under study, and subjects in a control group do not. Then, differences in responses between the two groups can be attributed to the presence of the single factor experienced by only those in the experimental group.
3. One disadvantage of the experimental method is that sometimes the situations seem artificial and so subjects may not respond naturally. Sometimes this problem can be addressed by conducting **natural experiments**, in which the experimenter conducts an experiment by measuring behavior as it occurs naturally without artificial manipulation. However, one trade-off that sometimes comes with increasing the naturalness of the experiment is the decrease in the amount of control the research can have over other factors not being studied.
4. **Correlational studies** reveal the degree to which two or more factors are be related to each other but they do not allow us to draw conclusions about cause and effect. Correlational studies are often used when one factor under study cannot be manipulated by the experimenter, for example, a person's age.
5. A **case study** is an in-depth investigation of one or at most a few people. Case studies can be valuable because they provide detailed information, but their drawbacks include their inability to prove that certain principles operate and the problem that the results based on the responses of a few subjects may not generalize, or pertain, to others.
6. Two approaches can be taken to studying developmental changes that occur across time. **Longitudinal studies** identify a group of subjects and then follow them for a period of time, often over several years. Thus, each person's development can be compared to his or her own development at an earlier age. In **cross-sectional studies**, researchers select subjects from among the different age groups they wish to study. Results from one age group are compared to those subjects of a different age. Cross-sectional studies are faster and less expensive, and there is less chance that the investigation itself will modify subjects' behavior. However, cross-sectional studies only estimate how behavior changes over time, whereas longitudinal studies actually record such changes. Also, in cross-sectional studies, people in different age groups grew up at different times in history, and, when the age differences are large, this may affect results.
7. The **cross-sequential study** incorporates aspects of both longitudinal and cross-sectional studies. Here, researchers start with groups of different ages, but also follow these subjects for a period of time.
8. Regardless of the research method used, data can be gathered in different ways. **Structured observations** are observations of people in structured or controlled environments. They permit researchers to standardize conditions and improve control, but they may also seem artificial

and may prompt subjects to behave in untypical ways. **Naturalistic observations** involve observing subjects in their own environments, thereby reducing artificiality. However, here behavior is limited to that which occurs naturally and therefore potentially important questions may not be answered. **Questionnaires** are written sets of carefully prepared questions to which subjects respond. They are often used when studying a very large group of people, but they may seem impersonal and superficial and researchers must be concerned about the honesty of responses. Face-to-face **interviews** reduce the impersonal nature of the questionnaire, but may also encourage more dishonesty in responses. **Standardized tests** can be used to measure many facets of human behavior and have been developed to be reliable and valid. However, tests may not be available to measure every trait in which a researcher is interested.

9. Researchers are concerned about ethical issues and follow a code of ethics which specifies certain guidelines: (1) the child's interest always comes first, not the researcher's; (2) children and usually parents must give informed consent; (3) researchers should not use deception unless it causes no psychological harm and there is no other way to collect that data; and (4) researchers should protect the privacy of all participants in their studies.

10. There are several bodies that insure the adherence to these ethical guidelines. These include ethics review boards at colleges and universities and governmental appointees who review all grant proposals to insure compliance with these ethical standards.

Self Test

A. Matching Questions

___ 1. Refers to those characteristics determined through heredity
___ 2. Focuses on the study of emotions
___ 3. Corresponds to the "nurture" side of the nature-nurture debate
___ 4. Focuses on "nature" side of the nature-nurture debate
___ 5. Focuses on behavior rather than feelings
___ 6. Focuses on the study of thought

a. nurture
b. psychoanalytic theories
c. cognitive theories
d. biological theories
e. behavioral learning theories
f. nature
g. social context

___

___ 7. The Oedipus and Electra complexes occur here
___ 8. Corresponds to the conscience
___ 9. Home of the libido
___ 10. First of Freud's psychosexual stages
___ 11. Psychic energy, often thought of as sexual
___ 12. Used by the ego to redirect the id's demands
___ 13. Corresponds to the ages of 5-12
___ 14. Process which gives rise to the superego
___ 15. Stage characterized by mature interest in opposite-sex peers

a. latent stage
b. libido
c. anal stage
d. phallic stage
e. id
f. oral stage
g. defense mechanisms
h. superego
i. identification
j. genital stage
k. ego

6 *The Study of Human Development*

___ 16. Focuses on the consequences of one's actions
___ 17. Fitting new information into an old category of knowledge
___ 18. Theory which focuses only on observable events
___ 19. Albert Bandura's work fits best here
___ 20. Basic categories of knowledge
___ 21. Equivalent to "reward"
___ 22. Involves a compromise between two processes
___ 23. The association of a new stimulus to a stimulus-response reflex
___ 24. Removal of some unpleasant stimulus
___ 25. Decreases the likelihood that the event it follows will be repeated

a. classical conditioning
b. punishment
c. observational learning
d. behaviorism
e. negative reinforcement
f. schemes
g. operant conditioning
h. social learning theory
i. accommodation
j. equilibration
k. positive reinforcement
l. assimilation
m. cognitive theory

___

___ 26. The procedure used to collect reliable, objective information
___ 27. Can be thought of as a biography
___ 28. Where same subjects are identified and followed across time
___ 29. Controlled observations of people
___ 30. Evaluates the degree to which two factors are related
___ 31. General term for the best method for discovering cause and effect
___ 32. Can be thought of as a combination of the experiment and naturalistic observation
___ 33. Where groups of subjects of different ages are compared to each other
___ 34. A written set of questions which subjects answer
___ 35. A face-to-face question-answer technique
___ 36. Includes groups of different ages and studies them across time
___ 37. An educated guess about the likely results of a study

a. natural experiment
b. correlational studies
c. questionnaire
d. scientific method
e. cross-sectional study
f. experiment
g. hypothesis
h. structured observations
i. cross-sequential study
j. standardized test
k. case study
l. interview
m. longitudinal study

B. Multiple Choice

Factual
Obj. 1
Moderate

1. The relationship between inborn temperament and learning is essentially the same as that between:
   a. id and superego
   b. assimilation and accommodation
   c. classical conditioning and operant conditioning
   d. nature and nurture

Factual
Obj. 1
Basic

2. "All of the elements of your environment" defines the construct called:
   a. social context
   b. human development
   c. nature
   d. assimilation

Factual Obj. 2 Moderate	3.	Which of the following theories focuses most closely on the development of emotions? a. Skinner's behaviorism b. Freud's psychoanalytic theory c. Piaget's cognitive theory d. Bandura's social learning theory
Applied Obj. 3 Moderate	4.	Bart tells his roommate that at times he feels very guilty about how he behaves and what he thinks about. Bart's experience corresponds most closely to the concept of: a. assimilation b. accommodation c. superego d. libido
Factual Obj. 3 Basic	5.	In the Electra complex, a girl develops sexual feelings for her ___ and ends up resolving the complex by identifying with her ___. a. father; father b. mother; mother c. father; mother d. mother; father
Applied Obj. 3 Moderate	6.	Julie believes that children learn appropriate sex roles by imitating and then adopting the attitudes and behaviors of their parents. Her belief corresponds most clearly to the concept called: a. ego b. identification c. assimilation d. accommodation
Conceptual Obj. 3 Advanced	7.	Frank explains personality as being like a wild horse which is directed and controlled by a skilled rider. In Freud's terms, the horse would be represented by the ___ and the rider would be represented by the ___. a. id; ego b. id; superego c. superego; id d. ego; id
Factual Obj. 3 Moderate	8.	The ego uses which of the following to repress or redirect the demands of the id? a. psychosocial stages b. defense mechanisms c. The Oedipus complex d. equilibration
Conceptual Obj. 4 Moderate	9.	Which of the following is an accurate statement reflecting the differences between the theories of Freud and Erikson? a. Erikson focuses more attention on early childhood than Freud. b. Erikson focuses more attention on ego processes than Freud. c. Erikson focuses more attention on the conflicts between id and superego than Freud. d. Erikson emphasized sexual development whereas Freud concentrated on social development.

8   *The Study of Human Development*

Factual
Obj. 4
Advanced

10. According to Erikson, the first period in human development revolves around which of the following conflicts?
    a. initiative versus guilt
    b. identity versus role confusion
    c. basic trust versus mistrust
    d. integrity versus despair

Applied
Obj. 5
Advanced

11. Judy ate sushi for the first time and almost immediately developed a terrible allergic reaction to it. Now Judy hates even the smell of a Japanese restaurant. This is an example of:
    a. accommodation
    b. observational learning
    c. operant conditioning
    d. classical conditioning

Conceptual
Obj. 5
Moderate

12. Which of the following types of consequences *decrease* the odds that the behavior it follows will be repeated again?
    a. positive reinforcement
    b. negative reinforcement
    c. punishment
    d. both negative reinforcement and punishment

Applied
Obj. 6
Moderate

13. Little Lucy watches as another child walks over to the sleeping dog which wakes up, barks loudly, and scares the child away. Lucy figures that waking up sleeping dogs isn't a very wise thing to do. This example highlights the main idea of the concept called:
    a. defense mechanisms
    b. observational learning
    c. equilibration
    d. classical conditioning

Factual
Obj. 7
Basic

14. The mental representations and patterns of action that structure a person's knowledge define the concept called:
    a. schemes
    b. temperament
    c. libido
    d. accommodation

Applied
Obj. 7
Advanced

15. John has played baseball for three years. Now, for the first time, he picks up a softball and, although it feels a little different from a baseball, throws it using the same motions he had learned earlier. This example most clearly demonstrates the principle of:
    a. assimilation
    b. accommodation
    c. equilibration
    d. identification

Conceptual 16. A thermostat works by trying to maintain a balance between hot and cold air. When the
Obj. 7   temperature gets too high, the air conditioning kicks on; when it's too cold, on comes
Advanced   the heat. The developmental process most like the thermostat is:
                a. observational learning
                b. accommodation
                c. assimilation
                d. equilibration

Conceptual 17. Dr. Tsuni believes that most of the differences in behavior between men and women
Obj. 8   today exist because, throughout human history, women have had to bear and nurture
Moderate   children whereas men were more responsible for securing food and safety. Her view is
                most consistent with those of
                a. sociobiologists
                b. behavioral geneticists
                c. social learning theorists
                d. cognitive theorists

Factual   18. Which of the following research methods provides the most information about cause?
Obj. 10   a. the correlational study
Basic   b. the case study
                c. the experiment
                d. the interview

Applied   19. Dr. Smith recruits a group of 3-year-olds, a group of 5-year-olds, and a group of 7-
Obj. 10   year-olds and will study their behavior now and again in two years. She is most likely
Advanced   using a method called:
                a. cross-sectional study
                b. cross-sequential study
                c. longitudinal study
                d. naturalistic experiment

Conceptual 20. Which of the following statements about ethical guidelines is **false**?
Obj. 12   a. The interests of the child must come before the interests of the researcher.
Moderate   b. Deception must never be used.
                c. Children and usually their parents must give informed consent before participating
                   in a study.
                d. Researchers must protect the privacy of all participants in their studies.

C. Essay Questions

INSTRUCTIONS

After reading and studying the text, read the question below and write your answer in the space provided. Do not refer to your text or to the Scoring Scheme or Model Answer on the next page.

1. The text describes the nature-nurture debate which considers how hereditary and environmental forces interact to produce human development. Using the psychoanalytic theories of Sigmund Freud and Erik Erikson, identify aspects of these theories in which their explanations reflect more nature-oriented process and components in which the environment plays a larger role.

Total Score ___

Scoring Scheme for Question 1

+2 points, up to a maximum of 4 points, for a description of any of the theoretical ideas that could be thought of as inherited or primarily the result of inherited features. These would include any of the constructs which are assumed to be present in all humans. These could include examples from the following categories:
   a. The idea that some components of personality are present from birth (e.g., the libido, the id, the life and death drives, etc.).
   b. The idea that all humans go through the same sequence of developmental events (e.g., oral, anal, phallic, latent, genital stages; the Oedipal and Electra complexes; the emergence of the ego and superego, etc.).

+2 points, up to a maximum of 4 points, for a description of any of the theoretical ideas that could be thought of as resulting from the specific experiences unique to an individual. These could include examples in the following categories:
   a. The idea that how a development event is treated (e.g., toilet training, the resolution of one developmental stage like basic trust vs. mistrust) can modify subsequent development.
   b. The idea that the unique people or situations one encounters can influence how one develops (e.g., if one's parents are overprotective, different responses will occur).

-2 points, up to a maximum of 8 points, for any event categorized under the wrong heading (e.g., an example of "nurture" discussed as an example of "nature."

Total: 8 points

Model Answer for Question 1

Freud's theory suggests that much of human nature is biologically driven, and thus the result of nature-oriented factors. For example, the libido is an inherent source of energy present in all people. Freud also believed that all humans go through a consistent developmental process. For example, we all go through a series of psychosexual stages focusing on different body parts at various ages. We also all develop an ego to help us control our id, and later, through the resolution of the Oedipus or Electra complex, a superego. Thus, because these developmental sequences are experienced regardless of the environment one experiences, they should be considered nature-oriented as well.

Freud also incorporated into his theory the idea that the environment in which we develop can affect how that development will occur. Some individuals, for example, resolve certain developmental milestones such as the Oedipus complex more successfully than do others, and their later development is permanently influenced by these accomplishments. Also, the specific morals and values one accepts will depend on with whom one identifies, again emphasizing the role of nurture. Erik Erikson's theory is clear in stating that the way a person resolves a former stage of development will influence how one can satisfy subsequent stages which again argues for the influence of the environment in development.

Thus, psychoanalytic theory can be seen as an example of the interaction of the forces of nature and nurture in the development of the individual.

The Study of Human Development

INSTRUCTIONS
After reading and studying the text, read the question below and write your answer in the space provided. Do not refer to your text, or to the Scoring Scheme or Model Answer on the next page.

2. Developmentalists are often interested in understanding how behavior changes across time. Describe three research methods that are used to address this issue, and point out the advantages and disadvantages of each.

Total Score ___

Scoring Scheme for Question 2

Characteristics of the longitudinal method:

+1 point (up to 3 points)
   a. The same people are always studied.

   b. These people have information gathered from them at repeated intervals.

   c. Information gathered at one time is compared to information collected at another time.

Characteristics of the cross-sectional method:

+1 point (up to 3 points)
   a. Groups of subjects of different ages are studied.

   b. Data on all subjects are gathered simultaneously.

   c. Subjects of one age are compared to different subjects of another age.

For the cross-sequential method:

+1 point (up to 3 points)
   a. Groups of subjects of different ages are studied.

   b. Subjects are also studied across a period of time.

   c. Subjects' data is compared with data collected on other subjects of a different age **and** with data collected on them at a different time.

+1 point each (up to 3 points) for mention of any advantages and disadvantages, such as:

   a. Cross-sectional studies are faster and cheaper than longitudinal studies.

   b. Subjects in cross-sectional studies have less chance that the data collection methods themselves will influence their behavior.

   c. Since cross-sectional studies involve comparisons among different groups of people, to the extent that the groups differ in background or experience the results will reflect this lack of control.

   d. The cross-sequential approach mixes the advantages and disadvantages of the longitudinal and cross-sectional approaches, being more efficient than a longitudinal study and gaining some measure of control over that of a cross-sectional approach.

Total: 12 points

Model Answer for Question 2

In the longitudinal method, a single group of subjects is identified and studied repeatedly at various intervals of time. Data collected on these individuals at one time can then be compared with data gathered on the same subjects at a different point in time.

In the cross-sectional method, different-aged groups of subjects are all studied at the same time. The data collected on subjects in one age group are then compared to the data collected on subjects of a different age.

The cross-sequential method combines elements of the longitudinal and cross-sectional methods. Here different-aged groups of subjects are studied at one time, as in the cross-sectional approach, and then these subjects are studied again at later times, as in the longitudinal method. Thus, data on subjects is compared both to data collected on other subjects of different ages and with data collected on themselves at different points in time.

Advantages of the cross-sectional method include that it is faster and cheaper to conduct, since all data is collected at the same time, and that, because no repeated measures are taken, there is less chance that the data collection methods themselves will influence the subjects' behavior. However, cross-sectional studies compare one group of people with a different group. Thus, to the extent that one group differs from the other in background or experience, the results obtained will reflect these differences in addition to the factors that change with age alone. The cross-sequential method mixes the advantages and disadvantages of the longitudinal and cross-sectional methods, and is therefore susceptible to both their disadvantages and advantages. Generally, it is more efficient than the longitudinal design and is better controlled than a study using the cross-sectional method.

Chapter 2

Conception, Heredity, and Prenatal Development

Preview of the Chapter

- I. **Human Conception**
  - A. Fertilization

- II. **Heredity: The Genetics of Life**
  - A. Genes and Chromosomes
  - B. The Genetics of Conception
  - C. Sex Determination and Differentiation
  - D. From Genotype to Phenotype
    1. Genes and the environment
    2. Separating genetic and environmental contributions
  - E. Genetic Abnormalities
    1. Down Syndrome
    2. PKU
    3. Sickle-Cell Anemia
    4. Tay-Sachs Disease

- III. **Preventing Abnormalities: Genetic Counseling and Prenatal Diagnosis**
  - A. Genetic Counseling
  - B. Prenatal Diagnosis

- IV. **Prenatal Development**
  - A. The Germinal Period
    1. Twins
  - B. The Embryonic Period
    1. Support Systems
  - C. The Fetal Period

- V. **Environmental Influences on Prenatal Development**
  - A. Nutrition and Development
    1. Malnutrition and the brain
  - B. Drugs
    1. Prescription and aspirin
    2. Marijuana, heroin, and cocaine
    3. Alcohol
    4. Nicotine
    5. Caffeine
  - C. Diseases
    1. Rubella
    2. Sexually transmitted diseases
  - D. The Rh Factor

16 *Conception, Heredity, and Prenatal Development*

      E. Environmental Hazards
      F. Fathers and Fetuses
      G. The Mother's Emotions
      H. Diseases

Learning Objectives

1. Describe the process by which conception occurs.

2. Describe the structure and function of genes and explain the genetic mechanisms by which hereditary traits are transferred.

3. Discuss the relationship between heredity and the environment, and suggest methods that can be used to determine the relative contributions of these factors.

4. Describe the causes and treatments of the major genetic diseases and disorders, including Down syndrome, PKU, sickle-cell anemia and Tay-Sachs disease.

5. Explain the intent and techniques of genetic counseling, describe the diagnostic procedures used in prenatal diagnosis, and comment on the ethical considerations involved in their use.

6. Describe the events which take place in the germinal, embryonic, and fetal periods and identify the structures which help support the embryo.

7. Define the term teratogen and discuss how teratogens affect development.

8. Evaluate the effect that malnutrition has on the developing baby.

9. Discuss the action and effects of the major teratogenic drugs.

10. Discuss the action and effects of the various diseases that can cause problems for unborn babies.

11. Describe how an incompatible Rh factor, environmental hazards, and the father's lifestyle can influence prenatal development.

Chapter Summary

    I. Human Conception
        1. The odds of a particular sperm fertilizing a particular ovum (egg) are extremely small. Yet, largely because each ejaculate contains hundreds of millions of sperm, a normal couple engaging regularly in intercourse without birth control can expect conception to occur in 3 to 6 months.
        2. Once ejaculated into the woman's vagina, the 300-400 million sperm begin their journey toward fertilization through the cervix, into the uterus, and down a fallopian tube where the ovum is. Although sperm propel themselves, they face several impediments including passing through a thick mucus plug in the cervix present except at the time of ovulation, the downward push of the cilia in the fallopian tube, and the attack by the woman's immune system. Only the rhythmic uterine contractions accompanying intercourse aid the sperm on their journey, and their numbers are reduced significantly as they make their way to the ovum. Recent research

suggest the egg may play an active role in attracting a given sperm. Conception occurs when the sperm is accepted into the egg.
3. Only one sperm is able to penetrate the ovum, and it is more likely coded to develop into a male than a female: for every 100 females conceived there are 160 males. Yet at birth the ratio is 100:105, indicating that throughout pregnancy, males succumb to stress more readily than females.

II. Heredity: The Genetics of Life

1. In the 19th century, Gregor Mendel's work disconfirmed the then-common belief that traits were inherited through a mixing of body fluids at conception. Now we know that traits are carried by **genes**.
2. Every normal human has 23 pair, or 46, chromosomes in the nucleus of every cell. Each chromosome contains about 20,000 genes, each in a specific place, or **locus**. James Watson and Francis Crick, in 1958, discovered that chromosomes were really long strands of **DNA (deoxyribonucleic acid)** shaped like a twisted ladder, with the rails consisting of sugar and phosphates and the rungs composed of four amino acids: adenine, thymine, cytosine, and guanine. All of the instructions held in the chromosomes depend on the order of these four nucleic acids.
3. Alternate genes for the same trait are called **alleles**, and since our chromosomes are paired, we have two alleles for each trait. A person who inherits the same alleles for a trait, say two alleles for blue eyes, is **homozygous** for that trait. A person who inherits two different alleles, say one for blue eyes and one for brown, is **heterozygous**. Some genes are **dominant**, and their characteristics will mask those of a **recessive** gene. Many diseases and defects are carried on recessive genes and are therefore only in evidence when the recessive trait is homozygous. Because homozygous traits are more commonly seen among related individuals, most societies prohibit marriages between close relatives. Most characteristics are **polygenic**, meaning many genes contribute to the trait.
4. Each ovum contains an X chromosome from the 23rd pair, or **sex chromosomes**. Two types of sperm are produced, and each carries either an X or a Y sex chromosome. Thus it is the sperm which determines the sex of the child: a Y sperm produces a male (XY) and an X sperm a female (XX). However, until the thirteenth week of gestation, male and female fetuses are structurally alike, and reproductive structures as well as brain differences between the sexes develop after this time.
5. The **genotype** is the set of genes one inherits; the **phenotype** refers to the observable traits that develop from the genes, but that also depend on the influence of the environment. Heavily **canalized** traits are those which are resistant to environmental influences, such as learning to talk. Genes establish a **reaction range**, or an upper and lower limit on development potential. The environment will determine where, within this reaction range, his phenotype will fall.
6. Genetic and environmental factors usually work together in one of three ways. First, in **passive** gene-environment correlations, the child is the passive recipient of genetic and environmental influences that work in the same direction. For example, she inherits a high genetic potential for intelligence and her parents stimulate her intellectual growth. Second, in **evocative** gene-environment correlations, the presence of the genetic potential causes the child to act in ways that evoke intellectual stimulation. For example, smart kids ask lots of questions and ask to be taken to the library. Third, in **active** gene-environment correlations, children who inherit genetic potential actively seek out activities that encourage or reward the development of that potential. For example, the intelligent child picks intelligent friends and seeks challenging projects.
7. One way researchers investigate the extent to which a trait is influenced by hereditary factors is to compare the traits of adopted children to the biological and adoptive parents. If the children more closely resemble their biological parents on trait, we conclude that heredity

plays a major role. If they are closer to their adoptive parents, we believe environment plays a more influential role. A second method involves comparisons between pairs of **identical twins**, who are genetically identical, and **fraternal twins**, who share similar environments but not identical genes. If correlations of the trait in question are higher between identical twins than fraternal twins, we conclude that heredity plays a role in the development of the trait. Today, developmentalists are no longer interested in how much of a trait is the result of heredity or the environment. Rather, they seek to understand how the genes and the environment work together to influence development.

8. Half of all conceptions are never implanted and 25 percent of implanted embryos are miscarried due, at least in part, to genetic defects. Genetic defects are more likely to show up in males since some negative traits are carried on the X chromosome. These **sex-linked** traits are more likely to be seen in men because the Y chromosome carries fewer genes and therefore is less likely to supply a dominant allele to counter a negative trait on the X chromosome.

9. **Down syndrome**, also called trisomy 21, is the result of an extra chromosome or piece of chromosome on the 21st pair. Its incidence increases sharply with increasing maternal age at conception, perhaps due to the aging of the ova. Recent research indicates that environmental influences are involved as well, and the incidence of Down syndrome also increases when the father is over 40 years old. People with Down syndrome have a characteristic physical appearance, some related medical problems, and are mentally retarded. Recent research, however, indicates the reaction range for Down syndrome victims is larger than previously thought, and researchers are studying ways of maximizing the potential of these individuals.

10. **PKU (phenylketonuria)** is a metabolic disorder caused when a child inherits a recessive gene from both parents. Without treatment brain damage results, but if the child is from birth placed on a phenylalanine-free diet, no damage occurs.

11. **Sickle-cell anemia** is a genetic disorder carried on a recessive gene. If only one sickle-cell gene is carried, the carrier is protected from malaria, but if two are present, medical problems occur. People whose ancestors lived in the tropics (Hispanic Americans and especially black Americans) are much more likely to have the recessive gene.

12. **Tay-Sachs disease**, found mostly among people descended from Eastern European Jews, is the result of a mutation which was confined to a small population due to few marriages outside this group. Although children born with Tay-Sachs seem normal at birth, they rarely live past their third birthday. Because Tay-Sachs can be detected in parents who carry the gene, prepregnancy counseling is helping to reduce the incidence of this disease.

III. Preventing Abnormalities: Genetic Counseling and Prenatal Diagnosis

1. Genetic counselors can recommend tests to determine if individuals carry certain genetic disorders. These tests involve producing from tissue a profile called a **Karyotype** of an individual's chromosomes. Thus, individuals can know whether they carry the possibility of producing a child with a genetic disorder, but the tests cannot predict if any given conception will be afflicted.

2. **Amniocentesis** is a test in which the cells of a fetus are examined for genetic disorders in the fourth month of pregnancy. It also reveals the sex of the child. **Ultrasonography** produces a picture, or **sonogram**, which can show some visible structural deformities. **Chorionic villis biopsy (CVB)** is a new technique which is about as risky as amniocentesis (complications in fewer than 1 in 1000 cases) and yields results earlier in pregnancy, usually between the 9th and 11th week. Maternal blood tests performed between the 14th and 20th week of pregnancy can be used to detect high levels of AFP (alpha-feto-protein) which may indicate the fetus has spinal or brain abnormalities. These abnormalities, then, can be confirmed with other tests.

IV. Prenatal Development

Conception, Heredity, and Prenatal Development 19

1. In humans, **prenatal development**, or development in the period before birth is relatively long compared to that of other animals. During this period of **gestation**, the period of prenatal development, genetic and environmental factors interact thereby shaping the course of development. Because of our long period of immaturity after we're born, each of us is exposed to different environments that contribute to individual differences.
2. The **germinal period** consists of the first two weeks of fetal development. Within hours after fertilization, the ovum and sperm fuse into the **zygote**, which travels from the fallopian tube to the uterus. Mitosis, or cell division, occurs and by day 4, the new organism consists of 60-70 cells arranged to form a hollow ball, the **blastula**.
3. The cells on the outer edge of the blastula join to become the **embryonic disk**, which will develop into the baby. Other cells become the placenta, umbilical cord and amniotic sac. After floating in the uterus a few days, the blastula attaches to its wall in a process called **implantation** in which the **villi**, the threadlike projections from the blastula, burrow into the uterine wall. **Monozygotic**, or identical, twins develop from the splitting of a single zygote, and therefore have identical chromosomes. **Dizygotic**, or fraternal, twins result from two separate zygotes, each resulting from its own distinct ovum and sperm.
4. The **embryonic period** (weeks 2-8) begins at implantation and is the period in which the development of physical structures occur.
5. The **placenta** is the organ in which the baby's and mother's blood exchange their nutrients and wastes. It also produces hormones that prevent menstruation, trigger milk production, and initiate labor contractions. The **umbilical cord** attaches the embryo to the placenta. The **amniotic sac**, filled with fluid, cushions the baby.
6. Three layers of cells develop in the first weeks of the embryonic period, the innermost **endoderm**, which will become the gut and related organs, the middle layer called the **mesoderm**, which will become the skeleton and muscles, and the outer layer, the **ectoderm**, which will become the skin and nervous system. **Differentiation**, the process by which cells develop into specific types and organs, is probably regulated by the chemical environment around the cells.
7. In the third week of gestation, the heart and neural tube begin to develop. In the fourth week, the neural tubes closes and the brain is forming. In the fifth week, the limb buds are beginning to form the rudiments of hands and feet and the eye cups have grown from the brain. In week six, the ears and teeth appear. By the end of the eighth week, the internal organs are in place and some are functioning, and the embryo resembles a human form, although it is only one inch long. If a serious developmental error occurs during the embryonic period a spontaneous abortion, or miscarriage, typically occurs.
8. The **fetal** period (from 8 weeks to birth) is characterized by growth and maturation, since differentiation occurred in the embryonic period. Fetuses can survive with medical intervention beginning at the seventh month. In the ninth and last month of gestation, the fetus typically engages, moving into a head-down, face to the mother's back position.

V. Environmental Influences on Prenatal Development

1. A **teratogen** is any substance, influence, or agent that causes birth defects. An example of a teratogen is **thalidomide**, a drug prescribed to pregnant women for nausea and sleeplessness and which caused limb malformation in 8,000 babies in the 1950's and 1960's. The most commonly ingested teratogen today is alcohol. The effects of a teratogen often depend on timing, and there are **critical periods** during which the effect of the teratogen produces its associated problems. Critical periods generally correspond to periods in which the organs involved are forming or developing, and therefore teratogens are generally most dangerous in the embryonic period. Even aspirin can harm a fetus. Women should not take drugs during pregnancy except those prescribed by a physician who is aware the woman is pregnant.

2. Malnutrition is associated with premature delivery and lower birth weight, and also affects the baby after it is born. Women whose diets have been poor before they become pregnant also tend to have low-birth-weight babies.
3. Nutrition affects brain development, which, for the first 6 months of pregnancy, involves cell division and, for the last 3 months of pregnancy and first two years of life, consists of cell growth. Malnourished children have both fewer and smaller brain cells. Malnutrition also disrupts **myelinization**, the laying down of the fatty sheaths that surround nerve cells and speed neural transmission, and this is associated with mental retardation.
4. At 15 days of age, babies in poor third world countries who had received a food supplement were more alert than those who had not. Malnourished babies also had, at ages 6-8, poorer social development, which may be due to their being less energetic and active early in life and therefore not being given as much stimulation. Nutrition interacts with social context: research shows that if maternal employment increases family income the infant benefits but, if it means the baby will be cared for by another child, the infant suffers. In the United States, 17 percent of children live in poverty, and the prevalence of low-birth-weight children is increasing, especially among African-Americans. The effects of early malnutrition can be partially corrected with adequate nutrition in childhood.
5. Evidence suggests the mother's use of illegal drugs is very hazardous to her baby. Marijuana may impair central nervous system development. Heroin addiction is passed on to the baby who after birth goes through withdrawal and later may exhibit behavioral problems. Cocaine is the most commonly used illegal drug among American women of childbearing age: 10 to 20 percent of babies are thought to be exposed prenatally to cocaine. Such babies are often premature, have neurological damage, develop language skills later, and are less securely attached to their mothers.
6. Alcohol is a teratogen, and, when ingested by the mother, it depresses the activity of the fetal neural system. Babies of alcoholic mothers often suffer from **fetal alcohol syndrome (FAS)** which involves symptoms of mental retardation, hyperactivity and other attention disorders, poor motor development, retarded growth, and an atypical facial appearance. FAS affects about 1 in 750 babies born in the U.S. Even social drinkers have higher-than-average risks of spontaneous abortion, stillbirths, and birth defects. Children of women who had one drink a day during pregnancy were more likely to have attention span disorders even at age 7.
7. Research shows that women who smoke are 30-50 percent more likely to have miscarriages or stillbirths, and their babies tend to be smaller at birth and be at risk for **sudden infant death syndrome (SIDS)**, from which some infants die for no apparent reason. Prenatal exposure to nicotine is linked to attention disorders which increase in childhood, and, indirectly, to achievement. Furthermore, these results were linked to the amount the mother smoked during pregnancy.
8. Although caffeine, the drug in coffee, tea, chocolate, and colas, crosses the placental barrier, it does not appear to be linked to birth defects. Research suggests that women who consume heavy doses of caffeine when pregnant tend to have low-birth-weight babies.
9. The placenta protects the fetus from most bacteria, but not from viruses. German measles, or **rubella**, has devastating effects on the fetus. Nowadays, a woman can be tested to see if she has had rubella and is therefore immune. If not, she can be vaccinated before becoming pregnant.
10. Sexually transmitted diseases (STDs) can affect a baby. **Chlamydia**, a common but little known STD, can infect a baby as it moves through the birth canal and cause conjunctivitis (eye inflammation) or pneumonia. It also increases the odds of prematurity and stillbirth. Chlamydia can be treated effectively with antibiotics, as can **gonorrhea** and **syphilis**. Syphilis bacteria can cross the placental barrier and infect the fetus, causing major birth defects such as blindness and deafness, especially during the critical period in the fourth month. Thus, early detection and treatment are critical. **Genital herpes** is a virus, but doesn't affect the baby unless it is

active at birth and the baby contracts it in the birth canal. Thus, its effects can be prevented through delivery by Caesarean section. **AIDS (acquired immune deficiency syndrome)** poses the gravest threat to unborn children since at present it is incurable and fatal. The AIDS virus can lie dormant for years and it appears to cross the placental barrier, affecting children of infected mothers. It may also be transmitted in breast milk. AIDS may be among the top 5 causes of death for United States children age 1 to 4 by the late 1990s.

11. In the United States, the poorer health status of certain ethnic groups translates into poorer health for their children as well.

12. The **Rh factor** is a protein found on red blood cells. When the father has the Rh factor (he is Rh positive) but the mother does **not** (she is Rh negative), and they produce an Rh positive child, the mother's body produces antibodies to attack the baby's Rh positive blood cells. Although these antibodies are not disastrous for the first child, they remain in her bloodstream and can cross the placenta to attack the blood cells of any subsequent Rh positive babies, producing serious birth defects or death. Today, the mother can receive an injection shortly after the birth of the first child that will prevent the formation of Rh antibodies and free future pregnancies from the risk of Rh incompatibilities.

13. Exposure to high levels of radiation causes chromosome damage and cancer in unborn children. Exposure to **industrial pollutants**, like lead, or **PCBs**, can also cause serious damage to the unborn baby.

14. Fathers' exposure to certain chemicals, such as lead, benzene, and other environmental pollutants, can also transmit increased health and developmental risks to their children. Fathers who smoke have children at greater risk for low birth weight and cancer.

15. Women who experience anxiety during pregnancy are at risk for vomiting, toxemia, and premature delivery. Also, their babies tend to be more irritable as well. Research suggests that the mother's anxiety may trigger the production of chemicals that reduce her bloodflow to the uterus or raise her blood pressure, thereby causing risk to the fetus. Support from friends and accurate information about what to expect from pregnancy and childbirth are the best treatments for maternal anxiety.

Self Test

A. Matching Questions

___ 1. Discrete units of hereditary information
___ 2. Alternative genes for the same trait
___ 3. Chemical substance of which chromosomes are composed
___ 4. Results in the production of sperm and ova
___ 5. When several genes influence a trait
___ 6. All normal humans have 46 of these
___ 7. Two matching alleles are described as this
___ 8. A gene that is expressed

a. genes
b. homozygous
c. chromosomes
d. heterozygous
e. DNA
f. dominant gene
g. meiosis
h. recessive gene
i. alleles
j. polygenic

22 Conception, Heredity, and Prenatal Development

___ 9. The upper and lower limits on development
___ 10. The observable traits that emerge during development
___ 11. Much more common in descendants of European Jews
___ 12. The 23rd pair
___ 13. They share identical chromosomes
___ 14. The extent to which a trait can be modified by the environment
___ 15. Caused by an extra chromosome on the 21st pair
___ 16. Can be treated with a special diet

a. canalization
b. reaction range
c. phenotype
d. identical twins
e. sex chromosomes
f. Down syndrome
g. fraternal twins
h. genotype
i. PKU
j. sickle-cell anemia
k. Tay-Sachs disease

___ 17. Technique that reveals an image of the fetus
___ 18. Its presence indicates a chance of spinal or brain abnormality
___ 19. Prenatal test done in the 4th month of pregnancy
___ 20. Prenatal test done in the 6th to 8th week after conception
___ 21. Profile of an individual's chromosomes

a. chorionic villus biopsy (CVB)
b. karyotype
c. amniocentesis
d. AFP (alpha-feto-protein)
e. sonogram
f. ultrasonography
g. genetic counseling

___ 22. Part of the blastula that will develop into a baby
___ 23. The time between conception and birth
___ 24. They accomplish implantation
___ 25. Last period of prenatal development
___ 26. Fraternal twins
___ 27. Corresponds to the first trimester of pregnancy
___ 28. A fertilized ovum
___ 29. Attachment of the blastula to the wall of the uterus
___ 30. Consists of a hollow ball of 60-70 cells
___ 31. Identical twins

a. germinal period
b. blastula
c. implantation
d. gestation
e. dizygotic
f. embryonic disk
g. villi
h. zygote
i. embryonic period
j. monozygotic
k. fetal period

___ 32. Exchanges nutrients and wastes between mother and baby
___ 33. Becomes the gut
___ 34. A dangerous teratogen
___ 35. Any substance that can cause birth defects
___ 36. Serves to cushion the baby from bumps
___ 37. Becomes the skeleton and muscles
___ 38. Converts cells that are all alike to cells with specific functions
___ 39. Time during which structures are most vulnerable
___ 40. Attaches baby to the placenta
___ 41. Becomes the nervous system and skin
___ 42. Laying down of fatty substance around the nerve cells

a. mesoderm
b. myelinization
c. umbilical cord
d. ectoderm
e. differentiation
f. amniotic sac
g. thalidomide
h. teratogen
i. endoderm
j. critical period
k. placenta

___ 43. May be linked to smoking during pregnancy
___ 44. The most common venereal disease in the U.S. today
___ 45. Is thought to be fatal in all cases
___ 46. An example of an industrial pollutant
___ 47. Another name for German measles
___ 48. Bacteria that crosses the placental barrier
___ 49. An incompatibility of this causes the mother's body to build antibodies that attack her unborn baby
___ 50. Symptoms include facial irregularities such as short eye slits and low nasal bridge
___ 51. Venereal disease which can be prevented in the baby by using the Caesarean section procedure

a. sudden infant death syndrome (SIDS)
b. chlamydia
c. cocaine
d. genital herpes
e. fetal alcohol syndrome
f. PCBs
g. syphilis
h. Rh factor
i. rubella
j. acquired immune deficiency syndrome (AIDS)

B. Multiple Choice

Conceptual
Obj. 1
Advanced

1. Which of the following *assists* the sperm in their journey from the vagina to the ovum?
   a. the movement of the cilia in the woman's fallopian tubes
   b. uterine contractions that accompany the woman's orgasm
   c. the woman's immune response
   d. the presence of a thick mucus plug in the cervix

Factual
Obj. 1
Moderate

2. For every 100 females conceived, about how many males are conceived?
   a. 80
   b. 98
   c. 105
   d. 160

Applied
Obj. 2
Basic

3. If we were to compare a chromosome to a strand of pearls, each individual bead would correspond to:
   a. a molecule of DNA
   b. a molecule of sugar
   c. a gene
   d. a molecule of phosphate

Applied
Obj. 2
Moderate

4. Suppose that Sandra inherits a gene for curly hair from her mother and a gene for straight hair from her father. This situation is best considered an example of a:
   a. homozygous trait
   b. heterozygous trait
   c. dominant gene
   d. recessive gene

Factual
Obj. 2
Basic

5. Traits which result from the effects of many different genes are called:
   a. heterozygous traits
   b. homozygous traits
   c. polygenic traits
   d. recessive traits

24 *Conception, Heredity, and Prenatal Development*

Conceptual
Obj. 3
Moderate

6. Canalization refers to:
   a. the extent to which a trait can be modified through experience
   b. the process of meiosis
   c. the degree to which a trait is dominant
   d. how strongly sex-linked a trait is

Applied
Obj. 3
Advanced

7. Mark inherits a high potential for intelligence and he therefore acts in ways consistent with his intellect. For example, he loves to engage older children in discussion and he asks many interesting questions. Mark's behavior is the result of:
   a. a wide reaction range
   b. a passive gene-environment interaction
   c. an active gene-environment interaction
   d. an evocative gene-environment interaction

Conceptual
Obj. 4
Moderate

8. Increasing maternal age at conception is most strongly linked to which of the following genetic diseases or abnormalities?
   a. PKU (Phenylketonuria)
   b. hemophilia
   c. Tay-Sachs disease
   d. Down syndrome

Applied
Obj. 5
Moderate

9. Lorraine is in her fourth month of pregnancy and has a diagnostic test performed to tell her if her baby is affected by Down syndrome. The test consists of the withdrawal of fluid surrounding the fetus and the preparation of a Karyotype. The test she had was:
   a. an amniocentesis
   b. ultrasonography
   c. a chorionic villus biopsy
   d. a test for AFP (alpha-feto-protein)

Factual
Obj. 5
Moderate

10. A high level of AFP (alpha-feto-protein) in an expectant mother's blood indicates a high likelihood that her baby will have:
    a. Klinefelter's syndrome
    b. Down syndrome
    c. Tay-Sachs disease
    d. spinal or brain abnormalities

Factual
Obj. 6
Moderate

11. The embryonic disk will eventually develop into the:
    a. baby
    b. placenta
    c. umbilical cord
    d. nervous system and skin

Conceptual
Obj. 6
Moderate

12. Twins that share identical genes are called ___; twins that are formed from the separate fertilization of two different eggs are called ___.
    a. monozygotic; identical
    b. identical; monozygotic
    c. monozygotic; dizygotic
    d. dizygotic; fraternal

Conception, Heredity, and Prenatal Development   25

Factual
Obj. 6
Moderate

13. The skeleton and muscles develop from which of the following embryonic structures?
    a. periderm
    b. ectoderm
    c. mesoderm
    d. endoderm

Conceptual
Obj. 6
Moderate

14. The major focus during the embryonic period is on ___; the major focus of the fetal period is on ___.
    a. differentiation; growth
    b. implantation; growth
    c. the nervous system; the rest of the body
    d. myelinization; differentiation

Applied
Obj. 7
Advanced

15. Suppose a research team finds that an experimental drug causes heart abnormalities in rats but only if it is given between day 7 and day 10 of gestation. These researchers have identified a(n) _____ period.
    a. germinal
    b. precocial
    c. critical
    d. altricial

Conceptual
Obj. 8
Moderate

16. Billy is a child with fetal alcohol syndrome. We should expect that he will exhibit all of the following characteristics except:
    a. being addicted to alcohol at birth
    b. mental retardation
    c. unusual facial appearance
    d. poor growth and motor development

Factual
Obj. 8
Moderate

17. Sudden infant death syndrome (SIDS) has been linked to which of the following teratogens?
    a. rubella
    b. alcohol
    c. cocaine
    d. nicotine

Conceptual
Obj. 9
Moderate

18. The effects on the fetus of which of the following diseases can be prevented if the delivery is performed by Caesarean section:
    a. syphilis
    b. genital herpes
    c. AIDS
    d. rubella

Factual
Obj. 10
Moderate

19. An injection that prevents the development of antibodies and that follows the delivery of the first child is the standard treatment for which of the following problems?
    a. rubella
    b. Rh incompatibility
    c. syphilis
    d. chlamydia

Conceptual
Obj. 11
Moderate

20. According to the text, which of the following is *not* associated with mothers who are highly anxious during pregnancy?
    a. babies who are more irritable
    b. lower risk of premature deliveries and a high rate of post-term deliveries
    c. a higher rate of toxemia
    d. more vomiting during pregnancy

C. Essay Questions

INSTRUCTIONS

After reading and studying the text, read the question below and write your answer in the space provided. Do not refer to your text or to the Scoring Scheme or Model Answer on the next page.

1. Name, explain, and give an example of the three types of gene-environment correlations that have been identified by Robert Plomin and his colleagues.

Total Score ___

Scoring Scheme for Question 1

+1 point each for correctly naming the three gene-environment interactions: passive, evocative, and active

+2 points each for correctly defining each of the three interactions

+2 points each for giving an appropriate example for each of the three interactions

Total: 15 points

Model Answer for Question 1

In the **passive** gene-environment correlation, the child is the passive recipient of genetic and environmental influences that work in the same direction. An example would be a child who inherits a high genetic potential for sociability from his highly social parents and, because the parents are also social, their actions bring her into many situations which encourage her to interact socially and develop her social skills.

In the **evocative** gene-environment correlations, children inherit a genetic potential, say for sociability, and because of this, they are more likely to act in ways that evoke social behavior from the people around them. For example, a girl who has a high genetic potential for sociability is likely to initiate social interactions with people she encounters. She may smile more and seek more attention than shy children, and therefore get more social attention which is reinforcing.

In the **active** gene-environment correlation, the child with a high genetic potential seeks and shapes the environment so that it fits her genetic predisposition. For example, a boy with a high genetic potential for sociability chooses play activities involving other children rather than solitary games, thus acting on his environment in a manner consistent with his predisposition.

INSTRUCTIONS

After reading and studying the text, read the question below and write your answer in the space provided. Do not refer to your text, or to the Scoring Scheme or Model Answer on the next page.

2. How does the concept of the "critical period" help us understand the varying effects of teratogens? Use an example of the effect of a particular teratogen to support your answer.

Total Score ___

Conception, Heredity, and Prenatal Development

Scoring Scheme for Question 2

+1 point each (up to 2 points) for demonstrating an adequate explanation of the terms teratogen and critical period.

+4 points for a clear and correct description stating that teratogens affect development during but not outside of critical periods.

+2 points for a clear and accurate example of a specific teratogen acting during a particular critical period.

Total: 8 points

Model Answer for Question 2

A critical period is the period of time in which a particular developing organ or body part is most vulnerable to environmental interference. Teratogens are substances that cause birth defects. The link between teratogens and critical periods centers on the idea that when teratogens disrupt development they are more likely to do so during a particular critical period, most likely when the organ or structure in question is forming. This is why teratogens are usually most dangerous during the embryonic period, in which most organs and structures are forming.

For example, the teratogen thalidomide is a drug that was given to pregnant women during the 1950s and 1960s to reduce the nausea and sleeplessness characteristic of some pregnancies. If the drug was taken during one particular period of time, for example the 38th to 46th days, a very specific birth defect occurred, in this case deformity of the arms. If the drug was taken at a different time, a different kind of disability, or perhaps no disability at all, resulted.

Thus, the effect of the teratogen was specific to a particular critical period. If the drug was taken during this critical period of time, the teratogenic effect occurred. If the drug was taken at a different time, that particular defect did not occur.

Chapter 3

Birth and the Newborn

Preview of the Chapter

I. **Preparing for Childbirth**
   A. Childbirth Classes
   B. Obstetricians and Nurse-Midwives
   C. Cultural Differences in Childbirth Practices
   D. Obstetrical Medication: Uses and Effects

II. **Labor and Delivery**
   A. The Signs of Labor
   B. Labor: First Stage
   C. Labor: Second Stage
   D. Labor: Third Stage
   E. Problems and Interventions

III. **The First Hours**
   A. Survival: The First Challenge
      1. The Apgar score
   B. First Contacts with Parents
      1. Fathers and birth

IV. **Behavior Patterns in Newborns**
   A. Crying
      1. The course of crying
   B. Reflexes
   C. States of Arousal
   D. The Brazelton Scale: Assessing Individual Differences
   E. Postpartum Depression

V. **The Competent Infant**
   A. The Newborn's Senses
      1. Vision
      2. Hearing
      3. Smell and Taste
   B. Newborns and Adults: A Natural Match
   C. Do Newborns Learn?

VI. **High-Risk Infants**
   A. Physical Characteristics of High-Risk Infants
   B. Behavioral Characteristics of High-Risk Infants
   C. Inequalities in Infant Mortality
   D. Prospects for Premature Infants
   E. Sudden Infant Death Syndrome

Birth and the Newborn

Learning Objectives

1. Explain the ideas on which prepared childbirth is based and describe how childbirth practices have changed over the past few decades.

2. Describe the conditions which indicate that labor is imminent.

3. Explain the major events in the three stages of labor.

4. Discuss the interventions available in cases of difficult labor and delivery.

5. Describe the typical infant's first experiences after birth.

6. Identify and discuss the behavior patterns present in newborns.

7. Describe the states of arousal experienced by the typical newborn.

8. Describe the functioning of the newborn's sensory abilities.

9. Discuss how newborns and adults interact with each other and influence each other's behavior.

10. Identify the types of learning of which a newborn is capable.

11. Identify the characteristics which place a newborn at risk and evaluate how advances in neonatology have affected at-risk babies.

12. Describe the physical and behavioral characteristics of infants at risk, and discuss the factors that affect their prospects for the future.

Chapter Summary

I. Preparing for Childbirth

1. Two generations ago, hospitalized childbirth was characterized by pain, ignorance, and sometimes pain-killing drugs. Nowadays, the acceptance of **prepared** (or **natural**) **childbirth** methods involves more information, preparation, and confidence.

2. Most physicians today recommend childbirth classes to expectant parents as a means of preparing them for the events of labor and delivery. Fernand Lamaze, a French obstetrician, believed that relaxation and abdominal massage could reduce childbirth pain. The **Lamaze method** does not discourage the use of pain-relieving drugs but does foster positive feelings toward labor and delivery.

3. Nurse-midwives are specially-trained nurses who attend women throughout labor and delivery. Although some women prefer nurse-midwives because they spend more time with the woman, obstetricians are trained to deliver babies in times of medical emergency.

4. Among different cultures, pregnancy and delivery are treated differently, from a medical condition to a normal condition. Even within the United States, different ethnic groups prefer and expect different practices.

5. Although anesthesia or other medication is sometimes used, it can have harmful effects on the baby because it rapidly crosses the placental barrier and takes a long time for immature liver and kidneys to metabolize. Risks to the infant are minimized when doses are small and administered close to the time of delivery.

II. GIVING BIRTH

1. Labor is a slow, painful process in which the closed cervix gradually widens to a diameter of about 10 centimeters (over 4 inches).
2. **Engagement**, or **lightening**, in which the fetus usually moves into a head-down position, is the first stage of labor. It may occur up to four weeks before birth, or may not occur at all. The **bloody show** generally occurs a few days before birth and consists of the expulsion of blood-tinged mucus that is released from the cervix as it begins to efface (grow thinner) and dilate (open). At this time, the baby may become less active, and the mother may lose a few pounds or have a spurt of energy. Oftentimes prior to delivery the amniotic membrane will break, releasing the amniotic fluid. Once the membrane breaks, infections can be transmitted vaginally to the now-unprotected fetus, so delivery is usually induced if it does not occur naturally within 24 hours. The clearest sign of labor is the beginning of rhythmic uterine **contractions** that will push the baby out of the uterus, through the cervix, and into the world.
3. The first stage of labor is the longest and lasts about 10–14 hours. In early first-stage labor, the cervix dilates to about 4 centimeters (1½ inches) and the amniotic membranes usually rupture. During the middle of this stage, contractions become longer, stronger, and closer together, and some women receive painkilling medication. During the last part of the first stage of labor, called **transition**, the cervix opens from 8 to 10 centimeters, and the women feel the urge to push. Transition lasts about one hour, and because the pain is most intense here and the woman feels the urge to push, she is usually very uncomfortable.
4. The second stage of labor begins when the cervix is fully dilated and ends when the baby is born. The mother is allowed to push the baby through the birth canal, and many physicians perform an **episiotomy**, a surgical incision below the vaginal opening, to enlarge the opening and prevent the tearing of vaginal membranes.
5. The placenta is delivered during the third stage of labor, and following this, uterine contractions stop and the uterus begins shrinking back to its normal size.
6. **Breech births**, in which the baby's feet or buttocks rather than its head point toward the cervix, or **transverse presentation**, in which the baby lies crosswise in the uterus, involve complications and, if these become serious, the baby is delivered via Caesarean section. When labor proceeds too slowly, a drug called **pitocin** can be used to speed and intensify contractions. **Anoxia**, the lack of oxygen in the fetus, can be detected with a **fetal monitor**, a device which measures fetal heartbeat and uterine contractions. In some cases of fetal distress, **forceps** or a **vacuum extraction** tube are used to pull the baby along, and in others a **Caesarean section** is performed.
7. A Caesarean section involves an incision in the mother's abdomen through the uterus. C-sections are becoming more common, presently accounting for about 25 percent of all births, due to improved surgical and fetal monitoring procedures and the higher risks of litigation for deliveries that result in birth complications.

III. The First Hours

1. When babies are born, they may be bruised and misshapen, and they are covered with **vernix**, which protected the skin in the uterus. The 10-point **Apgar test** is used to evaluate at 1 and at 5 minutes after birth the general physical condition. A low score indicates the need for assistance, but babies with low scores do not necessarily develop problems later in life, although they are at increased risk for sudden infant death syndrome.
2. Some research has shown that early mother-infant contact enhances maternal behavior as long as a year later. Other research, however, has failed to replicate this finding, and the text's conclusion is that early contact between some mothers and infants may sometimes enhance the bond between them. Fathers' involvement with their newborns is called **engrossment**.

IV. Behavior Patterns in Newborns

1. A newborn's first days are marked by instability and crying, and newborns sleep about two-thirds of each day and cry 4–15 minutes out of each hour.
2. A baby's cry is a distress signal, and healthy, normal infants' cries can sometimes be distinguished from those of infants with disorders. In most normal babies, crying increases from birth to six weeks, peaking at about 2¼ hours a day. As crying decreases, the number of crying episodes remains the same but the length of episodes diminishes. Some research suggests that babies who are carried a lot by their mothers cry less, but babies with **colic**, a condition of frequent, intense crying often associated with grimacing and gas, do not respond to extra holding.
3. A baby is born with several **reflexes**, which are motor behaviors not under the infant's control. Some reflexes remain throughout life, but others disappear at predictable times unless neurological damage interferes.
4. Newborns, like adults, experience **states of arousal** corresponding to different levels of activity or mood. Patterns of arousal states for babies tend to be consistent over time unless medical or behavioral problems are involved. There are some cultural differences in the states of arousal typical for infants. Parents' responses to their infant's dominant state are influenced by their own temperament and needs, and development proceeds most easily when there is a good fit between parental expectations and infant behavior.
5. The **Brazelton Newborn Behavioral Assessment Scale** is given at 10 days of age, and assesses the newborn's capacity for interaction and motor abilities. Among other things, it measures **state control**, the tendency to shift from one state of arousal to another. It is not, however, an accurate predictor or future development.
6. Twenty-five to 40 percent of new mothers experience postpartum depression, the emotional ups and downs that may be triggered by changing hormones and worry about coping with a new baby. Depressed mothers are less involved with their babies and their babies are accordingly less involved with them.

V. The Competent Infant

1. Because they are relatively under-developed at birth, human newborns are exposed to many stimulating experiences early in their development, and their senses function much better than we previously thought.
2. At birth, a baby's vision is about 20/600, or 20 times worse than a normal adults', but by 6 to 12 months of age, **visual acuity**, or clarity, has improved to normal (20/20). Normal vision is not achieved until age 3, however. Newborns can sense light and dark and can track objects as they move, but they do not have **binocular convergence**, the ability to focus both eyes on the same object, until later in development. They prefer to look at objects that are complex, three-dimensional, and patterned, and research supports the idea that they have inborn strategies for seeking information and are motivated to do so.
3. Human fetuses can hear before they are born, but as in vision, their hearing improves in the first months of life. Infants at birth have some ability to locate the source of a sound, called **sound localization**, but this ability is often lost during the first 2 to 3 months only to be regained at about 4 months of age, probably as a result of neurological control shifting from lower to higher brain areas. Infants prefer sounds in the same range as the human voice, and at 3 days can tell the difference between their mother's and a stranger's voice.
4. The newborn's sense of smell is sharp. It begins to develop at 3 days of age, and it remains relatively constant throughout life. Newborns orient more toward breast pads worn by their own mothers, indicating the ability to recognize their own mother's smell. Newborns also have a preference for sweet foods.

5. Adults and infants behave naturally in ways that are compatible, that enhance the ability to communicate and become attached. Furthermore, these compatible behaviors seem automatic and do not need to be specifically learned or executed.
6. **Learning** is a more or less permanent change in behavior that occurs as a consequence of experience. Newborns are capable of learning though classical conditioning, operant conditioning, and **observational learning**, the process of learning though observation and imitation. Researchers have shown that infants appear to be able to imitate adult facial expressions at just a few hours after birth.

VI. High-Risk Infants

1. **High-risk babies** are those whose physical and psychological well-being may be in jeopardy. Two conditions that place a baby at risk are **prematurity**, (being born **preterm**), in which the baby is born 3 or more weeks before the normal 38-week term of pregnancy is over, or having **a low birth weight** of less than 5½ pounds, compared to the average weight of 7½ pounds. (A very-low-birth-weight [VLBW] baby weighs less than 1,500 grams.) Factors which contribute to prematurity and low birth weight include: insufficient prenatal care, poor nutrition, the mother's age (over 35 or under 19), the mother's reproductive condition (too many pregnancies too close together), the mother's drinking and smoking habits, and the father's frequent exposure to teratogens. Furthermore, these factors cumulate, or add up, in increasing the risk of a given baby. Recent medical advances are keeping more very-low-birth-weight babies alive, most of whom have no major handicap. **Neonatology**, the branch of medicine that focuses on newborns, has achieved many advances which have improved survival rates for many at-risk babies. However, about 40,000 U.S. babies die in the first year, due in large part to conditions of poverty and lack of adequate prenatal care and to maternal drug addiction.
2. In comparison to normal babies, high-risk infants have smaller eyes, narrower, pointed heads, a relatively long distance between their nose and mouth, and are less physically attractive. Their greatest health risk stems from an immature respiratory system and they may develop **respiratory distress syndrome (RDS)**, also known as hyaline membrane disease. RDS is the leading killer of infants and results from the inability of fetuses younger than 35 weeks to manufacture the lubricating chemical **pulmonary surfactant**, which helps the lungs inflate properly without sticking together. A new treatment in which surfactant is dripped into the lungs of premature infants promises to reduce the death rate of preterm infants by 50%. High-risk babies also have trouble maintaining normal body temperature and are often placed in incubators, also called isolettes, in which temperature and air flow are controlled. Infants with weak sucking reflexes are usually fed intravenously.
3. High-risk babies do not have regular sleep patterns and cry more and in a more distressed manner than do normal infants. They also tend to smile less, to be less responsive in interactions with their parents, and to have a narrower band of arousal. Of course, there are many individual differences in responses of high-risk infants. Babies actively contribute to their own development; their behavior influences that of their parents which, in turn, influences them.
4. The United States infant mortality rate of 1 in 100 in the first year is among the highest in the industrialized world in spite of improvements in medical intervention. This high infant mortality is linked to poverty and poor prenatal care, and it is especially prevalent among African-Americans and, to a lesser extent Hispanic-Americans and Native Americans.
5. High-risk infants who receive early care, attention, and stimulation do better than those who don't receive extra stimulation. Infants whose parents attend support groups in which they share their feelings about their high-risk babies also benefit, probably because the help parents receive is passed on to the babies. If, however, the preterm infant's environment is difficult, the opportunity to catch up is limited.

36   Birth and the Newborn

6. **Sudden infant death syndrome (SIDS)**, or crib death is the leading nonaccidental cause of death between 1 month and 1 year. Most SIDS victims are between 2 and 4 months old. Most victims are low-birth-weight babies. Other risk factors include having a poor, single, teenaged mother who smoked, having a cold or diarrhea, being bottle-fed, and perhaps not sleeping with adults whose breathing the baby could imitate. Between 2 and 4 months, the control of breathing shifts from brain stem to cortex, and SIDS babies may have trouble in this transition.

Self Test

A. Matching Questions

___ 1. Used to measure fetal heartbeat and uterine contractions
___ 2. Discharge of the cervical mucus plug
___ 3. When the baby's feet or buttocks are delivered first
___ 4. Childbirth without anesthetics
___ 5. The last part of the first stage of labor
___ 6. A drug which intensifies labor
___ 7. Lack of oxygen
___ 8. Describes the father's involvement with their newborns
___ 9. Movement of fetus into the head-down position
___ 10. A surgical enlargement of the vaginal opening
___ 11. Involves relaxation and light massage
___ 12. When the baby is crosswise in the uterus
___ 13. 25 percent of all U.S. babies are delivered using this technique

a. engagement
b. Lamaze method
c. episiotomy
d. transition
e. bloody show
f. transverse presentation
g. contractions
h. prepared childbirth
i. pitocin
j. engrossment
k. anoxia
l. caesarean delivery
m. breech birth
n. fetal monitor

___ 14. Given at 10 days to evaluate arousal, responsiveness, and reflexes
___ 15. Protective coating around the newborn
___ 16. Palmar, Moro, and Stepping are examples
___ 17. Ability to focus the eyes on a single object
___ 18. Given at 1 and 5 minutes to evaluate infant distress
___ 19. Tendency to shift from calmness to crying, for example
___ 20. Varying levels of energy, attention, and activity
___ 21. A skill present at birth, lost at age 2 or 3 months, and regained around 4 months

a. states of arousal
b. Apgar test
c. Brazelton Newborn Behavioral Assessment Scale
d. binocular convergence
e. reflex
f. state control
g. vernix
h. visual acuity
i. sound localization

___ 22. Involves watching and imitating
___ 23. Corresponds to the 35th week of pregnancy
___ 24. Helps maintain body temperature
___ 25. Prematurity or low birth weight define this
___ 26. Also called hyaline membrane disease
___ 27. A change in behavior resulting from experience
___ 28. Branch of medicine focusing on newborns
___ 29. Failure to produce this causes respiratory distress

a. learning
b. pulmonary surfactant
c. high-risk infants
d. neonatology
e. low birth weight
f. respiratory distress syndrome
g. observational learning
h. premature baby
i. incubator
j. classical conditioning

B. Multiple Choice

Factual
Obj. 1
Moderate

1. Dr. Martin believes that the fear of childbirth pain produces more pain, and, therefore, she teaches her patients to relax and to understand the events of childbirth so they will be unafraid. Dr. Martin advocates the same ideas as:
   a. B.F. Skinner
   b. Fernand Lamaze
   c. Ivan Pavlov
   d. Sigmund Freud

Conceptual
Obj. 2
Moderate

2. Which of the following is not a sign that labor is about to begin?
   a. transition
   b. engagement
   c. contractions
   d. the bloody show

Applied
Obj. 3
Advanced

3. Lorraine has been in labor about 8 hours and her cervix is dilated about 7 centimeters. If hers is typical, which stage of labor is she in?
   a. early part of the first stage
   b. middle part of the first stage
   c. transition
   d. the second stage

Factual
Obj. 3
Moderate

4. An episiotomy is:
   a. a relaxation technique used in the Lamaze method of childbirth
   b. a surgical procedure used during a Caesarean section
   c. a new therapeutic technique used to treat infants with respiratory distress syndrome
   d. an incision made to widen the opening of the vagina

Applied
Obj. 4
Moderate

5. Julie's labor doesn't progress easily because her fetus is lying crosswise in the uterus. This condition is called:
   a. a transverse presentation
   b. a breech birth
   c. anoxia
   d. transition

Applied
Obj. 4
Advanced

6. Rosalyn is in labor, but her contractions are not strong enough or frequent enough for delivery to proceed as it should. Her physician would most likely:
   a. perform an episiotomy
   b. call in a neonatologist for help in diagnosing her condition
   c. administer pitocin
   d. give her an Apgar test

Factual
Obj. 4
Moderate

7. About what percent of the babies born in 1990 in the United States are delivered by Caesarean section?
   a. 1-2 percent
   b. 4-5 percent
   c. 10 percent
   d. 25 percent

38 *Birth and the Newborn*

Factual
Obj. 5
Moderate

8. The Apgar test is given to determine:
   a. how successfully the newborn responds to being born
   b. the states of arousal of a particular child
   c. the cognitive ability of the newborn
   d. the degree to which reflexes control behavior

Conceptual
Obj. 5, 7
Advanced

9. Which of the following tests is a good predictor of development in childhood?
   a. the Apgar test
   b. the Brazelton Newborn Behavioral Assessment Scale
   c. both the Apgar and the Brazelton tests
   d. neither the Apgar nor the Brazelton tests

Conceptual
Obj. 5
Moderate

10. According to the text, research studying the long-term effects of immediate physical contact between mother and baby is best summed up by saying that:
    a. this bonding enhances social development
    b. this bonding enhances cognitive development
    c. there may be some benefit to some children from early bonding
    d. it doesn't affect later development at all

Factual
Obj. 5
Basic

11. Fathers' involvement with their newborns is called:
    a. engagement
    b. transition
    c. engrossment
    d. gentle birth

Factual
Obj. 6
Moderate

12. Typically, normal babies of about what age spend the most amount of time crying?
    a. 1 week
    b. 1 month
    c. 6 months
    d. 1½ years

Applied
Obj. 6
Advanced

13. George notices that, if he gently strokes his newborn daughter's sole of her foot, she fans her toes outward and turns her foot inward. George has just discovered his daughter's:
    a. Moro reflex
    b. Babinski reflex
    c. stepping reflex
    d. placing reflex

Applied
Obj. 7
Moderate

14. Mark's son sleeps a lot and seldom cries. Larry's son sleeps very little, cries several hours a day, and is generally irritable. These two babies are quite different in their:
    a. states of arousal
    b. engrossment
    c. engagement
    d. Apgar scores

Factual
Obj. 7
Moderate

15. The Brazelton Newborn Behavioral Assessment Scale measures:
    a. physical health immediately after birth
    b. states of arousal and responsivity
    c. cognitive development
    d. the degree to which infants have bonded with their mothers

Applied
Obj. 8
Moderate

16. Doug notices that his newborn son's eyes don't appear to focus very well on objects, but rather they sometimes appear to be looking in different directions. A few weeks later, both eyes focus on objects. Doug is noticing in his son the development of:
   a. observational learning
   b. binocular convergence
   c. classical conditioning
   d. visual acuity

Factual
Obj. 11
Moderate

17. A low-birth-weight baby is defined as one who weighs less than:
   a. 7½ pounds
   b. 6½ pounds
   c. 5½ pounds
   d. 4½ pounds

Conceptual
Obj. 11
Moderate

18. If a premature baby is having breathing difficulties, these are probably due to the lack of:
   a. pitocin
   b. pulmonary surfactant
   c. vernix
   d. state control

Conceptual
Obj. 12
Moderate

19. Suppose Sarah's baby is born prematurely and weighs only 4½ pounds. At least for the first few days after birth, the most immediate and significant medical problem it will most likely face is difficulty in:
   a. breathing
   b. binocular convergence
   c. engrossment
   d. engagement

Conceptual
Obj. 12
Moderate

20. Which of the following is *not* a characteristic of a high-risk infant, as compared to a normal infant:
   a. they cry more in general
   b. their cries are more distressed
   c. they have a narrower band of arousal
   d. their sleep patterns are more regular

C. Essay Questions

INSTRUCTIONS
After reading and studying the text, read the question below and write your answer in the space provided. Do not refer to your text or to the Scoring Scheme or Model Answer on the next page.

1. Identify and describe four physical signs that indicate that labor is approaching.

Total Score ___

Scoring Scheme for Question 1

+2 points each (up to 8 points) for the correct description of any of the following signs of labor: a) engagement; b) bloody show; c) false labor; d) decreased fetal activity; e) energy spurt in the mother; f) breaking of the amniotic sac; g) uterine contractions.

Total: 8 points

Model Answer for Question 1

One sign that labor is approaching is the appearance of the **bloody show**, the appearance of blood-tinged mucus discharged from the vagina. During pregnancy, mucus seals over the opening at the cervix, but as the cervix begins to dilate with approaching labor, the mucus is dislodged, causing the rupture of some small blood vessels. This blood and mucus discharge indicates that labor will soon follow.

Another more gradual sign of impending labor is **engagement**, the final orientation of the baby in the "head down" position. Not all babies engage, however, so labor can begin before engagement occurs.

A third signal of labor involves the **breaking of the amniotic membrane** and the release of the amniotic fluid that has been surrounding the fetus. Because once this membrane is broken the fetus is unprotected from vaginal infections, if labor does not start on its own within 24 hours, it is usually induced.

A fourth sign of labor is the occurrence of rhythmic uterine **contractions**. These contractions are required to push the baby through the birth canal, and their presence indicates that labor is about to begin.

42 *Birth and the Newborn*

INSTRUCTIONS
After reading and studying the text, read the question below and write your answer in the space provided. Do not refer to your text, or to the Scoring Scheme or Model Answer on the next page.

2. At several points in this chapter, the text suggests that infant and parental behaviors influence each other and enhance the infant's chance of survival. Give two examples of this dynamic interaction pattern, and specify in each how the combined infant-parent behaviors affect the environment in which the child is raised.

Total Score ___

Scoring Scheme for Question 2

+4 points each (up to 8 points) for each clearly identified example. Examples must include either (1) the idea that parents' behavior affects infants' behavior and infants' behavior affects parents' behavior, or (2) the idea that infants are biologically prepared for certain activities or events and parents naturally respond with behaviors that maximize the infants' opportunities for developing these abilities.

Total: 8 points

Model Answer for Question 2

One example of an infant-parent interaction has to do with the sensory abilities first available to the infant. When born, the infant's eyes focus most clearly at a distance of about 6 to 13 inches, which is also the distance most parents hold their babies from their own faces. Thus, the parents allow the infant to maximize its interactions with the parent through eye contact, facial expressions and speech, and the infant responds favorably to this attention, thereby reinforcing and maintaining the parents' behavior. In similar fashion, adults make several adjustments in their speech and facial expressions when interacting with infants that match the infants' sensory abilities and preferences.

A second example has to do with variations in state of arousal preferences among babies. Some infants are simply fussier, more difficult, and more active than others from birth on, and the parent needs to adjust to the particular arousal patterns that characterize the baby. However, parents have different temperaments as well, and the match between the temperament of the parent and that of the child will influence the experience each of them has. When the fit is good, for example, when a parent expects and prefers an alert, active child that cries a lot and doesn't sleep much and his child turns out to have these characteristics, the match is good and both parent and baby benefit. If the parent is annoyed, however, by this same pattern of arousal states, he may become resentful of the infant's seemingly constant demands, and the infant's behavior is likely to become aggravated due to improper attention from the parent. Thus, a "mismatch" causes discomfort for parent and infant and probably escalates the problems they experience. Obviously, both parents and infants must be somewhat tolerant of each other, and flexibility here is probably of benefit to both parent and infant.

Chapter 4

Physical Development in Infancy

Preview of the Chapter

I. **Growth**
   A. Changes in Weight, Height, and Shape
   B. Changes in Proportion

II. **Motor Development**
   A. Developmental Trends and Principles
   B. Gaining Body Control
   C. Heredity and Environment
   D. Consequences of Motor Development

III. **Brain and Nervous System Development**
   A. Biology, Experience, and Brain Development

IV. **Physical Development and Nutrition**
   A. Breast- versus Bottle-Feeding
   B. Malnutrition: Causes and Effects
      1. Morasmus and kwashiorkor
      2. Malnutrition and cognitive and social development
   C. The Infant's Later Nutritional Needs
   D. Infant Obesity

Learning Objectives

1. Describe the physical changes that occur in the first two years of life.

2. Identify and define the principles that govern motor development.

3. Describe the process by which infants gain control of their bodies.

4. Explain the relationship between heredity and environmental influences in the process of development.

5. Identify the major events in brain and nervous system development that occur in the first two years of life, and suggest how hereditary and environmental events influence this development.

6. Describe the advantages and disadvantages of breast feeding and bottle feeding.

7. Describe the effects of malnutrition, and the consequences it has on development and suggest some remedial steps that can be taken to reduce malnutrition.

8. Describe the causes, symptoms, and consequences of marasmus and kwashiorkor.

46 *Physical Development in Infancy*

9. Discuss the nutritional needs of infants after they are weaned, and evaluate the research on infant obesity.

Chapter Summary

I. Growth
1. An average newborn weighs 7½ pounds, and growth in infancy and in puberty is very rapid in comparison to other times in the lifespan.
2. Weight gain in the first 9 months is mostly fat; after that it is mostly bone and muscle. A baby's weight triples in the first year, to 20-24 pounds, and by the end of the second year, he weighs about 30 pounds.
3. In two years, infants grow to about half their adult height: at one year they are about 20-30 inches tall and at age 2 they reach about 35 inches. After age two, growth slows down until puberty. African-American children grow somewhat faster and mature earlier than their white counterparts. Height at age 2 is predictive of adult height.
4. The **proportional phenomenon** refers to the idea that different parts of the infant's body grow at different rates. Generally growth occurs first at the head, and then proceeds downward. For example, a newborn's head comprises one-fourth of her body weight; by childhood it makes up 10 percent. Infant growth appears to occur in spurts.
5. The legs follow an opposite pattern of growth, from one-third of body length at birth to half of adult. As growth proceeds, the body's center of gravity shifts downward, making upright posture and walking easier.

II. Motor Development
1. Motor development is the increasing ability to control the body in purposeful motion. As in fetal development, motor skills develop from head to foot, a pattern called **cephalocaudal development**. Growth and control also proceed from the center of the body outward, a trend called **proximodistal development**. Another growth trend is **mass-to-specific development**, which implies the movement from large to small muscle control. **Differentiation** refers to the ability to make specific moves to specific goals, and it develops along with the maturing nervous and muscular systems.
2. Research suggests that even at 6 weeks, infants' kicking responses are coordinated in a way that resembles walking. Motor development proceeds through the exercise of **rhythmical stereotypes**, the apparently reflexive, repeated rhythmic movements that serve as transitions from more random to more controlled movements. The presence of these stereotypes suggests that certain behaviors, like crawling and walking, are "wired in" to the organism and these behaviors automatically produce the kinds of reflexive responses, like rocking, that will lead to the fully-developed behavior.
3. Motor skills do not appear suddenly, but rather appear first in rudimentary forms and in specific contexts, according to the principle of **developmental gradualness**. Gradually these early forms become more complex and wide-ranging. All infants follow the same general sequence of motor development, but the rate of development varies from infant to infant.
4. Wayne Dennis compared motor development between a group of Hopi Indian children who were restricted in infancy to cradle boards and a group who were allowed free movement. Both groups learned to walk at age 15 months, suggesting the influence of a genetic mechanism. In another study, however, Dennis discovered that Iranian babies raised in an environment of restricted visual and physical stimulation were delayed in motor development, indicating that genes alone do not influence development. Most babies, however, receive sufficient stimulation for the development of normal motor skills.

5. Other cross-cultural research has indicated that early practice can accelerate the rate of motor development, but too much stimulation can be counterproductive. Thus, heredity sets the sequence of motor development, but its expression in each infant is influenced by experience.
6. New motor skills, like sitting up, enlarge the baby's experience with the world and alter his social relationships with parents and others as well. For example, **haptic perception**, the ability to acquire information about objects by handling them, is enhanced when the infant can sit up and it, in turn, enhances the infant's knowledge of the world. Thus, motor skill development affects how the infant is treated; a busy, curious baby may cause an anxious mother more trouble. This treatment, in turn, influences the baby's subsequent development. Thus, infants influence their own development since their new motor skills affect the way others respond to them.

III. Brain and Nervous System Development

1. All motor skill development is influenced by the **nervous system**, which includes the brain, the spinal cord, and the nerves. All control is exercised through electrochemical impulses that pass through **neurons**, or nerve cells, and jump across the tiny spaces between neurons, called **synapses**.
2. The brain is composed of about 10 billion neurons. Its last part to develop is the outermost area, the **cerebral cortex**, which is not fully developed until adolescence. The cortex contains the areas of the brain responsible for motor behavior, sensory skills and higher-order cognitive functions.
3. From birth on, the number of connections among neurons increases, a process called **arborization**, although the number of cells remains constant. Also, myelinization occurs, in which a fatty sheath, called **myelin**, develops around neurons to insulate them and speed neural conduction. The voluntary control which begins emerging at 3 months of age is possible due to this arborization and myelinization.
4. Although genes determine the timing of changes within the brain, normal development is also based on adequate sensory experience and nutrition. For example, the right side of the brain develops faster than the left, perhaps because frequently used functions are located there. When damage occurs to a young brain, sometimes other brain tissue can substitute for the part damaged and lost functions can be recovered if the loss is not too severe. Sensory deprivation can hinder development, but most infants get the stimulation they need from normal experiences and do not need special experiences for normal development to occur.

IV. Physical Development and Nutrition

1. The study of nutrition provides a clear case in which to examine the interaction of heredity and environment. A child inherits a genetic potential for height, for example, but this potential includes a range within which the person's height can develop: the maximum will be achieved under ideal environmental conditions, the minimum under conditions of extreme deprivation.
2. Sometimes it is possible to compensate for short-term deprivation. For example, the growth of children who live under temporary near-famine conditions may slow down, but when conditions are restored to normal, they may experience a growth spurt and catch up with their never-deprived peers. Infancy is a critical time with respect to nutrition, since infants require twice the calories and three times the protein per pound as does an adult.
3. In 1971, 75 percent of U.S. babies were fed formula, mostly due to its convenience and dependability. Formula provides adequate nutrition if it is used properly. However, American opinion and practice has since swung back to breast-feeding, reversing the trend of two decades ago. Advantages of feeding breast milk include: it is sterile and of comfortable temperature; it is digested more easily and with fewer allergic reactions; its iron and other nutrients are more readily absorbed, it has more sugar and prevents constipation; it contains

antibodies to prevent minor infections; and, its nutrients are balanced to promote brain growth and myelinization. Breast-feeding is, though, less frequent among poor and minority women.

4. In the U.S., about one-fourth of all children under 6, and one-half of such black children, grow up in poverty, and are therefore at risk for malnutrition and several other problems. Malnutrition in infancy produces a slower rate of brain cell growth and reduces the number of brain cells that develop. Malnutrition in infancy has become more problematic as women in underdeveloped countries were encouraged to stop breast-feeding in favor of giving their infants formula. Unfortunately, formula was often over-diluted or mixed with contaminated water, producing malnutrition and health risks for the children.

5. **Marasmus** is a disease affecting infants under one year and is caused by insufficient and often contaminated food supplies. Its symptoms include zero weight gain or weight loss, emaciated appearance, diarrhea, and anemia. **Kwashiorkor** tends to affect children who are weaned at age 2 or 3 but who are not provided a nutritional substitute for the breast milk. Swollen stomachs, deteriorated muscles, and several other symptoms accompany this disease. Of course, the major cause of these diseases is poverty.

6. In 1972, Congress enacted the WIC (Women, Infants, and Children) program, which provides supplemental nutritional foods to these groups. The WIC program seems to be effective: birth weights have increased probably due to longer terms of pregnancy, and infants are healthier as children. Estimates suggest that every $1 spent on WIC saves $3 in future medical costs, but only about half of all eligible infants and children are receiving these benefits.

7. Severe malnutrition affects both cognitive and social development. Malnourished children are less responsive, more irritable, more easily frustrated, less socially involved, less active, more dependent on adults, and more anxious. They are also physically smaller, and less intelligent (as measured by IQ tests); and they had more trouble with schoolwork and more behavior problems.

8. Malnourished children, in addition to getting inadequate food, often get inadequate care. One study showed that even before they became malnourished, they received less social, emotional and cognitive stimulation from their mothers. Thus, like other developmental characteristics, different environments produce a particular kind of behavior, and that behavior influences the kind of treatment the child will receive.

9. Infants begin to require food in addition to milk when they reach about 12 pounds. New foods are usually introduced one at a time, beginning with cereal and fruit, followed by vegetables and meat and eggs.

10. Whether overfeeding in infancy leads to later obesity is debated, as is the connection between infant obesity and obesity later in life. Some research indicates that breast-feeding and introducing solid foods later may reduce obesity, but these results are questioned by others. Also questioned is the evidence that overfeeding leads to production of more fat cells which remain throughout life. Genetic factors are, however, involved in determining who will be overweight.

Self Test

A. Matching Questions

___ 1. The increasing ability to control the body in purposeful motion
___ 2. Growth from the center of the body outward
___ 3. Reflexive, repetitive movements that serve as a transition from random to controlled movements
___ 4. Growth pattern from large to small muscles
___ 5. The idea that the relative proportions of body parts changes with development
___ 6. Ability to make specific, goal-directed movements
___ 7. Pattern of growth from the head downward

a. proportional phenomenon
b. proximodistal development
c. differentiation
d. cephalocaudal development
e. motor development
f. mass-to-specific development
g. rhythmical stereotypes

___ 8. Increases the numbers of connections among nerve cells
___ 9. A nerve cell
___ 10. Linked to an insufficient amount of food in the first year after birth
___ 11. Works to make neural conduction faster and more efficient
___ 12. Social program to reduce infant malnutrition
___ 13. Results from the failure to replace breast milk with an adequate diet
___ 14. Most highly evolved part of the brain

a. cerebral cortex
b. marasmus
c. kwashiorkor
d. myelin
e. WIC
f. arborization
g. neuron

B. Multiple Choice

Factual
Obj. 1
Moderate

1. At birth, the average baby weights ___ pounds; at age one he weighs ___ pounds; and at age 2 he weighs ___ pounds.
   a. 7½; 22; 30
   b. 6½; 15; 30
   c. 8; 18; 28
   d. 7½; 25; 34

Conceptual
Obj. 1
Moderate

2. Growth is slowest during which of the following stags of the lifespan?
   a. the prenatal period
   b. infancy
   c. childhood
   d. puberty

Applied
Obj. 2
Advanced

3. Bob notices that his daughter's growth seems irregular in that some body parts grow most quickly at one time and other body parts grow most quickly at other times. Bob's observation is an example of the concept called:
   a. the proportional phenomenon
   b. arborization
   c. rhythmical stereotypes
   d. cephalocaudal development

50 Physical Development in Infancy

Applied
Obj. 2
Moderate

4. Janice observes that her son learns first to move his arms, then his legs and uses his hands before his feet. Her observation points out the central characteristic of:
   a. proximodistal development
   b. cephalocaudal development
   c. rhythmical stereotypes
   d. mass-to-specific development

Applied
Obj. 2
Moderate

5. Mark notices that his son learns to use his legs before his feet, and his arms before his hands. The principle which best describes this developmental pattern is:
   a. cephalocaudal development
   b. arborization
   c. proximodistal development
   d. the proportional phenomenon

Factual
Obj. 2
Moderate

6. The ability to make specific movements toward specific goals defines the concept called:
   a. arborization
   b. cephalocaudal development
   c. the proportional phenomenon
   d. differentiation

Applied
Obj. 3
Advanced

7. Baby Lou seems to move his arms in an unintentional, reflexive fashion over and over again. Gradually, these random movements become intentional and he is soon able to reach out to touch things that interest him. This is an example of:
   a. the proportional phenomenon
   b. arborization
   c. a rhythmical stereotype
   d. proximodistal development

Conceptual
Obj. 4
Moderate

8. Wayne Dennis conducted a study in which he compared the motor development of Hopi Indian children swaddled to cradle boards to that of similar children who were allowed free movement. Dennis found that the babies whose movement was restricted walked at about ___ months of age, and the unrestricted babies walked at about ___ months of age.
   a. 18; 12
   b. 15; 10
   c. 15; 15
   d. 10; 15

Conceptual
Obj. 4
Advanced

9. According to the text, what is the most accurate conclusion regarding the use of more than the normal amount of stimulation to accelerate development?
   a. Excessive stimulation will most likely slow down the rate of development.
   b. Excessive stimulation will not affect the rate of development.
   c. Excessive stimulation can accelerate development and should therefore be attempted.
   d. Excessive stimulation can accelerate development but can be counterproductive.

Physical Development in Infancy 51

Conceptual 10. According to the text, which of the following is *not* an accurate conclusion regarding
Obj. 4   motor development?
Moderate   a. All humans follow a similar sequence in their motor development.
              b. A serious lack of stimulation can retard motor development.
              c. All infants influence their own development through their behavior.
              d. Few infants receive enough stimulation to ensure normal motor development unless their parents specifically structure their environments.

Factual   11. A synapse is:
Obj. 5   a. a space between two neurons in a neural pathway
Basic   b. a chemical involved in neural transmission
              c. the longest, thinnest part of the neuron
              d. one of the regions of the brain where problem solving occurs

Conceptual 12. During infancy, the neurons in the brain develop an increasingly elaborate set of
Obj. 5   connections with other neurons. This process is called:
Moderate   a. arborization
              b. proximodistal development
              c. myelinization
              d. the proportional phenomenon

Conceptual 13. The main effect of the development of myelin is to:
Obj. 5   a. increase the number of brain cells
Moderate   b. speed neural conduction
              c. increase the size of brain cells
              d. increase the number of connections among hair cells

Factual   14. Which of the following statements about breast milk is *not* true?
Obj. 6   a. It contains antibodies to help fight infections.
Moderate   b. It contains less sugar than formula.
              c. Its iron and nutrients are more readily absorbed than those in formula.
              d. Its nutrients are balanced to promote brain myelinization rather than muscle growth.

Factual   15. In the United States today, about what percent of children under the age of 6 grow up
Obj. 7   in poverty?
Moderate   a. 5 percent
              b. 15 percent
              c. 25 percent
              d. 40 percent

Factual   16. Which of the following conditions is *not* linked to poverty?
Obj. 7   a. slower rate of growth of brain cells
Moderate   b. lower number of brain cells
              c. obesity at age 2 due to high starch diets
              d. being underweight at birth

Factual   17. Severe malnutrition that occurs in infants less than a year old is called:
Obj. 8   a. scurvy
Basic   b. arborization
              c. kwashiorkor
              d. marasmus

Physical Development in Infancy

Applied
Obj. 8
Moderate

18. Jennifer is doing a research report on babies who suffer severe malnutrition after they are weaned from breast milk. She is studying the problem called:
    a. marasmus
    b. myelinization
    c. arborization
    d. kwashiorkor

Factual
Obj. 9
Moderate

19. Which of the following foods is most likely to be introduced as the first solid food given to a baby?
    a. eggs
    b. cereal
    c. vegetables
    d. meat or fish

Factual
Obj. 9
Moderate

20. Which of the following situations has been shown to be linked to infant obesity?
    a. bottle feeding
    b. breast feeding
    c. waiting until later in infancy to introduce solid foods
    d. having overly thin parents

C. Essay Questions

INSTRUCTIONS

After reading and studying the text, read the question below and write your answer in the space provided. Do not refer to your text or to the Scoring Scheme or Model Answer on the next page.

1. Using motor development as an example, explain how heredity and environment interact to produce a particular developmental outcome. Cite research findings to support your answer.

Total Score ___

Scoring Scheme for Question 1

+2 points for noting that developmental sequences are established through heredity.

+4 points for explaining that heredity determines a range of possible developmental outcomes, but that environmental influences will determine where in that range the behavior will occur.

+2 points for a relevant example of research supporting this conclusion (see pp. 140-142 in the text).

Total: 8 points

Model Answer for Question 1

Heredity and environment both affect motor development in infancy. One way that hereditary influences act is that they program into the developmental plan a particular sequence of developmental events which are common to all members of a species. For example, human infants all roll over before they crawl, crawl before they walk, and so forth. Furthermore, heredity establishes the upper and lower limits within which a developmental event will occur. The specific time at which the event does occur will fall somewhere in that range, however, its exact occurrence will be determined by environmental factors. If the environment is favorable, the event will occur optimally. If the environment is poor, the event may occur near the bottom of the range of possibilities.

Wayne Dennis' research on infants provides a good example of these hereditary and environmental influences. Dennis compared two groups of Indian children on the age at which they learned to walk. One group spent most of its time bound to cradle boards, which seriously limited the infants' opportunities to move. The other group was allowed to move freely at will. If environment was playing a key role in the development of walking, you would expect the more active children to walk at earlier ages, yet this was not the result. In fact, both groups of children walked at the same age.

Subsequent research, however, did show that an impoverished environment can have a debilitating effect on the development of motor skills. Again, Dennis compared two groups of children. On group was raised in what we would consider a fairly normal environment in which the infants could interact freely with the people and objects around them. Infants in the other group were left to lie in their cribs, which were surrounded with sheets that limited their ability to interact with their environment even further. They were seldom picked up or talked to, and they had limited time in which they had any human contact. Here, the children in the deprived conditions showed dramatic developmental delays in sitting up, walking, and other motor behaviors. Thus, in this situation of profound deprivation, environmental circumstances did affect the development of motor behavior.

Perhaps the best way to understand the effects of heredity and environment is to consider heredity to set the limits on the developmental events in question, and to view environment as the determinant of where, within those limits, the actual development will occur.

INSTRUCTIONS

After reading and studying the text, read the question below and write your answer in the space provided. Do not refer to your text, or to the Scoring Scheme or Model Answer on the next page.

2. Describe two major biological changes that occur in the brain during infancy, and suggest how, in general, sensory experiences and nutrition affect the development in infancy of the brain.

Total Score ___

Scoring Scheme for Question 2

+4 points for correctly describing the process of arborization (the name need not be mentioned).

+4 points for correctly describing the process of myelinization (the name need not be mentioned).

+4 points for the idea that sensory or nutritional deprivation can interfere with normal brain development and limit arborization and myelinization.

Total: 12 points

Model Answer for Question 2

Biology affects the development in infancy of the brain in several ways. First, during the period of infancy, the connections among the 10 billion neurons of the brain increase. This process is called **arborization**, and occurs most in the cerebral cortex, the part of the brain most responsible for thinking and sensory and motor functions. The second major development in infancy is the manufacture of **myelin**, a fatty substance that surrounds and insulates neurons and increases the speed and efficiency of neural conduction.

Sensory experiences and nutrition influence the development of the brain in that, if the infant is deficient in them, arborization and myelinization are limited. Thus, infants deprived of adequate experiences or of adequate nutrition may not, if the effects are severe enough, develop a normal brain structure.

Chapter 5

Cognitive and Language Development in Infancy

Preview of the Chapter

I. **Attention, Perception, and Memory**
   A. Attention
   B. Perception
      1. Color Perception
      2. Face Perception
      3. Perception and social and emotional growth
   C. Cross-model Transfer

II. **Cognitive Development: Piaget and Beyond**
   A. Sensorimotor Intelligence
   B. A New Look at Piaget
      1. The 3-month transition: From reflex to accidental discovery
      2. The 8-month transition: From accidental discover to intentional behavior
      3. The 12-month transition: From intentional behavior to systematic exploration
      4. The 18-month transition: From sensorimotor functioning to symbolic thinking
   C. Complete Object Permanence

III. **Language Development**
   A. Prelinguistic Communication
   B. Early Sounds
   C. The First Words
   D. Two-word Sentences
   E. Individual Differences in Language Development
      1. The role of experience
      2. Cultural and socioeconomic differences in parents' speech to infants
      3. The role of health and genetics
   F. Talking to Infants Effectively: Motherese and Expansion

IV. **Assessing Infant Development**
   A. Gesell Development Schedules
   B. The Bayley Scales
   C. The Value of Infant Tests
   D. Infant Tests and Beyond: Predicting Later Development

Learning Objectives

1. Describe the development of attention in infancy.

2. Describe the development of perception in infancy, paying special attention to color perception and face perception.

58 *Cognitive and Language Development in Infancy*

3. Discuss the development of cross-modal transfer and memory.

4. Explain the basis of Piaget's theory of development, focusing on the sensorimotor stage.

5. Discuss the transitions in development that occur at the ages of 3, 8, 12, and 18 months.

6. Define the concept of object permanence and explain how it develops.

7. Identify and explain the characteristics of prelinguistic communication.

8. Describe the acquisition of first words and two-word sentences.

9. Evaluate the roles of experience, social and economic conditions, and health and genetics in the development of language.

10. Describe how mothers talk to their infants and explain how these patterns influence the baby's language learning.

11. Describe the tests which are used to assess infant development and evaluate their usefulness.

Chapter Summary

I. Attention, Perception, and Memory

1. **Representation thinking**, the ability to use one object to stand for or symbolize, another, is a major turning point in the development of cognitive abilities. Transitions in the growth of cognitive and linguistic skills occur at about 3, 8, 12, and 18 months of age.
2. In the first 2 months, newborns like familiarity, but by 2 months they can process more information and they prefer novelty, as long as the new experience doesn't overwhelm them. Thus, they seek an optimal, or intermediate, level of novelty—a balance between the familiar and unfamiliar. Infants also seek an optimal level of **complexity**, which refers to the number of intricacy of traits like color of pattern in a stimulus, in the objects with which they interact.
3. These conclusions are based on research that measures how long infants look at objects of varying levels of familiarity and complexity. Since they spend more time looking at objects intermediate in these dimensions, researchers conclude that they prefer objects of intermediate familiarity and complexity.
4. Lev Vygotsky argues that children's intellectual development advances when they are stimulated through interactions with people more capable than they are, a notion he calls the **zone of proximal development**. Children whose parents respond to them by interacting and stretching their base of knowledge grow up to be more competent intellectually.
5. From birth, infants prefer color, and by 3 months, they stare longest at red, yellow, green, and blue. After 3 months, they make finer distinctions, and by 4 months, they can perceive both similarities and differences between colors. This ability to sort colors or other stimuli into categories of similar objects is called **equivalence**, and its development assists the infant understand the world around them.
6. The loss of interest in a stimulus is called **habituation**, and its opposite, called **dishabituation**, occurs when a new stimulus excited a baby's attention. Perceptual studies in infants use these two principles. When a picture is presented, researchers record how long the infant stares at it. By comparing responses to pictures of different levels of novelty or complexity, researchers can determine what kind of stimuli infants prefer.

7. During their first 3 months, infants stare mostly at the borders of a face. At 3 months, they become more interested in the eyes. At 4 months, infants begin to prefer pictures of whole faces to those of isolated features and prefer normal-looking faces to those with scrambled or unattractive features. This shift illustrates a major principle in perceptual development: Perception has moved from the part to the whole. In the next two months, infants will learn to discriminate among different faces and recognize familiar faces.
8. New perceptual abilities make possible **social referencing**, which is the process of looking to someone else to find an emotional response for oneself. Infants often observe their mother's reaction in novel situations and respond in the same way she does.
9. Piaget believed that information from the different senses is processed separately by the infant and that only after much experience is the baby able to integrate information from different sensory channels. Now, however, researchers have found evidence that these **cross-modal abilities**, which involve the transfer of data from one sensory system to another, are present almost from birth.
10. During that first year, infants habituate faster and faster to a familiar stimulus, indicating faster and more efficient memory processes. Long-term memory seems to be functioning to some degree by 6 months of age. However, most adults cannot remember any events from infancy, perhaps because these memories are buried as a result of neural reorganization of the brain.

II. Cognitive Development: Piaget and Beyond

1. Jean Piaget was a Swiss psychologist who believed that biology and experience work together in cognitive development and that all humans go through a series of distinct stages of cognitive development that unfold naturally as the person interacts with the environment.
2. The first two years of life form the first of Piaget's stages of development, the **sensorimotor** stage, which is based on the senses and motor actions. As they move through the sensorimotor stage, infants gain three basic cognitive abilities: **decentration**, the understanding that they are separate from their surroundings, **intentionality**, the ability to plan and coordinate their actions, and **object permanence**, the understanding that things exist even when they can't be seen or sensed.
3. Piaget divided the sensorimotor stage into six substages which occur in the same sequence in every child although children spend differing amounts of time in each substage. Each stage lays the foundation for the next, but the earlier skills are incorporated into later stages and are retained for future use if they are needed.
4. A new proposal suggests that sensorimotor development progresses through four substages, occurring at 3, 8, 12, and 18 months, and corresponding to changes in the brain.
5. For the first month after birth, infants' behavior is governed by reflexes. As these reflexes begin to be modified to match experiences marks the beginning of sensorimotor intelligence. The next step occurs at about 3 months with the discovery of **circular reactions**, the intentional repetition of an action. The first circular reactions, called **primary circular reactions**, center around the infant's body and first occur by accident. They signal the earliest awareness of cause-and-effect, and form the foundations for later development.
6. From 6 to 12 months, the infant's patterns of repetition include objects as well as parts of her own body, and these are called **secondary circular reactions**. The emergence of secondary circular reactions marks the start of decentration, a key achievement of infancy. **Intentional behavior**, or learning that one's own actions cause separate results, is acquired toward the end of the first year.
7. By about 8 months, babies begin to acquire object permanence, which develops gradually in the second half of the first year.
8. The 12-month transition is marked by active, purposeful, trial-and-error exploration. Whereas in the first year, the infant's discoveries occurred by accident, in the next 6 months, she

actively seeks out situations in which to explore. Increasing object permanence aids this experimentation.
9. The 18-month shift is from infant intelligence to symbolic thinking, the ability to represent things mentally. This ability, called **representation thinking**, involves the mental manipulation of images, or symbols, and makes mental experiments, called **mental combinations**, possible. **Deferred imitation**, the duplication of behavior seen earlier, becomes possible as memory skills grow.
10. Children who can think symbolically can solve the most advanced object permanence problem, in which an object in the hand is hidden and then the empty hand is moved to other locations. By 24 months, children can find the object, even if they must search several locations, indicating that they know it exists somewhere and that object permanence is complete.

III. Language Development

1. **Prelinguistic communication** includes all the means by which parents communicate with their babies before language develops. Many of these prelinguistic games and gestures involve **turn-taking**, in which the parent and infant take turns in responding to each other's behavior. This turn-taking, especially if the parent responds to the infant as if his actions had meaning, fosters the development of intention, or purposefulness, in the baby's use of language.
2. Regardless of the parents' language, all babies make the same sounds at about the same age, and the sounds they make occur in the same order, for example, lip sounds ("p" or "b") before tongue sounds ("d" or "n"). Even babies of deaf parents follow this same pattern, which suggests that these early sounds are biologically programmed. By 2 or 3 months, infants begin cooing, or repeating the same vowel sound. By 5 months, they add consonants producing a pre-speech pattern called **babbling**.
3. By 15 months, the typical infant has mastered about 10 words, and by age two, have a vocabulary of about 200 words. However, language comprehension, or understanding, precedes language production, or talking, so children can understand more complicated language than they themselves can produce.
4. First words are likely to be names of familiar or important things, and English-speaking babies usually say nouns, verbs, and pronouns before adjectives, adverbs, and other modifiers. Early on, babies' speech is characterized by **underextension**, the use of a general word like "truck" to represent a narrowly defined object like "my favorite red truck.' Later, children's language is characterized by the opposite process, **overextension**, in which a word is used too broadly. Also, early speech is often composed of **holophrases**, in which a single word stands for a more complicated whole thought.
5. Most children start using two-word sentences by 24 months and the structure of these sentences follows the same general pattern as does adult language. Language is now a **symbolic system**, meaning that it represents and labels elements of the world and their interrelations. Two-word sentences tend to belong to one of five standard categories: recurrence ("More juice."), attribution ("Big dog."), possessive ("Dada hat."), action agent ("Barbara cry."), or action object ("Throw rattle.").
6. There is considerable individual variation in the age at, and the way in, which children learn language. Some children even use **compressed sentences**, in which several words are slurred together, before they use single words. Research shows that early talkers tend to have mothers who accepted their early speech as meaningful.
7. This research conducted by Katherine Nelson also suggests that there are two styles of language learning in young children. The first words of **referential** children are usually names of objects rather than people. The early words of **expressive** children expressed something about their involvement with people. The vocabulary of expressive children grows at a slow and steady rate, whereas referential children start slowly and then speed up. Both groups acquire their first 50 words by the same age, but at age two and one-half, referential children

Cognitive and Language Development in Infancy **61**

have larger vocabularies and expressive children have more facility informing two-word combinations. Referential children tend to be first-borns in middle-class homes and have mothers who frequently label things and events. Expressive children tend to be later-borns with less-educated parents who speak to them conversationally. Also, children who were more linguistically advanced at age 3 also had a more secure emotional bond to their mother at age 1.

8. Across cultures, mother-infant interactions involve mothers' response to their babies' content vocalizations with imitation but respond to distressed vocalization with nurturance. However, there are some differences in how mothers from various cultures interact verbally with their infants. Also, parents from higher social classes generally are more verbally responsive and stimulating with their infants. Across cultures and socioeconomic groups, though, infant cognitive and language development is facilitated by responsive, verbally stimulating interaction.

9. Frequent ear infections in infancy have been linked to speech delays between ages 2 and 3 since the infection interferes with hearing and understanding speech sounds. Another study which demonstrated the effect of experience on language learning showed that adoptive mothers who were more responsive to their infant's vocalizations raised more linguistically skilled babies. Genetic factors, however, also play a role in language acquisition.

10. Regardless of style, most mothers and other adults speak to their babies in **motherese**, a style of speaking that is slow and high pitched and uses exaggerated intonation. Sentences are short, well-formed, and grammatically simple, and tend to hold infants' attention. Motherese seems to be used in all languages, and infants prefer it to other forms of speech. Motherese reinforces language learning by exaggerating the differences between sounds and by expanding and elaborating on things the infant has said, a technique called expansion.

IV. Assessing Infant Development

1. The **Gesell Development Schedules** provide standardized observational procedures for evaluating a child's development from 1 month to 6 years. The Gesell Schedules were developed to provide normative information about average rates of development in four areas: motor (e.g., movement), adaptation (e.g., alertness), language (e.g., vocalization), and personal-social behavior (e.g., feeding).

2. The **Bayley Scales** focus on two areas of development, the mental scale which measures cognitive abilities like perception, learning, and language, and the motor scale, which assess fine and gross motor capacities and coordination. Infants are given two scores, the Mental Development Index (MDI) and the Psychomotor Development Index (PDI) which are compared to scores of infants of the same age. The average score, called a **developmental quotient** or **DQ**, is 100, so advanced children have scores higher than 100 whereas children who are slower to develop would score lower than 100.

3. Infant tests are used for two purposes: assessing development at the time of the test and predicting the infant's future functioning. Except in cases of neurological impairment, the tests are better at assessing that predicting.

4. New tests of an infant's **visual recognition memory** (how he remembers things he's seen) can be given as early as 2 months and are strongly predictive of intelligence test scores later in childhood. Apparently, the ability to discriminate those things which have been seen before is a very basic cognitive processing ability and underlies later cognitive development. The value of early prediction is that it can signal the need for early intervention to the extent that experience can influence cognitive development.

Self Test

A. Matching Questions

___ 1. Adaptation to an unchanging stimulus
___ 2. Recognition that similar stimuli belong to the same category
___ 3. Involves the transfer of data from one sensory system to other sensory systems
___ 4. The number and intricacy of traits in a stimulus
___ 5. Reaction to a new stimulus
___ 6. The interpretation of sensations

a. perception
b. dishabituation
c. cross-modal abilities
d. habituation
e. equivalence
f. complexity

___ 7. Knowing that something exists even if it can't be sensed
___ 8. For example, kicking the legs to make a mobile move
___ 9. Going to the drawer, taking a spoon, going to the refrigerator, and getting some yogurt, as an example
___ 10. Development away from focusing on one's physical self
___ 11. Duplication of behavior seen or performed earlier
___ 12. Repetition of an action that originally occurred by chance
___ 13. Purposeful coordination of activity toward a goal
___ 14. Involves the mental manipulation of symbols and marks the end of the sensorimotor period
___ 15. The first of Piaget's stages of development
___ 16. Behavior that is goal-directed

a. decentration
b. secondary circular reaction
c. object permanence
d. deferred imitation
e. primary circular reaction
f. sensorimotor
g. intentional behavior
h. intentionality
i. mental combinations
j. representational thinking

___ 17. Phrase made up of several words slurred together into one
___ 18. Oo-oo-oo-oo-oo, for example
___ 19. Yields a Mental and a Psychomotor Development Index.
___ 20. Too restrictive a use of words
___ 21. Score on the Bayley Scales based on scores of children of the same age
___ 22. Conversational give-and-take
___ 23. Using "dog" to describe all medium-sized, four-footed, furry animals, for example
___ 24. "Here, let Mommy help you," for example
___ 25. The best predictor of later IQ
___ 26. Ba-ba-ba-ba-ba, for example
___ 27. Using "mine!" to mean "That is mine. Don't touch it!", for example
___ 28. Examples include games, gestures, sounds, and facial expressions

a. underextension
b. turn-taking
c. symbolic system
d. visual recognition memory
e. holophrase
f. Gesell Development Schedules
g. babbling
h. compressed sentences
i. developmental quotient
j. prelinguistic communication
k. motherese
l. overextension
m. cooing
n. Bayley Scales

B. Multiple Choice

Conceptual
Obj. 1
Advanced

1. During the first two months, newborns prefer to look at things that are ___ familiar. At six months, they prefer to look at things that are ___ familiar.
   a. not at all; very
   b. moderately; very
   c. very; moderately
   d. very; not at all

Applied
Obj. 2
Moderate

2. Bill is showing baseball cards to his son, one at a time. At first the boy pays attention to each new card, but after a while, he gets bored and is no longer interested in this game. The son's boredom represents the concept called:
   a. habituation
   b. equivalence
   c. turn-taking
   d. overextension

Applied
Obj. 2
Moderate

3. Dr. Spear is showing slides of different colors to 4-month-old babies. She finds that most babies respond differently to red and blue and become excited when they see a new color. Her research shows that these babies have acquired the concept called:
   a. dishabituation
   b. intentionality
   c. equivalence
   d. habituation

Applied
Obj. 2
Moderate

4. Mike falls down and looks at his mother to see if she is upset. If she is, he'll cry; if not, he'll get up and start playing again. Mike's behavior is an example of:
   a. habituation
   b. object permanence
   c. deferred imitation
   d. social referencing

Applied
Obj. 3
Advanced

5. Suppose you conducted an experiment in which you showed infants two films, one of a man mowing the lawn, and one of a man listening to the radio. Generalizing from an experiment described in the text, you would expect the infants to look longest at the lawn-mowing film if they heard the ___ sound track with it; and longest at the radio-listening film if they heard the ___ sound track with it.
   a. radio-listening; lawn-mowing
   b. lawn-mowing; radio-listening
   c. radio-listening; radio-listening
   d. lawn-mowing; lawn-mowing

Factual
Obj. 4
Moderate

6. According to Piaget, which of the following is *not* one of the three basic cognitive abilities acquired in the sensorimotor stage?
   a. perception
   b. decentration
   c. object permanence
   d. intentionality

64 *Cognitive and Language Development in Infancy*

Conceptual
Obj. 4
Moderate

7. Babies tend to spend all of their time focused on their own bodies and how they interact with other things. Older children are able to focus on events apart from themselves. This change is an example of:
   a. intentionality
   b. object permanence
   c. cross-modal abilities
   d. decentration

Applied
Obj. 5
Advanced

8. Baby Jeff gets excited and moves his arms. When he sees his hand, he is fascinated and so he moves his arms again and again, trying to gain other looks at his hand. Jeff's behavior is best thought of as an example of:
   a. habituation
   b. a primary circular reaction
   c. a secondary circular reaction
   d. turn-taking

Factual
Obj. 5
Moderate

9. Repetitions of actions that trigger responses in the external environment are called:
   a. cross-modal abilities
   b. primary circular reactions
   c. secondary circular reactions
   d. overextensions

Conceptual
Obj. 6
Advanced

10. Susan is interested in a rattle held by her father. As she reaches for it, her father moves it under a piece of paper, and, as soon as he does so, Susan acts as if the rattle never existed. If Susan's behavior is typical of children her age, how old would she be?
    a. 5 months
    b. 8 months
    c. 15 months
    d. 20 months

Factual
Obj. 5
Moderate

11. The mental manipulation of images or symbols is called:
    a. a mental combination
    b. representational thought
    c. visual recognition memory
    d. object permanence

Applied
Obj. 5
Moderate

12. Chris sees a movie that shows two witches mixing up a magic potion. Two days later, Chris' mother overhears him playing in the kitchen and asks him what he is doing. He says, "I'm making a magic potion and I'm a witch!" This is best thought of as an example of:
    a. deferred imitation
    b. object permanence
    c. a secondary circular reaction
    d. overextension

Factual
Obj. 6
Basic

13. The development of object permanence is completed at about what age?
    a. 12 months
    b. 18 months
    c. 2 years
    d. 6 years

Cognitive and Language Development in Infancy 65

Applied
Obj. 7
Basic

14. John's baby is starting to make sounds like "ba-ba-ba-ba-ba" and "goo-goo-goo." These sounds are an example of:
    a. underextension
    b. motherese
    c. babbling
    d. cooing

Conceptual
Obj. 8
Moderate

15. The development of which of the following most clearly indicates that a baby is forming mental categories and classifying events which belong to them?
    a. underextension
    b. overextension
    c. holophrases
    d. motherese

Factual
Obj. 8
Basic

16. The use of a single word that stands for a whole thought is called:
    a. underextension
    b. habituation
    c. object permanence
    d. a holophrase

Conceptual
Obj. 9
Advanced

17. In comparison to referential children, which of the following characteristics is typically associated with expressive children?
    a. Their first words usually refer to their involvement with people.
    b. Their acquisition of language starts slowly and then speeds up.
    c. They have larger vocabularies at age two and one-half.
    d. They tend to be first-borns.

Conceptual
Obj. 9
Moderate

18. Infants all learn to talk at about the same time, yet the specific words they learn depend on the kind of language to which they are exposed. The first part of this statement points out the role of ___; the last part emphasizes the role of ___.
    a. overextension; underextension
    b. underextension; overextension
    c. environment; heredity
    d. heredity; environment

Factual
Obj. 11
Moderate

19. The two scores given on the Bayley Scales correspond to:
    a. personal and social development
    b. intelligence and creativity
    c. behavior that is predictive of social problems and behavior that is predictive of emotional problems
    d. mental and psychomotor development

Conceptual
Obj. 11
Moderate

20. According to the text, a measure of which of the following characteristics would be the best predictor of intelligence later in life?
    a. how well babies can remember what they have already seen
    b. the age at which they acquire object permanence
    c. the size of their vocabulary at age two
    d. the age at which they begin using two-word sentences

C. Essay Questions

INSTRUCTIONS
After reading and studying the text, read the question below and write your answer in the space provided. Do not refer to your text or to the Scoring Scheme or Model Answer on the next page.

1. Define the concept of object permanence and describe the manner in which the infant acquires this concept. In your answer, be sure to identify and give an example of the behavior typical of a 4-month-old, a typical 8-month-old, a typical 16-month-old, and a typical 2-year-old.

Total Score ___

Scoring Scheme for Question 1

+2 points for a correct definition of object permanence.

+2 points each (up to 8 points) for a correct explanation of object permanence at each of the four ages. To be correct, the answers must include:
   a. at 4-months: the idea that the baby will not search when the object is hidden
   b. at 8-months: the idea that the baby will search if part of an object can be seen **or** the idea that the baby will keep looking at the place where the object disappeared
   c. at 16-months: the idea that the baby will look behind objects if she sees the object moved there.
   d. at 24-months: the idea that the baby understands that objects exist even when they can't be sensed.

+1 point each (up to 4 points) for an accurate example for each of the four ages.

Total: 14 points

Model Answer for Question 1

Object permanence is the understanding that objects exist separate from one's perception of them. The typical 4-month-old has no concept of object permanence. For example, a baby of this age might start reaching out for a rattle you held in your hand, but if you moved your hand behind a pillow, the baby would stop reaching, because she would no longer be able to hold in her memory the idea that the rattle could still exist if she couldn't see it.

At 8 months, if you hide an object, the baby will look at the spot where it disappeared. But, in the example given above, he will not reach behind the pillow to get the rattle unless he can see a little part of it sticking out. At this age, then, the baby is beginning to develop an idea that objects exist apart from his experience, but he has not yet really grasped this idea.

At 16 months, the baby understands that objects are separate from the things that happen to them. Now, if the rattle is placed behind a pillow, the baby will reach behind the pillow or push it away in order to find the hidden rattle. Object permanence is limited, however, at this age in that the infant must see the rattle being moved to its position, but as long as the rattle is seen, the baby can follow it, even if it is moved more than once.

At 2 years, children can solve the most advanced object permanence problems and can follow the movement of an object even if it is hidden from their view. For example, if a coin is hidden in the hand, the hand is moved behind a series of three pillows, and then the empty hand is shown to the child, she will search for the coin behind the three pillows. Thus, by age two, the child has learned that objects exist, even if they can't be sensed. They can now represent objects mentally.

Cognitive and Language Development in Infancy

INSTRUCTIONS
After reading and studying the text, read the question below and write your answer in the space provided. Do not refer to your text, or to the Scoring Scheme or Model Answer on the next page.

2. Cite two pieces of evidence that support the idea that language is influenced by heredity. Cite two pieces of evidence that the environment plays a role in language learning.

Total Score ___

Scoring Scheme for Question 2

Evidence for Hereditary Influences:

+3 points each (up to 6 points) for answers which include such points as:
   a. All humans learn language in the same steps in the same sequence.
   b. All humans learn language at the same time.
   c. All normal babies babble the same sounds, regardless of the language of their parents.
   d. Even babies of deaf parents babble the same way as other babies.

Evidence of Environmental Influences:

+3 points each (up to 6 points) for answers which include such points as:
   a. Children learn the particular language they hear, not one they've never heard spoken.
   b. The way mothers talk to infants affects the babies' language development (specific examples can be given and can count as separate pieces of evidence).
   c. Mothers in different cultures use language differently with their children.
   d. Children have different patterns of language development depending on the social class of their parents.

Total: 12 points

Model Answer for Question 2

Language learning is influenced by both heredity and environment. The fact that all children learn language in essentially the same sequence of steps, even though they are raised in widely varying environments, is strong evidence that we inherit the predisposition to learn to talk. Also, the fact that all normal humans learn language at the same time suggests that linguistic ability is a genetically programmed human characteristic.

Yet, the environment does have an effect on language learning. After all, humans speak hundreds of different languages and children learn the one which is spoken in their environment. Also, research has shown that the way that mothers talk to their children makes a difference in the way language is learned. For example, mothers who accept their children's early speech as meaningful are more likely to have children who talk early, thus suggesting that environment plays a role in language learning. Similarly, the kinds of words first learned by children and the speed at which they are learned seem to depend on environmental variables, such as how the mother speaks to them, their position in the family, and their social class background. Thus, environment, too, seems to play a role in language learning.

Chapter 6

Social and Emotional Development in Infancy

Preview of the Chapter

- **I. Infant Temperament**
  - A. Dimensions of Temperament
    1. Three Types of Babies
  - B. Temperament, Heredity, and Malleability
  - C. Temperament and Development
    1. The evocative effects of temperament, or how babies affect their own treatment
    2. Choosing their own activities
  - D. Goodness of Fit

- **II. Landmarks in Social and Emotional Development**
  - A. Changes in Emotional Expression
  - B. Smiling and Laughing
    1. Where do smiling and laughter come from?
  - C. Stranger Wariness
  - D. Separation Protest

- **III. Attachment Relationships**
  - A. Defining the Attachment Relationship
  - B. Theories of Attachment
    1. Attachment and exploration: The "secure base"
  - C. Differences in Attachment
    1. The strange situation
  - D. Explaining Differences in Attachment
  - E. Consequences of Infant-Mother Attachment
    1. A foundation of security or insecurity
  - F. A Long View: Attachment Relationships Over the Life Span
  - G. The Infant-Father Relationship

- **IV. Relations with Peers**
  - A. Differences in Sociability with Peers

- **V. Learning to Say "I": The Emerging Self**
  - A. Growing Toward Independence: Autonomy and the "Terrible Twos"
    1. Embarrassment, pride, and shame
    2. Autonomy and toilet training

Social and Emotional Development in Infancy

Learning Objectives

1. Define the concept of temperament and explain its dimensions according to the work of Chess and Thomas.

2. Discuss the influences of heredity and environment on the development of temperament.

3. Describe the development of emotions during infancy.

4. Define the concepts of stranger wariness and separation protest and explain the factors that influence their development.

5. Define the attachment relationship and describe the various theories that explain it.

6. Explain the different patterns of attachment and discuss their causes and consequences.

7. Describe how early attachments affect behavior at later stages of development.

8. Compare the father-infant relationship to the mother-infant relationship.

9. Discuss the development of sociability in infancy and suggest why individual differences in social behavior exist.

10. Describe the development of the self-concept in infancy, paying special attention to the views of Margaret Mahler and Erik Erikson.

Chapter Summary

I. **Temperament**
   1. **Temperament** is the unique, inborn pattern of responsiveness and mood which characterizes each of us. **Personality**, on the other hand, is the combination of behavior and response patterns that are developed through experience. Because they haven't had much experience, newborns don't have much personality, but they do have temperaments, which vary considerably from one infant to another.
   2. Stella Chess and Alexander Thomas have studied longitudinally a group of 140 children from infancy through adolescence. Their findings, published in the **New York Longitudinal Study (NYLS)**, involved the rating of these children on dimensions of infant temperament, which have now been reduced to three: emotionality, activity level, and sociability.
   3. All children possess these three central traits in varying degrees. The **difficult child's** temperament is best characterized by negative emotionality, and they cry a lot, are easily distracted, are fearful of new things, have irregular schedules, and are active. They also may be low in sociability. The **easy child** has little negative emotionality and high sociability, and is calm, predictable, adaptable. Easy children also have regular schedules and approach rather than are upset by new experiences. Children who are described as **slow-to-warm-up** are distressed by new things but will adapt if given time, and their reactions tend not to be intense. About 40 percent of the babies in the Chess and Thomas study were classified as easy, about 10 percent were difficult, and about 15 percent were slow-to-warm-up. The concept of infant temperament should help parents understand that much of their infant's disposition results from hereditary programming and that they should not feel responsible for difficult behavior in their

child. Instead, parents should focus on adapting their own styles to the temperaments of their children.
4. Studies suggest that temperament is inherited, especially those traits of activity level, sociability, attention span, fearfulness, and fussiness. However, experience moderates and shapes temperament, and can have a substantial impact on how a child develops.
5. Temperament affects development in two ways: It influences the responses babies evoke, or cause, from others, and through the activities they choose for themselves.
6. Infant temperament and parental characteristics interact, or influence each other, in the process of development. The term **goodness-of-fit** refers to how well the parents' expectations and responses match the temperament of the baby. Although temperament strongly influences development, it does not determine development, since so many other factors enter in.

II. Landmarks in Social and Emotional Development
1. All humans, regardless of culture, recognize certain sets of facial characteristics as representing particular emotions. Some psychologists accept this universality of emotional expression as evidence of their inborn nature. However, knowing whether an infant's expression is accompanied by an adult-like emotional experience is difficult to know. Researchers have found that the facial expressions for distress, disgust, and interest are present in the newborn, and that by 3 months joy, sadness, and anger appear.
2. Newborns make responses that look like smiles, but **social smiles**, which reflect feelings of pleasure, don't develop until 6 to 9 weeks of age. By 4 months, babies smile selectively and begin to laugh. Social smiling is a biologically-timed event, appearing at a particular gestational age, or age since conception rather than birth, and being present in blind babies who could not benefit from imitation. However, social reinforcement can increase the frequency of smiling, and unstimulating, institutional environments can delay the development of social smiling.
3. **Stranger wariness**, or fear of strangers, develops at about 7 months, and, like social smiling, is a major landmark of emotional development. It develops as the result of the baby's developing cognitive skills, which now allow him to tell the difference between familiar and unfamiliar situations, which cause fear.
4. According to Jerome Kagan, fear develops when the infant has developed the abilities to raise questions about an unfamiliar event, but is unable to answer them. Stranger wariness is reduced when the baby is in a familiar setting, when she is physically close to her mother, and when she has lots of experience with strangers. Babies also are less fearful of strangers who approach slowly, are female, or are children rather than adults, perhaps because of their smaller size.
5. **Separation protest** is the infant's reaction, based on fear, to separation from the mother or caregiver, and it is present from about 10 to 12 months of age. Kagan argues that this protest results from confronting the child with a situation he can't figure out: Where is Mommy going? This explanation is supported by the research finding that infants are more distressed when the mother goes into a closet (an unusual behavior) than into the next room. Infants experience less distress if parents explain when they will be back and if they leave quickly rather than prolonging the leave-taking activity.

III. Attachment Relationships
1. Through repeated, shared experiences, a baby and a caregiver develop a relationship, a combination of behaviors, interactions, feelings, and expectations that are unique to these two people. By the end of the first year, most babies raised in families develop one or more attachment relationships, usually with the mother and perhaps with a few additional caregivers.
2. **Attachment** is a close, significant emotional bond between mother (or father) and infant. Although Freud and some others see first attachments as extremely important in setting the

Social and Emotional Development in Infancy

context for later life, many modern psychologists believe that later experiences can influence the effects of early attachment.

3. Freud believed that attachment grew from the mother's ability to satisfy the baby's hunger drive. Through repeated feedings, the baby comes to associate the pleasure of feeding with the presence of the mother. Learning theorists also focus on feeding and see milk as a reinforcer. Since the mother is associated with the milk, she becomes a **secondary reinforcer** and her presence alone can elicit the pleasure response. However, research with rhesus monkeys demonstrated that physical comfort, not milk, was more important in mother-infant attachment.

4. **Ethological theory**, based on the theory of evolution, holds that attachment enhances the survival value of the individual, and, hence, the species and has therefore become an ingrained pattern of human behavior, as are smiling, clinging, crying, stranger wariness, and separation protest.

5. By age 1, the child's need to stay near her mother, her **secure** base, is balanced by her desire to explore. John Bowlby, a proponent of ethological theory, sees both attachment and exploration as having been necessary for the survival of the species.

6. The security of attachment is the extent to which the child can count on his mother to meet his needs. Mary Ainsworth studied individual differences by putting babies under social stress in a **strange situation**, an experimental procedure used for observing attachment patterns. In the strange situation a mother and infant enter an unfamiliar room, a stranger enters, the mother leaves and comes back, the stranger leaves, the mother leaves, the stranger returns and finally the mother returns. Throughout, the child's behavior is observed. Based on research of this sort, Ainsworth classified attachment patterns as being **secure attachments**, in which infants are distressed when the mother leaves and are comforted when she returns, **anxious-resistant attachments**, in which children push the mother away when she returns, or **anxious-avoidant attachments**, in which the child is indifferent to the mother. There are some cross-cultural differences in the proportion of children in each attachment style.

7. One way of explaining the differences in mother-infant attachment is to focus on the mother's sensitivity in responding to her infant's needs. Research supporting this view suggests that maternal sensitivity and the moderate amount of stimulation does seem to promote secure attachment. Also, infant temperament is bound to affect the mother's behavior. Infants prone to distress who receive insensitive care are likely to develop insecure-resistant attachments; those who get sensitive care develop secure attachments. On the other hand, infants not prone to distress tend to develop insecure-avoidant attachments when they have insensitive mothers and secure attachments when they have sensitive mothers.

8. Erik Erikson sees as the developmental task of infancy the establishment of a sense of **basic trust** which, if well developed, sets the stage for a successful childhood at which the basic psychosocial issue becomes one of **autonomy and initiative**, the ability to be independent, resourceful, and self-motivated. Insecurely attached infants, then, have not learned that their environments are stable and supportive, and are, therefore, likely to be less socially skilled. Research shows that insecurely attached infants grow up to have more trouble in school, and to be more tense, helpless, and fearful. In one study, 40 percent of the boys classified as insecurely attached showed signs of psychopathology, or abnormal behavior, at age 6.

9. Although mother-infant attachment sets the stage for later development, other experiences also shape a child's future.

10. Research has shown that by 18 months, most infants have formed attachments to their fathers. Also, children who are securely attached to both parents appear more competent than those attached to one parent, and those attached to only the mother seem more competent than those attached to only the father. Research also shows that fathers can be equally good as mothers in being sensitive and responsive, but their play with infants tends to be physical whereas mothers' play is more likely verbal or with toys. Although mothers spend more time with infants than fathers, infants prefer to play with their fathers. When fathers are the primary

parent, they respond in a more motherly style, although, of course, every parent has a style uniquely his or her own.

IV. Relations with Peers
1. Even 3-month-olds stare at each other, but true social behavior begins at about 6 months. During the second year, imitation occurs along with complementary-reciprocal play such as run and chase in which players have opposite roles. Later in the year, play becomes cooperative imaginative, in which children pretend and imagine together, and includes games such as playing "house" or playing "school."
2. All normal infants experience the same sequence in the development of social behaviors, but children do differ from each other in the degree to which they are social. Furthermore, these early differences in sociability seem to persist in later development.

V. Learning to Say "I": The Emerging Self
1. At age 1, a child with rouge on her nose will not recognize herself in a mirror. By age 2, though, nearly all children reach for their noses, thereby indicating that she understands that she exists as a separate person.
2. Margaret Mahler has argued that the young infant's experience is one of **symbiosis**, the inability to distinguish herself from her mother. As they grow older, they gradually strive toward independence and a sense of separate self, which Mahler called **individuation and separation**. Sometimes children form attachments to **transitional objects**, like a blanket or teddy bear, as they move toward establishing their own distinct sense of self. Generally, by age 4 or 5, children leave these transitional objects behind.
3. Erik Erikson described the toddler's major developmental crisis as one of **autonomy versus shame and doubt**. This crisis is characterized by the desire for independence but, at the same time, the fear of giving up security.
4. At about 18 months, children develop the capacity to be embarrassed as they begin to understand that they are a unique individual separate from their parents. Toward the end of the second year, or into the third, the child also develops standards about what is good. At this point, pride can develop, as well as shame. Research suggests that children cooperate best when mothers provide guidance or guidance and control. Children were most defiant when mothers used negative control. Thus, parents who negotiate rather than battle with their children foster cooperation, self-worth, autonomy, and social skills that lead to high self-esteem.
5. Toilet training is seen as an example of the toddler's desire to let go (eliminating) and her desire to hold on (retention). Toilet training calls for parents' sensitivity so that children gain a sense of self-control without a loss of self-esteem and in this way encourage the child to develop a positive self image rather than a sense of impotence and lasting doubt and shame.

Self Test

A. Matching Questions

___ 1. Included about 40 percent of the children studied
___ 2. Behavior and responses developed through experience
___ 3. A shy child might be considered to be in this category
___ 4. Describes the idea that mothers influence children and children influence mothers
___ 5. Included about 10 percent of the children studied
___ 6. An inborn pattern of responsiveness and mood
___ 7. Characterized by irregular schedules and negative emotionality

a. personality
b. goodness-of-fit
c. difficult child
d. temperament
e. slow-to-warm-up child
f. easy child
g. New York Longitudinal Study

___ 8. Idea that the evolutionary past is an important determinant of development
___ 9. Anything associated with reducing a need
___ 10. First seen between 6 and 9 months of age, although many mothers notice its reflexive forms much earlier
___ 11. An attachment object from which the baby explores
___ 12. Baby cries when mother leaves, for example
___ 13. Fear of unfamiliar people
___ 14. An emotional bond
___ 15. Experimental procedure for observing attachment patterns

a. secondary reinforcer
b. separation protest
c. attachment
d. ethological theory
e. social smile
f. strange situation
g. stranger wariness
h. secure base

___ 16. A central event here is toilet-training
___ 17. When distressed, these children seek their mother and then express anger and resentment toward her
___ 18. Failure to separate self from another
___ 19. Movement toward independence and a separate sense of self
___ 20. Object to which an infant transfers attachment
___ 21. When distressed, these children show indifference to the mother
___ 22. Erikson's first developmental task
___ 23. When distressed, these children seek their mother

a. basic trust
b. secure attachment
c. transitional object
d. anxious-resistant attachment
e. symbiosis
f. individuation and separation
g. insecure attachment
h. autonomy versus shame and doubt
i. anxious-avoidant attachment

B. Multiple Choice

B.   Multiple Choice Questions

Factual   1.   The combination of behavior and response patterns each of us develops as we grow and
Obj. 1   learn is called:
Basic   a. goodness-of-fit
               b. temperament
               c. our secure base
               d. personality

Social and Emotional Development in Infancy 77

Applied
Obj. 1
Moderate

2. As a baby, Michelle was very sociable and had regular schedules, was calm and adaptable. According to chess and Thomas' research, Michelle would be described as:
a. easy
b. slow-to-warm-up
c. anxious-avoidant
d. anxious-resistant

Conceptual
Obj. 1
Advanced

3. In the New York Longitudinal Study, of those children classified, which group made up the largest percentage of children?
a. difficult children
b. easy children
c. slow-to-warm-up children
d. about equal numbers of children were placed in each group

Applied
Obj. 2
Moderate

4. D. Thomas tells parents that their experience with their child will be somewhat determined according to how well their expectations correspond to the basic temperament of their child. D. Thomas is emphasizing the central idea of the concept called:
a. symbiosis
b. attachment
c. personality
d. goodness-of-fit

Factual
Obj. 3
Moderate

5. The expression of which of the following emotions is the first to be observed in a newborn?
a. joy
b. distress
c. sadness
d. anger

Factual
Obj. 3
Moderate

6. The first social smile appears at about the age of:
a. 1 week
b. 3–4 weeks
c. 6–9 weeks
d. 3–4 months

Conceptual
Obj. 3
Moderate

7. Social smiling occurs at the same gestational age for normal babies, yet those raised in unstimulating institutions are sometimes delayed in the age at which they first smile. The first part of this sentence supports the influence of ___; the second part points out the influence of ___.
a. parents; poor nutrition
b. secure attachments; the separation protest
c. environment; heredity
d. heredity; environment

78   *Social and Emotional Development in Infancy*

Applied
Obj. 4
Moderate

8. Little Whitney is playing with some toys in the physician's office. When the nurse comes in, Whitney immediately moves over and sits by her father's feet. Whitney's behavior is best thought of as an example of:
   a. separation protest
   b. stranger wariness
   c. an anxious-resistant attachment
   d. an anxious-avoidant attachment

Conceptual
Obj. 4
Moderate

9. According to Kagan, the separation protest is the result of:
   a. an anxious-resistant attachment
   b. an anxious-avoidant attachment
   c. increasingly well-developed cognitive skills
   d. having a difficult or slow-to-warm-up temperament

Factual
Obj. 5
Moderate

10. According to Freud, attachment develops from:
    a. the hunger drive
    b. the Oedipus or Electra complex
    c. the superego
    d. fear of the unknown

Conceptual
Obj. 5
Moderate

11. John Bowlby, an ethological theorist, believes that attachment results from:
    a. fear of the unknown
    b. the mother's becoming a secondary reinforcer due to her association with the pleasurable event of satisfying a primary drive
    c. the fact that in our evolutionary history, its presence helped preserve the species
    d. the mother's ability to satisfy the hunger drive

Applied
Obj. 6
Moderate

12. Roberta and her son participate in an experiment in which they come into a room, play for awhile, and then Roberta leaves and an unfamiliar person comes in. Finally Roberta returns. This experiment is most closely associated with the term:
    a. individuation and separation
    b. transitional object
    c. strange situation
    d. goodness-of-fit

Applied
Obj. 6
Advanced

13. Bart's mother leaves him alone with a stranger and then returns. When she leaves, Bart is greatly distressed, and when she returns, he acts angry with her and ignores her. Which term best describes Bart's behavior?
    a. anxious-avoidant attachment
    b. anxious-resistant attachment
    c. symbiosis
    d. slow-to-warm-up

Factual
Obj. 6
Basic

14. Which of the following forms the basis for a baby's secure attachment to the mother?
    a. trust
    b. activity level
    c. stranger wariness
    d. autonomy

Conceptual 15. Little Robert's temperament is characterized as high in negative emotionality and his
Obj. 6   mother responds to him in a sensitive, responsive manner. Which of the following types
Moderate   of attachments is Robert most likely to form?
   a. insecure-resistant
   b. insecure-avoidant
   c. secure
   d. insecure-negative

Factual   16. According to Erik Erikson, the major task of infancy is:
Obj. 10   a. the establishment of basic trust
Basic   b. the formation of a secure attachment
   c. symbiosis
   d. to acquire an easy temperament

Factual   17. Which of the following statements about infant-father relationships is *true*?
Obj. 8   a. Very few infants become attached to their fathers before two years of age, although
Moderate   nearly all are attached by age 3.
   b. Infants prefer fathers' play to mothers' play.
   c. Infants attached to both their mother and father tend to be less competent than those
      attached only to their mother.
   d. The birth of a second baby usually leads to less involvement of the father with the
      infant, since he has other things to do.

Factual   18. At about what age do infants begin imitating the social behavior of their little friends
Obj. 9   and playing games such as hide-and-seek and run-and-chase?
Advanced   a. 10 months
   b. 15 months
   c. 2 years
   d. 3 years

Applied   19. Dr. Carlson believes that when babies are born, they have no view of themselves as
Obj. 10   being separate creatures from their mothers. This idea is best described by the concept:
Moderate   a. individuation
   b. secure base
   c. attachment
   d. symbiosis

Applied   20. Laura can't go to sleep without her stuffed bunny. When her parents visit their friends
Obj. 10   and forget "Bun-bun," Laura cries and cries. This example most clearly points out the
Moderate   importance of:
   a. transitional objects
   b. secure attachments
   c. goodness-of-fit
   d. temperament

Social and Emotional Development in Infancy

C. Essay Questions

INSTRUCTIONS
After reading and studying the text, read the question below and write your answer in the space provided. Do not refer to your text or to the Scoring Scheme or Model Answer on the next page.

1. Name and describe the three classification groups used by Chess and Thomas in the New York Longitudinal Study, and suggest two ways that temperament affects development.

Total Score ___

Scoring Scheme for Question 1

+1 point each (up to 3 points) for correctly naming the three categories: difficult, easy, and slow-to-warm up.

+2 points each (up to 6 points) for correctly describing each category. Each description should include at least two characteristics, and one point should be given for each.

+2 points for the idea that temperament evokes different responses from caregivers.

+2 points for the idea that temperament influences the kinds of activities in which the baby will engage.

Total: 13 points

Model Answer for Question 1

Chess and Thomas developed a method of observing children on nine dimensions, and, based on these observations, were able to classify children into three groups. **Easy children** were those with regular schedules, and little negative emotionality. They were calm, predictable, and adaptable. **Difficult children** were high on negative emotionality and tended to be low on sociability. They cried a lot, kept irregular schedules, were very active, were easily distracted, and were fearful. **Slow-to-warm-up children** were distressed by new things but did eventually accept these new experiences. Their behaviors were unlike those of the difficult child in that they were calmer and less extreme.

One way temperament affects development is that babies with differing temperaments evoke, or bring out, different responses in others. For example, a difficult baby may be hard to satisfy and may cause her mother to be upset with her and even avoid her, whereas an easy baby may get more attention because she is nicer to be around.

A second way temperament affects development is through the activities babies choose for themselves. For example, an active child likely will have more experiences than will one who is content to do less, but may also be less able to pay attention for long enough to learn from these experiences. Thus, the temperament, to some extent, determines the type of experiences the baby will have.

Social and Emotional Development in Infancy

INSTRUCTIONS
After reading and studying the text, read the question below and write your answer in the space provided. Do not refer to your text, or to the Scoring Scheme or Model Answer on the next page.

2. Are fathers as competent as mothers in establishing attachment relationships with their babies? What similarities and differences exist in the way fathers and mothers treat their infants?

Total Score ___

Scoring Scheme for Question 2

+4 points for the idea that some research evidence suggests fathers are not as strongly attached to their infants or that infants attached to fathers are not as competent.

+4 points for the idea that some research evidence suggests that fathers interact with their infants with similar sensitivity and as competently as do mothers.

+2 points for an example of a way in which fathers and mothers respond similarly.

+ 2 points for the finding that fathers' play is more physical and/or vigorous than mothers' play.

Total: 12 points

Model Answer for Question 2

It is difficult to assess whether fathers are as competent as mothers in establishing attachments with their infants since mothers are the ones who generally give infants their primary care. Research shows that most infants by 18 months show attachment to their fathers, but it also suggests that in general they attach earlier to their mothers. Also, research shows that infants securely attached only to their mothers seem more competent than those attached securely to their fathers. These studies, then, indicate that fathers may not foster as successfully as mothers secure infant attachments.

Other research, however, shows that fathers can be as sensitive to their babies' needs as mothers, and can respond to their infants in much the same way. For example, fathers can be equally good as mothers in interpreting the signals given by a newborn.

Thus, the answer to the question of whether fathers can be as effective as mothers in establishing attachment seems to be a qualified yes. The differences in attachment that do seem to exist may result from the fact that, in general, mothers spend more time with infants than fathers do.

In general, fathers and mothers treat infants in much the same way. One difference does exist, however, and that is in the way fathers and mothers play with their babies. Fathers are more likely to engage in vigorous, physical play whereas mothers are more likely to play games, to play with toys, or just talk to their babies. Interestingly, infants tend to prefer playing with their fathers.

Chapter 7

The Social Context of Infancy

Preview of the Chapter

I. **The Family as a System**
   A. How Infants Affect Marriages
      1. Adoption
      2. Husbands and wives with handicapped infants
   B. How Marriages Affect Infants
   C. Infants and Siblings
   D. Extended Families and Infant Development

II. **Beyond the Family**
   A. Parents and Infants in Social Networks
   B. Infant Day Care

III. **Class and Culture**
   A. Social Class, Parenting, and Infant Development
   B. Cultural Differences in the Context of Infancy
      1. Asia and the West: Interdependence versus Independence

Learning Objectives

1. Describe the changes that occur to a husband-wife relationship upon the birth of a first child.

2. Identify and describe the factors that affect how parents adjust to having a baby.

3. Discuss how an adopted child influences family life.

4. Describe how families adjust to the birth of a handicapped child.

5. Discuss how marriages affect infants.

6. Compare the adjustments required by a second child to those by the first and comment on the role played by extended families.

7. Describe how social networks influence parenting.

8. Analyze the effects of day care on infants and children and describe the features of high quality day care.

9. Explain how social class affects infant development and how it is related to parenting styles.

10. Describe how different cultures approach the task of parenting and comment on the effects that culture may have on infant development.

Chapter Summary

I. The Family as a System

1. Every family is a **system**, an interacting and interdependent group that functions as a whole. Because the birth of a baby changes the **social context**, or environment, in which the family members interact, this effect has major implications for the family, regardless of its specific structure.
2. Couples confront four kinds of problems when they have a baby: physical demands, strains in the husband-wife relationship, due largely to the substantial demands of the baby's schedule, emotional costs, and the loss of freedom and opportunities.
3. These strains on parents can strain their marriages: Overall satisfaction with marriage tends to drop after parenthood begins. Wives' satisfaction drops more than husbands' due to their larger role in child care, and all marriages, whether previously satisfying of not, seem to experience the same kind of decline in satisfaction: Those that were most happy before the baby were also most happy after the baby, although the overall level of satisfaction dropped.
4. The added work that accompanies parenthood often results in a more traditional division of labor and produces more dissatisfaction among women, and especially career women, than men since they oftentimes perform more of the new work. Stress with parenthood is greater when the couple has a romanticized view of parenthood, when their in-laws give too much unwelcome advice, or when the couple is newly married or very young. Also, babies with difficult temperaments or who are more prone to illness produce more stress in their parents.
5. Becoming a parent can also have positive effects and bind parents to their marriage partners. Also, with parenthood often come feelings of maturity, accomplishment, and less selfishness.
6. Infertility problems can cause problems for both individuals and couples. If the couple chooses to adopt a child, they must cope with an uncertain timetable as well as many other concerns. However, most studies show that marital satisfaction increases with adoption, and adoptive parents tend to be less controlling and authoritarian than biological parents. These findings may reflect the careful screening given to adoptive parents, their older ages, or their longer marriages. Babies form secure attachments with their adoptive mothers if they are adopted in their first 4 to 6 months of life, before they have formed secure attachments to another caregiver.
7. Caring for a handicapped child can be particularly demanding because of the extra work and responsibility and because the baby does not match the parents' expectations. Research shows that both mothers and fathers are less involved with and less responsive to a handicapped child. The effect of having a handicapped child depends on the severity of the handicap, the quality of the marriage, the context of the specific situation, and the availability of support and relief from relatives or people in the community who can protect the family from some negative effects.
8. A close husband-wife relationship encourages a father's interest in his baby: Fathers who rank high in marital communication show high involvement with their infants, and the mother's marital satisfaction is related to the security of the infant-mother attachment. The relationship among parenting, marital adjustment, and infant development occur in a pattern of **reciprocal feedback**, with each relationship affecting and being affected by the others.
9. Siblings make the family system more complex. Babies with secure attachments to their mothers are more tolerant of attention given to older children; securely attached older children have less conflict with a new baby than those with insecure attachments.

10. **Extended families** include relatives in addition to the child's parents. Some psychologists argue that our theories of mother-infant attachment are too Western and view as "abnormal" family situations in which the mother is not the primary caregiver. For example, research shows that African-American youngsters who have frequent contact with extended family members are emotionally better off than those who grow up in environments stressing religious and moral values.

II. Beyond the Family

1. Social networks support parents in three ways: they provide emotional support, instrumental assistance, including help and advice, and social expectation, or guidelines for childrearing. However, if the values of the parents and the values of the community are different, their interaction can do more harm than good. Generally, though, mothers who see friends often are the most effective parents, being more verbally and emotionally responsive to their babies.
2. Many European countries give both new mothers and fathers time off from work with pay to make the adjustments a new baby requires. In the U.S., women are guaranteed 12 weeks of unpaid leave.
3. Half of all American mothers with babies less than 1 year old work either full- or part-time. For children under 2, 57 percent were cared for by a father or other relative, 20 percent were in a family day care home, and 14 percent were in child care centers.
4. Until 1980, research on the effects of day care showed no associated disadvantages, probably because the day care centers studied were of the highest quality. More recent research suggests that some infants in day care appear to be less securely attached to their mothers, and some boys appear to be less securely attached to their fathers. Other research suggests that nonparental care in the first year may be linked to aggression, disobedience, and low tolerance for frustration in children. These results do not apply, however, to all children.
5. Caution must be taken in interpreting day care studies because not all children experience difficulty, researchers disagree on whether some behaviors are adaptive or not, and children raised in day care also experience other living situations different from home care children that may, in fact, be causing the difficulties rather than the day care experience.
6. Parents should look for the following when choosing a high quality day care arrangement:
   - A nurturant caregiver is the top priority.
   - A caregiver should be trustworthy, easy to talk to, and generous with time and information.
   - Stability and consistency are important.
   - The number of children per adult should be small.
   - The setting is the least important consideration.
   - Infants need time for adjustment.
   - Infants can thrive in the care of others.

III. Class and Culture

1. Compared to American middle-class babies, babies born to low-income parents have two-to three-times greater chance of dying in the first year, due to the associated high rate of teenage pregnancy, insufficient diets, and lack of prenatal care. Death rates are even higher in underdeveloped countries.
2. Social class is also associated with values and behaviors. As compared to lower-class mothers, middle-class mothers talk more and stimulate their babies, give them more freedom to explore, and encourage them to be independent, curious and achieving. Lower-class mothers also believe that control and discipline are extremely important, which may be linked to a fatalistic view of life.
3. These differences in parenting may be linked to later differences in child development. Social class differences begin to show up around the end of the second year, when tests of intellectual

88 The Social Context of Infancy

ability begin to rely on language skills. Perhaps the extra verbal stimulation given to middle-class children encourages and reinforces their use of language. However, even though studies consistently show that parents with more educational, economic, and occupational resources provide more cognitively stimulating care, they do not imply that lower-class parents love their children less. When caregiving is compromised, it is usually the result of the stress of poverty which saps the emotional resources needed to provide quality care.

4. Enrichment programs to aid poor families better care for their children can be successful, benefitting both parents and children. Helping mothers be more sensitive and providing support helps babies, too.
5. The culture into which one is born has a strong effect on development, and there are many significant differences among different cultures. Erik Erikson, Jerome Kagan, and others believe that we treat our infants according to the values of our culture, and therefore culture is transmitted to children from parents.
6. In Japan, babies are thought to be too independent, so, until age 5, dependency is fostered. Japanese mothers spend more time with their infants than American mothers do.
7. In China, babies sleep with their mothers and breast-feed on demand. When the baby is about 1 month old, the mother returns to work, leaving the infant with an older female relative or family friend.
8. The Rajput of northern India believe that a child's fate is determined by forces outside human control. Therefore, parents do not attempt to influence their children's lives.
9. In the United States, parents emphasize individual effort, overcoming obstacles, and achieving personal goals. Thus, Americans foster independence and autonomy in their children.
10. Both our inborn temperament and the genes we inherit and the social context in which we grow up continuously interact to shape and modify our development.

Self Test

A. Matching Questions

___ 1. The environment in which a person grows up
___ 2. Brother or sister
___ 3. A measure of income, education, and occupation
___ 4. An organized, interacting, interdependent group, functioning as a whole
___ 5. People who provide parents with support
___ 6. Pattern of mutual, interdependent influences in which each person affects and is affected by the others

a. system
b. stage one
c. reciprocal feedback
d. sibling
e. social context
f. stage two
g. social class

___ 7. Country in which mothers sleep with infants, breast-feed on demand, and return to work at 1 month leaving babies with older female caregivers
___ 8. Culture which encourages children to be independent and focused on cognitive development
___ 9. Culture which considers babies too independent
___ 10. Culture that believes that fate, not parents, influence children's development

a. Japan
b. the Rajput of northern India
c. China
d. United States

B. Multiple Choice

Conceptual
Obj. 1
Moderate

1. All of the interpersonal, community, and cultural influences to which each person is exposed combine to form that person's
   a. system
   b. social context
   c. reciprocal feedback mechanism
   d. social class

Applied
Obj. 1
Moderate

2. Greg describes his family as an interacting and interdependent group of individuals who make decisions and live together as a group. His description of his family emphasizes the concept called:
   a. system
   b. social class
   c. altruism
   d. authoritarianism

Factual
Obj. 1
Moderate

3. According to the text, which is *not* one of the four kinds of problems married couples typically face when they have their first child?
   a. physical demands that require more work
   b. less time for or interest in sex
   c. doubts about competence that cause stress
   d. boredom

Factual
Obj. 2
Moderate

4. In the last part of pregnancy and first six months of a child's life, the level of marital satisfaction reported by mothers ___ and the level reported by fathers ___.
   a. decreased; increased
   b. increased; decreased
   c. decreased; decreased
   d. increased; increased

Conceptual
Obj. 2
Moderate

5. According to research reported in the text, which of the following would you expect to experience the greatest decline in marital satisfaction following the birth of a baby?
   a. a career-oriented father
   b. a career-oriented mother
   c. a traditional father
   d. a traditional mother

Conceptual
Obj. 2
Moderate

6. On the basis of research reported in the text, which of the following couples would you expect to have the greatest adjustment to the birth of their child?
   a. Ann and Dave, who have romanticized parenthood and looked forward to its joys
   b. Bob and Carol, who are in their late 20s
   c. Ted and Alice, who have been married 8 years
   d. Fred and Irene, whose baby has an easy temperament

Factual
Obj. 3
Advanced

7. In comparison to couples who conceive their own children, couples who adopt babies are more likely to:
   a. have a greater decline in marital satisfaction after the child arrives
   b. be more authoritarian parents
   c. be younger
   d. be less controlling and intrusive parents

The Social Context of Infancy

Conceptual
Obj. 4
Moderate

8. In comparison to parents of normal children, the fathers of handicapped children tend to interact with their babies ___ and the mothers interact with them ___.
   a. less; less
   b. less; more
   c. more; less
   d. more; more

Factual
Obj. 5
Basic

9. The idea that each person affects and is affected by other members of the family is central to the concept called:
   a. reciprocal inhibition
   b. reciprocal feedback
   c. cooperative context
   d. ethological interdependence

Applied
Obj. 6
Moderate

10. Suppose your friend has two children, Matt, age 4, and Jill, age 1. Generalizing from research in the text, which of the children will be more interested in the other, and which will teach the other more?
    a. Matt will be more interested in Jill and will teach her more.
    b. Matt will be more interested in Jill, but Jill will teach him more.
    c. Jill will be more interested in Matt and will teach him more.
    d. Jill will be more interested in Matt, but Matt will teach her more.

Applied
Obj. 6
Moderate

11. Barbara and Doyle live with their mother, their grandmother, two aunts, and an uncle. The word that best describes this living arrangement is:
    a. extended family
    b. reciprocal feedback
    c. sibling-to-sibling network
    d. parent-to-sibling network

Applied
Obj. 7
Moderate

12. Jeff complains to his wife that, since their son was born, her parents have been driving him crazy with unwelcome advice about how to be a good father. According to the text, Jeff is having trouble with which of the following aspects of social networks?
    a. emotional support
    b. social expectations
    c. instrumental assistance
    d. reciprocal feedback

Conceptual
Obj. 7
Moderate

13. According to research presented in the text, new mothers who see their friends often and get support from them:
    a. are less verbally responsive to their babies
    b. are less emotionally responsive to their babies
    c. are more likely to experience the symptoms of depression
    d. are the most effective parents

Factual
Obj. 8
Moderate

14. According to the text, which of the following countries gives the least amount of leave with pay after the birth of a baby?
    a. Austria
    b. the United States
    c. France
    d. England

Factual Obj. 8 Moderate	15.	Approximately what proportion of American mothers with children under a year old work part- or full-time? a. one-fourth b. one-third c. one-half d. two-thirds
Conceptual Obj. 8 Moderate	16.	According to the text, which of the following is not a major difficulty in interpreting the results of studies on the effects of day care? a. Researchers don't agree on what kind of behavior constitutes "healthy" adjustment. b. Children placed in day care also are more likely to experience other problems in their family life at home. c. The effects of day care are different for different children. d. Such studies usually involve very complex research designs and statistics and are therefore very difficult to understand.
Factual Obj. 8 Moderate	17.	Which of the following is *not* considered good advice to be given to parents who are trying to select a high quality day care center. a. The number of children per adult should be small. b. Caregivers should be warm and affectionate with children rather than adhering tightly to rules and procedures. c. Parents should be prepared to stay at the center each morning until their child stops crying and begins to play. d. Few changes in routine or caregivers are desirable.
Conceptual Obj. 9 Moderate	18.	In comparison to middle-class mothers, which of the following is a characteristic that applies more to lower-class mothers? a. They talk more to their babies. b. They encourage curiosity and independence. c. They use more discipline. d. They try to teach their children that they can do anything if they just try hard enough.
Factual Obj. 9 Moderate	19.	According to the text, when do social class differences in cognitive functioning begin to appear? a. at about 6 months b. at about 1 year c. around the end of the second year d. at about age 4
Applied Obj. 10 Moderate	20.	Suppose you read an article on child care that discusses the fact that most mothers in this country do not attempt to affect their children's development in any way because they believe that fate, rather than parents, determines how a child's life will turn out. From the information presented in the text, your best guess is that the country being described is: a. Japan b. China c. the United States d. India

C. Essay Questions

INSTRUCTIONS

After reading and studying the text, read the question below and write your answer in the space provided. Do not refer to your text or to the Scoring Scheme or Model Answer on the next page.

1. Define and give a specific example of the concept called reciprocal feedback.

Total Score ___

Scoring Scheme for Question 1

+4 points for an accurate definition.

+4 points for an example in which it is clear that all members of the family affect and are affected by every other member.

Total: 8 points

Model Answer for Question 1

Reciprocal feedback is the pattern of interactions among family members in which each member affects and is affected by every other member. An example of reciprocal feedback can be found when a baby is born into a family. The mother and father have a relationship in which each affects the other, and now a baby is born, which affects them both. They both, in their care of the baby, affect her behavior and the behavior of each other in new ways. If the baby's temperament is easy, the parents will have an easier time taking care of her. If she is difficult, they may experience more difficulty, may get more tired, and may argue more with each other. If the baby puts stress on their marriage, each of them might be unhappier, and this might lead to different treatment of the baby and of each other. For example, the parents might leave the baby with sitters more, the mother may return to work sooner, the parents may argue more, and so forth. Thus, each member of the family affects the other members and each member is affected by them as well.

The Social Context of Infancy

INSTRUCTIONS
After reading and studying the text, read the question below and write your answer in the space provided. Do not refer to your text, or to the Scoring Scheme or Model Answer on the next page.

2. Based on research discussed in the text, describe three differences between the way middle-class and lower-class mothers interact with their babies that appear to affect infant development.

_____
_____
_____
_____
_____
_____
_____
_____
_____
_____
_____
_____
_____
_____
_____
_____
_____
_____
_____
_____

Total Score ___

Scoring Scheme for Question 2

+4 points each (up to 12 points) for accurate description of social class differences that affect development, such as:
    a. middle-class mothers talk more to their infants.
    b. middle-class mothers stimulate their infants more.
    c. middle-class mothers give their babies more freedom to explore.
    d. middle-class mothers are more encouraging of independence, curiosity, and achievement.
    e. lower-class mothers are more controlling and use more discipline.
    f. lower-class mothers may hold more fatalistic attitudes and be less encouraging of their infant.

-4 points if the answer suggests that lower-class mothers love their children less.

Total: 12 points

Model Answer for Question 2

One difference between middle-class and lower-class mothers is in how much the mother talks to and stimulates her baby. Middle-class mothers generally interact more in these ways with their babies. Middle-class mothers also set fewer limits on their baby's exploration. Rather than keeping him in a restricted area like a playpen, a middle-class mother is more likely to let her baby move around the house and explore. Finally, middle-class mothers are less likely to tightly control or discipline their babies. Instead of focusing on absolute adherence to the rules, middle-class mothers are more encouraging of their children to develop their own potential. This may reflect the middle-class belief that effort will contribute to one's success.

Chapter 8

Physical, Cognitive, and Language Development in Early Childhood

Preview of the Chapter

I. **Physical Development**
   A. Size and Growth Rates
      1. Growth and nutrition
      2. Growth abnormalities
   B. Brain Growth
   C. Motor Development

II. **Cognitive Development: Piaget and Beyond**
   A. Piaget's Approach
   B. Preoperational Thought
      1. Centration
      2. Reversibility
      3. States and transformations
      4. Conservation
   C. Current Research on Children's Cognitive Ability
      1. Appearance and reality
      2. States and transformations
      3. Conservation
      4. Understanding of number
      5. Causal reasoning
      6. Theory of mind

III. **Information Processing**
   A. Memory Development: Recognition and Recall
   B. Thought and Language

IV. **Language Development**
   A. Building Vocabulary
   B. Grasping the Rules of Grammar
   C. Communicating
   D. Self-Communication: Inner Speech
   E. Bilingualism and Language Learning

V. **Children's Art: A Silent Language**
   A. From Scribbles to Pictures

Physical, Cognitive, and Language Development in Early Childhood

Learning Objectives

1. Describe the growth in physical size and shape that occurs between the ages of 2 and 7.

2. Discuss the changes that occur in brain growth and motor development during the preschool years.

3. Describe the characteristics of the preschoolers' cognitive abilities, focusing on the principles of centration, reversibility, and conservation.

4. Discuss the young child's developing ability to understand number.

5. Explain how young children understand and use causal reasoning and how egocentrism influences their thinking.

6. Describe how memory develops during the preschool years and how the development of language and thought are related.

7. Describe the changes that accompany the development of language in the preschool years.

8. Discuss how children learn to communicate with others and how they use self-communication to direct their own activities.

9. Explain the advantages and disadvantages that accompany bilingualism.

10. Identify and explain the typical changes that occur in artwork as children grow from age 2 to age 7.

Chapter Summary

I. Physical Development

1. Between 2 and 3, children gain fewer pounds than any period until after puberty. Two-year-olds weigh about 20 to 25 pounds, and over the next three years gain 6 or 7 pounds and grow 2 to 4 inches per year. Height in childhood correlates with adult height.
2. Height varies across races, demonstrating its hereditary component, with children of African descent being the tallest in the U.S., followed by Caucasians, Hispanics, and Asians. Nutrition, an environmental factor, also influences growth. Children in upper socioeconomic groups and who grow up in urban areas are usually taller, due to wider availability of adequate nutrition and health care. Children are quite able to regulate their own diets and their consumption of food is relatively consistent from day to day.
3. Kwashiorkor, caused by prolonged protein deficiency, can cause irreparable physical and mental retardation. Obesity is increasing among U.S. children, due to more junk food and TV and less exercise.
4. Growth problems can result from hormone deficiencies. **Growth hormone deficiency**, which is sometimes linked to problems with the pituitary gland, slows growth from birth, affects 1 in 10,000 people, and is four times likelier in boys than girls. When diagnosed efficiently, it can be treated with injections of growth hormone during childhood. A deficiency of **Thyroxin**, a hormone made by the thyroid gland, can cause cretinism, which is characterized by stunted growth and mental retardation.
5. By age 2, the brain has grown to 75 percent of its adult size; by age 5, it totals 90 percent. Body size grows at a much slower rate: a child is at about half his adult weight at age 10. The brain grows throughout childhood, and myelin, the fatty sheath surrounding neurons which speeds neural transmission, develops until puberty. **Cerebral lateralization**, the process by

Physical, Cognitive, and Language Development in Early Childhood **99**

which brain functions become located in one hemisphere, also continues to puberty, and brain waves and the speed of neural transmission also develop in childhood. Brain development in childhood is characterized by **plasticity**, or flexibility, meaning that a different part can sometimes take on the function that was present in a damaged part of the brain. Brain development is fastest during periods of rapid growth in speech, physical coordination, and cognitive and social development. Brain development and skill development are reciprocal: new stimulation promotes brain development which, in turn, allows new skills to be developed.

6. **Lead poisoning**, caused by too much exposure to lead through living with lead-based paint, being close to a lead plant, or having parents who work around lead, can severely affect brain development in early childhood. It is most prevalent among poor children and is linked to poor performance on IQ tests and in school.

7. **Gross motor skills**, which involve large-muscle groups, improve during childhood due to increasing muscle strength, better coordination, and improved balance resulting from better body proportions.

8. **Fine motor skills**, which involve small-muscle groups, also improve. Although some toddlers prefer the use of one hand over the other, clear **hand dominance** may not appear until age 5. Children with a clear preference for one hand are more coordinated than those with inconsistent hand preferences. Boys are somewhat stronger and have better gross motor skills, but girls are usually better at fine motor skills, perhaps due to practice.

II. Cognitive Development: Piaget and Beyond

1. Although more recent work has qualified some of Jean Piaget's ideas, his theory is still influential in our understanding of cognitive development. Piaget called the period from about ages 2–7 the **preoperational period**, which spans the time between the end of the sensorimotor period and the rule-governed thought of school-aged children. Recent research suggests that Piaget underestimated the cognitive abilities of preschoolers.

2. The hallmark of the preschool years is the development of **symbolic thought**, the ability to represent the world mentally, which begins at about age 2. Symbolic thought develops in two ways: first, children learn to use mental images to solve problems, and second, children begin to use external symbols such as words or pictures to stand for objects or events. Symbolic thinking is also seen as pretend play, which begins at about 18 to 24 months of age.

3. Piaget believed that preschoolers' thought is characterized by **centration**, the inability to focus on more than one aspect of a stimulus at a time. Thus, a cat wearing a dog mask becomes, for the preschooler, a dog, since he focuses only on the face.

4. Preschoolers have trouble with **reversibility**, the idea that an action can be done and undone. Also, their thinking is limited about **states and transformations**, the idea that objects and states can be transformed and rearranged. **Conservation** is the term Piaget used to describe the child's knowledge that the basic physical dimensions of a stimulus remain the same, even if there are superficial changes in the way it appears. For example, if five cookies are laid in a row and then spread out, the preoperational child may conclude that there are more cookies now than before, indicating the inability to mentally reverse the spreading out process and demonstrating the failure to conserve number.

5. Recent research indicates that preschool children may have more ability in these areas than Piaget thought and also that training can teach children to do better at these tasks than Piaget believed was possible. For example, although 3-year-olds confuse appearance and reality, 5-year-olds do not, indicating that between age 3 and 6 preschoolers develop a theory of the mental world in which they distinguish between appearance and reality. Other studies suggest that preschoolers can attend to transformations and can learn reversibility. It appears that children can employ conservation skills earlier than Piaget thought and can learn these skills as well.

6. Even though cognitive development can be speeded up by supplying children with optimal learning experiences, many researchers believe that such formal and competitive instruction stifles normal curiosity and intellectual growth. As David Elkind warns, academic gains may lead to personal losses, and life itself provides more than enough of a curriculum for young children.

7. Contemporary researchers have found that young children's thinking is less limited by centration, appearances, and nonreversible thinking than Piaget thought, and that they can conserve number and count spontaneously and systematically. Rochel Gelman argues that number abilities may be inborn and universal as evidenced by the findings that preschoolers associate one number per each object counted; that they use names for numbers in a consistent, though not always accurate, way; that they seem to believe anything is countable; that, unlike names, counted objects can be rearranged without changing the total; and that they seem to have an intuitive understanding of adding and subtracting. Many children by age 3 or 4 have acquired these five principles.

8. Preschool children often confuse cause and effect in their logic, and infer causality in situations in which it does not apply. However, they are less likely to confuse cause and effect when analyzing situations with which they have had experience. Children use **animism** in their thinking, which is the practice of assigning qualities of living organisms to nonliving entities, for example, saying a tree might get lonely.

9. Piaget found that when children looked at a three-dimensional construction of three mountains, they responded that a child seated in different locations would see the mountains the same way they did, thus ignoring the fact that position alters one's point of view. Piaget called this inability to consider others' perspectives **egocentrism**. Again, more recent research suggests children are not so egocentric as previously thought.

10. The term "theory of mind" refers to the child's understanding of mental states, such as beliefs, emotions, desires, intentions, and dreams. Contrary to Piaget's original view that children know nothing about thought, recent research suggests that young children actually have a fairly sophisticated theory of mind, especially by age 4 or 5, but their thinking is not so advanced as is adult thinking.

III. Information Processing

1. An **information processing** approach to the study of development is one that emphasizes the growth of basic cognitive processes over time.

2. As preschoolers get older, both their **recognition memory**, or memory for previously seen objects, and their **recall memory**, or memory in the absence of strong retrieval cues, improves. However, recognition memory is the stronger of the two throughout development.

3. Young children appear to organize their memories into **scripts**, or sequences of day-to-day activities, and find it humorous when there are departures from the sequence of activities in a given script. Children probably remember familiar events by incorporating them into scripts based on experience, which may lead to difficulty when they try to remember a specific instance of a particular activity.

4. Preschoolers sometimes use **memory strategies**, or plans that aid recall, to help them remember important information. They also engage in **rehearsal**, or repetition, if this strategy is suggested to them. Children can also use the strategy called **interactive imagery**, or **elaboration**, which involves thinking back to the event which needs to be remembered and trying to reconstruct it in memory. Usually, until children are 5 or 6, they don't use many memory strategies unless they are specifically instructed to remember something. However, as they get older, they become increasingly aware of the usefulness of memory aids, and they begin to develop **metacognition**, the ability to understand and control their own thinking.

5. For Piaget, language develops naturally as the result of the developing ability to think symbolically. A. R. Luria, a Russian psychologist, takes the opposite view that language

develops first and directs and organizes thinking. Lev Vygotstsky and Jerome Bruner accept an interactionist view, believing that language skills and cognitive growth interact and influence each other. Thus, separating thought from language is impossible, as evidenced by preschoolers "inner speech" in which they tell themselves out loud what to do in a given situation. However, studies with deaf children who have little language facility but normal cognitive abilities somewhat contradicts this interactionist view.

IV. Language Development

1. During the preschool years, children learn as many as two to four new words each day, and at age 6, vocabulary totals between 8000 and 14,000 words. The words children use the most are the "five Ws," what, where, who, when, and why.

2. One common error children make in the early stages of language development is **overextension**, using the same word to stand for a number of similar things. Although 2-year-olds have trouble generating compound words, like "fishat," 3- and 4-year-olds use compound words almost as often as adults do.

3. A second way of filling in gaps in vocabulary is **fast-mapping**, in which she relates a new word to a general meaning the first time she hears it and only later comes to understand its exact meaning. **Mutual exclusivity**, where children assume that a word can refer to only one object, also helps children acquire larger vocabularies.

4. Children learn words that help them express relationships among objects, and these words emerge in a predictable order. They also use words which express time order, like "tomorrow," but their understanding of the exact meaning of these words is often fuzzy. Although some 3-year-olds confuse words referring to spatial relations, like "more-less," by age 5, most children understand these words and use them correctly.

5. Grammar is the set of rules that governs the use of words in language. Young children learn many rules of grammar automatically, and in a fairly predictable pattern. When children apply a standard rule of grammar, for example, plurals are formed by adding an "s," to an exception to the rule ("foots" instead of "feet"), they make the error called **overregularization**. Overregularizations indicate that children are, in fact, learning grammatical rules.

6. Children also have trouble understanding past, present, and future, and in a compound sentence, may mistakenly assume that the first thing mentioned in the sentence is necessarily the first action in the series. Preschoolers also can be confused by sentences that depart from the subject-verb-object order that is commonly used. For example, in the sentence "the dog is chased by the cat" they may believe that the dog, which is mentioned first, is doing the chasing. By age 5, children no longer make these errors, and even younger children do not make errors that are meaningless interpretations.

7. There is some evidence that both first and second languages are learned most easily and fluently in early or middle childhood, perhaps due to brain maturation. Experience influences language development as well: Children whose parents correct their grammatical errors learn grammar at an earlier age, and there are some ethnic differences in early language development, although socioeconomic status seems more important in this regard than racial differences.

8. **Referential communication** is communication that refers to something specific. Preschoolers often fail to give adequate descriptions of things they talk about and may describe events in terms of their own experience, which may be meaningless to the listener. Piaget believed that these difficulties with referential communication result from egocentrism, the inability to understand what the other person knows. Newer research, however, suggests that preschoolers are better at communicating than Piaget thought, and that communication at this age is limited more by difficulty with processing information and coordinating communication skills than by egocentrism.

9. Preschoolers use simpler language when talking to younger children than when talking with adults. They also are sometimes aware of what confuses them in a conversation and can clear it up by asking for more information. Although preschoolers seem to have most of the abilities required for communication, these skills have not yet become automatic for them and so have some difficulty coordinating all the information-processing demands imposed in the communication process.
10. Preschoolers sometimes give themselves verbal directions to help them regulate their own behavior. This vocal self-communication is called **inner speech**, and in childhood it gradually changes from out-loud commands to silent thoughts, often moving through a period of whispering or mouthing words silently. Teaching preschoolers to talk out loud through the steps in solving a problem helps memory, increases patience, and improves schoolwork.
11. When young children learn two languages at the same time, they at first tend to mix the two languages, thus developing an "interlanguage" system. In time the two languages become separate, and at age 3 or 4, children become aware that they are speaking two languages.
12. Problems are most likely to occur when one language is learned at home and another is learned through acquaintances, thereby producing interference between the two languages. Even if problems occur, bilingual children usually catch up in language learning by the early elementary years, and studying a second language may actually enhance general cognitive development.

V. **Children's Art: A Silent Language**
1. Children's artwork can reflect both their emotional states and their general cognitive development. For example, insecurely attached children depict their mothers as overly prominent or as insignificant in their art.
2. Until about age 3, children are more interested in the process than the product of drawing, and their pictures are scribbles. Rhoda Kellogg has identified four stages in the development of drawing: the **placement stage**, or scribbling; the **shapes stage** (ages 3 to 3½), where marks are combined into complex shapes; the **design stage** (from 3½ to 4) where marks become recognizable geometric shapes; and the **pictorial stage** (ages 4 or 5 on) where children begin to represent objects in their art. Also, by age 4 or 5, children have developed their own style of drawing.

Self Test

A. Matching Questions

___ 1. Can be linked to cretinism
___ 2. Related to the idea that the brain becomes less flexible with age
___ 3. Buttoning, lacing shoes, coloring, for example
___ 4. Focusing on one aspect of a stimulus
___ 5. Laying down of functions into the left and right sides of the brain
___ 6. These use the large muscles of the body
___ 7. Between the sensorimotor stage and rule-governed thought
___ 8. Endocrine disorder often associated with pituitary disfunction
___ 9. Representing the world mentally

a. plasticity
b. hand dominance
c. growth hormone deficiency
d. centration
e. gross motor skills
f. preoperational period
g. thyroxin deficiency
h. symbolic thought
i. cerebral lateralization
j. fine motor skills
k. kwashiorkor
l. reversibility
m. lead poisoning

___ 10. Inability to see any perspective except one's own
___ 11. Knowledge that basic physical characteristics don't change even if superficial appearances do
___ 12. "The sun shines when it is happy," for example
___ 13. Memory based on something that was previously experienced
___ 14. The hallmark of cognitive development in early childhood
___ 15. Sequences of day-to-day activities
___ 16. Understanding that what can be done can also be undone
___ 17. Memory in the absence of strong retrieval cues

a. reversibility
b. animism
c. recall memory
d. egocentrism
e. states and transformations
f. scripts
g. symbolic thought
h. recognition memory
i. conservation

___ 18. A message that refers to something specific
___ 19. A specific kind of memory strategy
___ 20. Repetition done to aid memory
___ 21. Ability to understand and control one's thinking skills
___ 22. The rules of language
___ 23. Talking out loud as a means of regulating one's own behavior
___ 24. Plans that aid recall
___ 25. "I sawed two gooses," for example

a. interactive imagery (elaboration)
b. overregularization
c. rehearsal
d. referential communication
e. memory strategies
f. inner speech
g. metacognition
h. grammar

B. Multiple Choice

Factual
Obj. 1
Moderate

1. Between the ages of 2 and 6, children gain about how many pounds per year?
   a. 2 or 3
   b. 4 or 5
   c. 6 or 7
   d. 8 or 10

Conceptual
Obj. 1
Advanced

2. Which of the following statements about growth patterns of children is **true**?
   a. Children growing up in densely populated urban areas are usually larger than children from rural areas.
   b. In the United States, Caucasian preschoolers tend to be a little taller than children of African descent.
   c. Children in upper socioeconomic groups are shorter but heavier than those in lower groups.
   d. Children in western Europe grow more in the fall and winter than the spring and summer.

Applied
Obj. 1
Moderate

3. Jennifer's parents were told she has a tumor on her pituitary gland. Her parents should also be told that, because of the tumor, she may experience which of the following problems?
   a. kwashiorkor
   b. anorexia
   c. thyroxin deficiency
   d. growth hormone deficiency

104 *Physical, Cognitive, and Language Development in Early Childhood*

Conceptual
Obj. 2
Moderate

4. Brain damage is often less severe if the person affected is a child rather than adult. This finding is most consistent with the concept called:
   a. reversibility
   b. plasticity
   c. centration
   d. animism

Applied
Obj. 2
Basic

5. Which of the following is the best example of a gross motor skill?
   a. being able to skip
   b. being able to type
   c. being able to tie your shoes
   d. being able to copy letters and numbers

Conceptual
Obj. 2
Moderate

6. According to research presented in the text, children with which of the following characteristics are most likely to be uncoordinated?
   a. those who have a strong preference for either hand present by age 3
   b. those with a strong preference for their right hand
   c. those with a strong preference for their left hand
   d. those who have inconsistent hand preferences

Factual
Obj. 3
Basic

7. The child's mental representation of the world defines the concept called:
   a. animism
   b. egocentrism
   c. inner speech
   d. symbolic thought

Factual
Obj. 3
Moderate

8. Piaget called the stage between the sensorimotor stage and that characterized by rule-governed thought the:
   a. preoperational period
   b. stage of concrete operations
   c. stage of referential communication
   d. stage of states and transformations

Applied
Obj. 3
Moderate

9. When Marjorie saw her dad in a gorilla mask, she became frightened because she thought her dad had really turned into a gorilla. This story is best thought of as an example of:
   a. animism
   b. centration
   c. overregularization
   d. metacognition

Applied
Obj. 3
Moderate

10. David watches his mother pour his juice from a small glass to a bigger glass. When his mother asks him how far the juice came up on the side of the small glass, he can't remember. David's problem is best thought of as a lack of:
    a. centration
    b. egocentrism
    c. reversibility
    d. metacognition

Applied
Obj. 3
Moderate

11. Julia knows that five pencils laid closely together are still the same number when they are spread apart. She has mastered the concept called:
    a. metacognition
    b. conservation
    c. animism
    d. elaboration

Conceptual
Obj. 4
Moderate

12. According to Gelman's discussion of the development of the understanding of number presented in the text, it is most accurate to view the acquisition of this understanding as resulting from:
    a. lots of repetition and reinforcement
    b. the increase in egocentrism that characterizes the preschool years
    c. an inborn and universal ability
    d. cerebral lateralization

Factual
Obj. 5
Moderate

13. The kind of reasoning that credits nonliving things with human qualities forms the basis for the concept called:
    a. centration
    b. animism
    c. metacognition
    d. egocentrism

Applied
Obj. 5
Moderate

14. Rachael walks over to her little brother and grabs the toy he is holding. When her father scolds her, she acts as if it never occurred to her that her brother was interested in the toy, only that she wanted it. Rachael's behavior is best thought of as an example of:
    a. transduction
    b. centration
    c. conservation
    d. egocentrism

Factual
Obj. 6
Moderate

15. Our memories for sequences of day-to-day activities are called:
    a. scripts
    b. metamemories
    c. inner speech
    d. metacognitions

Conceptual
Obj. 6
Moderate

16. According to research presented in the text, preschool children ___ usually organize and rehearse information on their own, and, if specific memory strategies are suggested to them, they ___ use them.
    a. do; do
    b. do; do not
    c. do not; do
    d. do not; do not

Factual
Obj. 7
Moderate

17. By the age of 6, most children have a vocabulary of about how many words?
    a. 800
    b. 2,000
    c. 11,000
    d. 27,500

Applied
Obj. 7
Moderate

18. Michael says, "I sawed two mouses today at preschool!" Michael's language demonstrates the concept called:
    a. animism
    b. overregularization
    c. metacognition
    d. transduction

Conceptual
Obj. 9
Moderate

19. Which of the following statements about bilingualism is **false**?
    a. Young children tend to mix the two languages together when they first learn them.
    b. Learning two languages has been shown to enhance the general cognitive development of bilingual children.
    c. Bilingual children generally have more language problems if they use one language at home and the other with peers.
    d. Bilingual children generally don't realize they are speaking two different languages until about the time they enter first grade.

Applied
Obj. 10
Advanced

20. Craig's drawings consist of rather elaborate geometric shapes like triangles and circles which are connected together in interesting ways. His artwork is typical of which of Rhoda Kellogg's stages?
    a. the placement stage
    b. the shapes stage
    c. the design stage
    d. the pictorial stage

C. Essay Questions

INSTRUCTIONS

After reading and studying the text, read the question below and write your answer in the space provided. Do not refer to your text or to the Scoring Scheme or Model Answer on the next page.

1. Children's understanding of grammar can be inferred from the kinds of errors they make in their speech. Define and give an example of two of these kinds of errors, overregularization and misinterpretation of sentences which depart from the simple subject-verb-object structure. What do these errors tell us about how children learn language?

Total Score ___

Scoring Scheme for Question 1

+2 points for the idea that overregularization involves applying grammatical rules too stringently.

+2 points for the idea that young children confuse the actor and the object when sentences depart from the standard form.

+3 points each (up to 6 points) for accurate examples of each of the errors described above.

+2 points for the idea that these errors in speech demonstrate the developmental nature of language acquisition.

Total: 12 points

Model Answer for Question 1

Overregularization is the application of general grammatical rules to exceptional cases where they don't apply. For example, in English we usually form the past tense of a verb by adding -ed to the present tense form, as in "Stop" and "Stopped." However, some verbs have an irregular past tense, like "run" and "ran." Young children often apply the past tense rule to these exceptional cases, using words like "runned" or "ranned," thereby committing the error of overregularization.

Children also get mixed up when a sentence departs from a simple subject-verb-object form, and they usually assume that the first noun that appears in the sentence is the actor and that the second noun is the object of the action. For example, in the sentence "Jill was chased by Jack," young children often make the mistake of believing that Jill is doing the chasing.

Errors of speech like those described above indicate that children learn the rules of grammar not by repetition but rather as part of a development process. Thus, children's learning of language seems to develop automatically without formal instruction or reinforcement.

INSTRUCTIONS
After reading and studying the text, read the question below and write your answer in the space provided. Do not refer to your text, or to the Scoring Scheme or Model Answer on the next page.

2. Describe the four stages through which children develop as they learn to draw pictures. Explain how the development, reflected in children's drawings, is related to their cognitive abilities.

Total Score ___

Scoring Scheme for Question 2

+1 point each (up to 4 points) for accurate descriptions of the four stages: placement, shapes, design, and pictorial. The names of the stages need not be mentioned to receive credit, but they must be described in the correct order.

+2 points for the idea that early on the child is more interested in the drawing process, and later becomes interested in the product.

+2 points for the idea that the ability to draw objects means that the child can hold mental representations of them, which is a cognitive ability that develops in childhood.

Total: 8 points

Model Answer for Question 2

Children begin drawing at about age 2 or 3, and their first drawings are scribbles. This is the **placement stage**, and here children are more interested in the activity of drawing than in the finished product or in what the drawing looks like. In the next stage, called the **shapes stage**, children combine marks to create simple designs like circles or crosses. The next stage, called the **design stage**, is marked by the combination of marks into more complex designs in which parts of the design are connected to other parts. Finally, at about age 4 or 5, children enter the pictorial stage, where they begin drawing pictures that represent things, like people, animals, and so forth.

Children's artwork corresponds directly to their level of cognitive development. The emergence of the child's ability to draw pictures of real things tells us that the child can now mentally represent visual images of things. Thus, like the acquisitions of words as labels for objects, the ability to draw pictures of objects tells us that the child can now imagine how things look even though the object being drawn is not physically present, but is only a mental idea.

Chapter 9

Social and Emotional Development in Early Childhood

Preview of the Chapter

I. **The Growing Self**

II. **Sex-Role Development**
   A. Masculinity and Femininity: A New View
   B. Gender Identity
   C. Sex Stereotypes
   D. Differences in Boys' and Girls' Behavior
   E. Nurture/Nature and Sex-Typed Differences
      1. Biological explanations
      2. Psychoanalytic explanations
      3. Cognitive explanations
      4. Social learning explanations
      5. Television, books, and sex roles
   F. How Do Sex Differences Matter?

III. **Developing Social Skills**
   A. The Development of Prosocial Behavior
      1. Attachment explanations
      2. Cognitive explanations
      3. Social learning explanations
   B. Controlling Aggression
      1. Cognitive explanations of aggression
      2. Social learning and aggression
   C. Peer Relations: Making Friends
      1. Individual differences in peer relationships
      2. Enhancing social skills

IV. **The Work of Play**
   A. From Solitary to Social Play
      1. Individual differences in style
      2. Playfulness

Learning Objectives

1. Describe the major developmental advances that occur as the child moves through the preschool years.

2. Define what is meant by the term sex roles and explain the basis of masculinity and femininity in our culture.

112 *Social and Emotional Development in Early Childhood*

3. Explain how gender identity is established, and discuss the development of sex stereotypes.

4. Describe the differences typical of boys and of girls.

5. Explain the origin of sex-typed differences according to biological, psychoanalytic, cognitive, and social learning perspectives.

6. Describe the influence of television, books, and role models on sex-role development and comment on the significance of one's sex role.

7. Describe the emergence of prosocial behavior and explain its development according to explanations emphasizing attachment, cognition, and social learning.

8. Describe how psychologists view aggressive behavior in children and explain its development according to cognitive and social learning views.

9. Explain how children go about making friends and discuss how children differ from each other in their social skills.

10. Describe the development of play behavior and discuss individual differences in how children play with others.

Chapter Summary

I. The Growing Self
1. The conflict at age 2 centers around becoming separate from one's mother, which Erikson discussed as the crisis between autonomy versus shame and doubt. By age 3, the main issue is growing up in relation to mother, father, and the adult society.
2. Erikson refers to this crisis as one of **initiative versus guilt**, in which the child balances the wish to do things against the prohibitions against doing them. Children who emerge from this period with a sense of initiative feel confident that their behavior will be judged appropriate by others. Children who experience a sense of guilt, on the other hand, are inhibited and anxious about the appropriateness of their actions. This stage is also called the "anticipation of roles," since by imagining themselves as adults they learn the rules of adult society.

II. Sex-Role Development
1. **Sex roles** are the tasks and traits that society assigns to females and males, and **sex-role development** is the process by which children come to behave in ways that are masculine or feminine.
2. Traditionally in Western culture, masculinity, with its associated traits of independence, competitiveness, self-confidence, strength, and dominance; and femininity, with its traits of gentleness, helpfulness, kindness, empathy, appreciativeness, and sentimentality, were seen as opposites. One was either masculine or feminine, but not both. Psychologists now emphasize that the traits we call masculine and feminine exist to some extent in both sexes.
3. **Agency** refers to active, assertive, and self-confident behavior we do independently; **communion** refers to supportive, helpful, and empathic behavior that we do with or for others. People with many **agentic** traits are considered masculine, those with mostly **communal** traits are considered feminine, and people strong in both agentic and communal traits are called **androgynous**.
4. At the age of 2 or 3, most children understand their **gender identity**, their knowledge that they are a male or a female. At this age, they begin to use the terms boy and girl reliably to

differentiate males and females, an ability called **gender labeling**. But they do not understand that their sex will never change, called **gender constancy**, until they are about 6 or 7.

5. By age 3, boys and girls are aware that certain toys and activities are more appropriate for one sex than the other, and by age 5 they often express distaste for things associated with the opposite sex and have **sex stereotypes**, or social expectations for how men and women behave, about the appropriateness of certain careers: for example, girls are nurses and boys are truck drivers. Young children stereotype personalities as well: across cultures women are believed to be gentle and men to be robust. These stereotypes occur in children whose mothers worked, indicating that stereotyped thinking may be the foundation of nonstereotyped thinking.

6. Although there are wide individual variations in behavior, in general, most boys are more active and aggressive than most girls. Their play is rougher, they try harder to dominate their peers, they are more antisocial, they respond to assault with physical force, they are more curious and do more exploring, and they work harder to get around barriers. Girls handle frustration and control their impulses better than boys, are more nurturant and compliant, but are also more anxious and timid. These behavior differences emerge once children are firmly aware of their gender identity, by age 4 or so.

7. In every mammalian species, including humans, males are more aggressive than females, beginning early in life. This finding suggests a biological link in sex-role development and may be related to the presence of **androgens**, or male hormones. Research supporting this idea shows that girls who have been exposed prenatally to androgens exhibit more masculine behaviors. Even though the relationship between aggression and masculinity seems clear, it is not clear as to what causes what.

8. For Freud, the conflict of the preschool years centers on the biological urges of genital sexuality. During this **phallic stage**, children wish to "possess" their opposite-sex parent, but fear retaliation from the same-sex parent. Freud called this conflict in boys the Oedipus complex and labeled the fear of the father's punishment **castration anxiety**. The Oedipus complex is resolved when the boy represses, or removes from consciousness, his desire for his mother and **identifies** with his father, accepting his attitudes, behaviors, and beliefs. Girls experience the parallel conflict, called the Electra complex, in which they repress their desire for their fathers and identify with their mothers. Freud believed that part of the Electra complex is the girl's envy of the penis, but many psychologists now prefer to interpret this penis envy in a figurative sense as the envy of masculine power and independence. Some theorists argue that girls have an easier time than boys in identification because their mothers see them as similar to themselves. Thus, boys do not develop the capacity for closeness and intimacy that girls do.

9. According to psychoanalytic theory, when children internalize the attitudes and behaviors of the same sex parent, they also internalize that parent's attitudes and behavior of the same sex parent, they also internalize that parent's moral standards thus creating the superego, or conscience. Appropriate sex-typing occurs when the same-sex parent is accepting, warm, and nurturing and when the opposite sex parent encourages sex-appropriate behavior. Children who do not have a same-sex parent or someone of the same sex with whom to identify may have greater difficulty in developing appropriate sex-typed behavior.

10. Cognitive theories of sex-role development suggest that this development is dependent on general cognitive development. For example, Lawrence Kohlberg believed that sex-role development begins by age 3, when children first label themselves as girls or boys. Gender constancy can be thought of as a conservation problem, like conservation of number or mass. Then, once children have identified their sex, new information gets sorted by gender: girls do this, boys do that. This is why examples showing nontraditional gender behavior, like boys playing with dolls, are often remembered in a gender-appropriate form—as boys playing with trucks. Thus, a few exposures to nontraditional gender situations is not likely to influence their sex-role expectations.

11. Social learning theorists believe that children learn sex roles through direct reinforcement of their gender-appropriate behavior and through modeling, or imitation. Sex-based messages begin early: parents of baby girls see them as more feminine than boys, even though observers who don't know the sex of the baby see no differences. Fathers "see" more differences than mothers. Parents also treat sons differently than daughters, reinforcing sex-appropriate behaviors. Although parents do not play with boys more or nurture girls more, they do expect boys and girls to select different toys and do different household chores.

12. Theorists believe that **modeling**, or imitation, plays an important role in shaping sex-roles, and in many families mothers still do the majority of the domestic work. However, mothers who are employed have daughters with less stereotyped ideas about family roles, careers, and toy preferences. Boys who prefer female sex-typed behavior are treated more harshly than girls who prefer boys' activities; but most children prefer to play with others of the same sex.

13. Women characters are greatly underrepresented in all television programming and are most often portrayed in sex-stereotyped roles, although some exceptions to this sex typing in the media exist.

14. No one theory can fully explain sex-role development, and there is considerable overlap among theories. Psychoanalytic theories emphasize feeling, cognitive focus on thinking, social learning highlights behaving, and all of these are influenced by the inborn, biologically based characteristics of each child.

15. If we lived in a nonindustrial culture, traditional sex roles might produce a productive division of labor. However, in our industrialized society, both sexes have more-or-less the same roles to play and it makes more sense for differences in sex roles to be deemphasized. Since the beginning of the women's movement in the 1970s, attention has focused on the appropriateness of the traditional sex roles in our culture and has made us aware of the potential both sexes have for the full range of human behavior and emotion.

III. Developing Social Skills

1. A child's ability to **empathize**, or know what another person is feeling, may be present from about 1 year, or even earlier, as evidenced by the finding that babies cry when they hear others crying. Two-and three-year-olds will offer gifts to others and help each other, and empathy increases in the preschool years. Furthermore, children who are more empathetic at early ages tend to remain more empathetic as they develop.

2. **Prosocial behavior** consists of positive, helping acts. Prosocial behavior is not linked to birth-order, economic background, or sex. Prosocial behavior is linked to sociability and the frequency of expression of positive emotions. Prosocial children tend to be more assertive and well-adjusted, and they tend to cope well with stress.

3. Prosocial behavior may arise from secure mother-infant attachments. Cognitive explanations for prosocial behavior center on the child's cognitive ability to take another's perspective rather than seeing the world only from his own point of view. Social learning explanations emphasize imitation and reinforcement of prosocial behavior as the primary means by which children learn.

4. Although boys tend to be more aggressive than girls at all ages, they show the same developmental trends. For example, as all children get older and their verbal skills develop, they rely more on talking, and less on pushing, to settle their disputes. Also, they exhibit both **instrumental aggression**, which arises from conflicts over ownership, territory or rights, and **hostile aggression**, which is directed at another person and can be both physical and verbal. Children who are the most aggressive at early ages tend to also be the most aggressive at older ages, although situations can influence behavior to reduce aggression.

5. Cognitive theorists emphasize the importance of one's interpretation of a situation in the decision to react aggressively. Aggressive children often misperceive accidents as intentional insults and they also tend to act aggressively without considering other ways to act. Social

learning theorists again focus on modeling and reinforcement in explaining aggression. Aggressive responses are often reinforced, either by getting what one wants or by getting attention. However, rewards can also be made contingent on nonaggressive behavior, thereby limiting aggression. Attachment theory stresses the link between children's experiences in the family and the way they expect others to treat them. All three theories of development—cognitive, social learning, and attachment—are useful in helping us explain the full range of social behavior.

6. Preschoolers choose their friends because of their physical qualities, common activities, possession of interesting things, and physical closeness. By the end of the preschool years, they begin valuing social support and affection in their friends. Also, children from the ages of 2 to 11, and especially boys, prefer friends of the same sex.

7. Although physical attractiveness is an advantage and physical handicaps and learning disabilities are liabilities, the most important determinant in how well liked a child is is that child's behavior. Popular preschoolers are more friendly and socially skilled than other children and engage in less disruptive, antisocial behavior. Thus, their pleasant behavior gets them what they want and also garners for them the respect and liking of their peers. Unpopular children have more trouble communicating, thereby maintaining their reputations as unpopular and disliked.

8. Knowledge of what emotions are appropriate under given circumstances is also linked to social skill. And, although sociability varies from infant to infant, family situations also influence a child's behavior. For example children with secure attachments as infants often have better social skills as preschoolers. Unpopular boys tended to have fathers who were least likely to play with their sons or who tended to be overstimulating in play. Also, popular children tended to have supportive families who did not use physical aggression to settle disputes at home.

9. Children's interpersonal behavior can be improved by decreasing the frequency with which they engage in aversive behavior and by increasing the frequency with which they engage in sharing and cooperative activity. Teachers can model appropriate behavior, explain more effective strategies for getting what the child wants, and reinforce the child whose behavior improves.

IV. The Work of Play

1. Play provides a setting for social, emotional, and cognitive development, and its activities are directly related to the level of the child's cognitive development.

2. At about 12 to 18 months of age, children engage in **parallel play**, in which they play in proximity to others but really focus only on their own activities. With time, they begin to acknowledge each other by making eye contact, the characteristic associated with **parallel-aware play**. Eventually, in **simple-social play**, they begin talking with each other, smiling, and exchanging toys.

3. At about age 2, **complementary and reciprocal play**, which is characterized by active, turn-taking, begins to emerge. At about age 3, in **cooperative social pretend play**, children act out complementary roles in a make-believe scenario, such as doctor/nurse or teacher/student. Later, in **complex social pretend play**, children not only act out the roles but also converse about the roles they are playing.

4. From about age 4 on, planning how to play usually precedes playing itself. Play planning provides a way of directing and monitoring oneself in relation to others and helps children solidify their identities.

5. The shift from playing alone to playing cooperatively happens gradually and, from time to time, older children prefer the kind of solitary or parallel play they developed earlier. From ages 2 to 5, however, children spend less and less time in parallel and parallel-aware play and more time in cooperative and complex social pretend play. Children who choose more advanced play at earlier ages are often more socially advanced as well.

116 Social and Emotional Development in Early Childhood

6. By age 2, children prefer different styles of play, with some being patterners, whose play is tied to the properties of the materials they are using, and others being dramatists, whose play consists more of social interactions. Also, some children are more playful than others, and these children are also more verbal and like to engage in social and imaginative play. Parents can encourage play by being interested in the child's activities, and children do not need expensive toys to engage in hours of creative, satisfying play.

Self Test

A. Matching Questions

___ 1. Supportive, helpful, and empathic behavior
___ 2. Process by which children learn to be masculine or feminine
___ 3. Having both masculine and feminine traits
___ 4. Knowledge that one is either male or female
___ 5. Active, assertive, and self-confident behaviors
___ 6. Traits assigned to males and females
___ 7. When a child emerges successfully from this period, she feels confident that her behavior is consistent with others' expectations

a. agency
b. initiative versus guilt
c. androgynous
d. autonomy versus shame and doubt
e. gender constancy
f. sex-role development
g. communion
h. sex roles
i. gender identity

___ 8. Psychoanalytic description for the preschool period
___ 9. Conscience
___ 10. Social expectations about how males and females behave
___ 11. Little boys' fear of their fathers
___ 12. Repression of desire for father and identification with mother
___ 13. Male hormones
___ 14. Imitation
___ 15. Repression of desire for mother and identification with father
___ 16. Process of accepting the values and behavior of the same-sex parent

a. sex stereotypes
b. Electra complex
c. castration anxiety
d. modeling
e. androgens
f. superego
g. Oedipus complex
h. phallic stage
i. identification
j. penis envy

___ 17. To know what another person is feeling
___ 18. Taking a desired toy away from another child, for example
___ 19. Children playing in the same place but focused on their own activities
___ 20. Children who prefer play that manipulates objects, like blocks
___ 21. Aggression that is deliberately harmful to another person
___ 22. Play in which children act out roles in a make-believe setting
___ 23. Positive, helping acts
___ 24. "Run and chase" is a common game in this stage of play

a. hostile aggression
b. patterners
c. parallel play
d. social pretend play
e. empathize
f. instrumental aggression
g. dramatists
h. complementary and reciprocal play
i. prosocial behavior

Social and Emotional Development in Early Childhood 117

B. Multiple Choice

Factual
Obj. 1
Basic

1. According to the text, the crisis involved in the balancing of the wish to do with the prohibitions against doing is the center of which of the following of Erikson's stages?
   a. initiative versus guilt
   b. autonomy versus shame and doubt
   c. group versus cooperative play
   d. generativity versus stagnation

Conceptual
Obj. 2
Moderate

2. Which of the following concepts is most closely related to the development of ideas about what constitutes appropriate masculine and feminine behavior?
   a. development of gender constancy
   b. development of gender identity
   c. sex-role development
   d. androgyny

Applied
Obj. 2
Moderate

3. Mark's behavior is usually very helpful and empathic, and he tries to be supportive and thoughtful of his friends. The term which best describes his behavior is:
   a. agency
   b. androgyny
   c. feminine
   d. communion

Applied
Obj. 2
Moderate

4. Jennifer has some traits that are masculine and some that are feminine. The word which best describes her is
   a. communion
   b. androgynous
   c. agency
   d. prosocial

Applied
Obj. 3
Moderate

5. Jason has just discovered that no matter what he does or what he wants, he will always be a male. He has just acquired the concept called:
   a. gender identity
   b. a sex stereotype
   c. gender constancy
   d. a sex role

Conceptual
Obj. 4
Moderate

6. Which of the following is the most accurate statement about how sex stereotypes have changed since the women's movement of the 1970s.
   a. Today's children hold fewer sex stereotypes.
   b. Today's children hold less rigid stereotypes about women, but have not changed their stereotypes about men.
   c. Today's children hold less rigid stereotypes about men, but have not changed their stereotypes about women.
   d. Sex stereotypes have not changed much at all.

Conceptual
Obj. 4
Moderate

7. Which of the following characteristics pertains more generally to girls than to boys?
   a. better control of impulses
   b. more aggressive
   c. more active
   d. more antisocial

118 Social and Emotional Development in Early Childhood

Applied
Obj. 5
Moderate

8. Dr. Johnson argues that sex-typed differences result from the resolution of the child's fear of the same-sex parent and the subsequent acceptance of that parent's attitudes, behavior, and values. Dr. Johnson's view is most similar to that expressed in:
   a. the psychoanalytic perspective
   b. the social learning perspective
   c. the biological perspective
   d. the cognitive perspective

Factual
Obj. 5
Moderate

9. The development of the superego corresponds most closely to the development of:
   a. castration anxiety
   b. the conscience
   c. parallel play
   d. gender constancy

Conceptual
Obj. 5
Moderate

10. Research which showed that children cannot establish gender constancy before they master other principles of conservation would be most consistent with which of the following views of sex-role development?
    a. the social learning view
    b. the cognitive view
    c. the biological view
    d. the psychoanalytic view

Applied
Obj. 5
Advanced

11. Martin believes that male homosexuality results when little boys are rewarded for imitating their mothers. His belief is most consistent with which of the following perspectives/
    a. the psychoanalytic view
    b. the biological view
    c. the cognitive view
    d. the social learning view

Factual
Obj. 5
Moderate

12. Which of the following is an accurate statement of the differences in treatment given to boys and girls by their parents?
    a. Both parents play more with boys.
    b. Both parents nurture girls more.
    c. Fathers play more with their sons and mothers are more nurturant with their daughters.
    d. Both parents expect boys and girls to play with different toys and assign them different chores.

Applied
Obj. 6
Basic

13. Samuel learns about being male by imitating the behavior of his father. This imitation is called:
    a. modeling
    b. reinforcement
    c. agency
    d. communion

Factual
Obj. 6
Moderate

14. According to the text, which of the following theoretical perspectives provides the best explanation for the development of sex roles?
    a. the biological and psychoanalytic theory taken together
    b. the social learning theory
    c. the social learning theory and cognitive theory taken together
    d. all of the theories provide meaningful, helpful explanations

Applied
Obj. 7
Moderate

15. Tommy offers to share his cookie with his friend who just dropped his in the mud. This example serves to demonstrate that Tommy has the ability:
    a. to model
    b. to empathize
    c. for functional play
    d. for associative play

Applied
Obj. 7
Moderate

16. Suppose you discover that preschool children who have just seen an adult share a toy with a child are now more able to share a toy themselves than are children who don't see the adult share. This example is most clearly related to which of the following perspectives?
    a. the biological view
    b. the psychoanalytic view
    c. the social learning view
    d. the cognitive view

Factual
Obj. 8
Moderate

17. Aggression which arises out of conflicts over ownership, territory, or perceived rights is called:
    a. emphatic aggression
    b. hostile aggression
    c. instrumental aggression
    d. functional aggression

Factual
Obj. 9
Moderate

18. The most important factor in determining how children are regarded by their age-mates is:
    a. their physical attractiveness
    b. their intelligence
    c. their behavior
    d. the parenting style used by their parents

Factual
Obj. 10
Moderate

19. Which of the following is the correct order of the stages of play through which children develop?
    a. parallel-complementary and reciprocal-social pretend
    b. social pretend-complementary and reciprocal-parallel
    c. parallel-social pretend-complementary and reciprocal
    d. complementary and reciprocal-parallel-social pretend

Factual
Obj. 10
Moderate

20. Fantasy and acting out of roles are major characteristics in which of the following types of play?
    a. parallel
    b. social pretend
    c. complementary and reciprocal
    d. parallel-aware

C. Essay Questions

INSTRUCTIONS
After reading and studying the text, read the question below and write your answer in the space provided. Do not refer to your text or to the Scoring Scheme or Model Answer on the next page.

1. Briefly describe how each of the four theoretical perspectives—the biological, the psychoanalytic, the cognitive, and the social learning—explain how children learn appropriate sex-typed behavior. For each of the four views, cite one piece of evidence that is supportive.

Total Score ___

Scoring Scheme for Question 1

+3 points each (up to 12 points) for accurate descriptions of the theoretical viewpoints. For full credit, the answer should include the following:
- biological: differences in hormones
- psychoanalytic: accurate description of the Oedipus and/or Electra complex, and an accurate explanation of identification
- cognitive: sex-role development is dependent on general cognitive development
- social learning: focus on modeling and reinforcement (both should be mentioned)

+1 point each (up to 4 points) for an accurate and appropriate example of supportive evidence.

Total: 16 points

Model Answer for Question 1

The **biological** perspective argues that sex-roles are, at least to some extent, determined by biological differences between the sexes. For example, the androgenic, or male, hormones may be linked to the greater aggressiveness seen in males of all mammalian species. Even females who are exposed to androgens prenatally develop more aggressive tendencies in childhood, indicating that these hormones may be linked to aggression.

The **psychoanalytic** view suggests that children go through the Oedipus complex (for boys) or the Electra complex (for girls). Here the child at first desires his or her opposite-sex parent and fears the same-sex parent. As development progresses, the child represses this desire for the opposite-sex parent and identifies with the same-sex parent. It is through this identification that the child copies and comes to value the behavior of the same-sex parent, including those behaviors that are sex-typed. Evidence supporting this view comes from research showing that boys who do not have a strong male figure with whom to identify sometimes have more trouble with the development of their own sexual identity.

Cognitive explanations view the development of sex-typed behavior to be linked to general cognitive development. A child learns appropriate sex roles when he or she comes to understand that gender is a permanent characteristic, in much the same way that other forms of conservation are learned. Evidence for the cognitive view comes from research that shows children tend to remember events involving boys playing with girl's toys as boys playing with boy's toys. Thus, they reinterpret situations in a way consistent with their own cognitive viewpoints.

Social learning theorists focus on imitation and reinforcement as the means by which sex roles are learned. Evidence for this perspective centers on the idea that in our culture little girls are reinforced for feminine behavior whereas little boys are reinforced for masculine behavior. This differential reinforcement transmits appropriate sex roles to the next generation.

122 *Social and Emotional Development in Early Childhood*

INSTRUCTIONS
After reading and studying the text, read the question below and write your answer in the space provided. Do not refer to your text, or to the Scoring Scheme or Model Answer on the next page.

2. Explain how children learn to play with each other by describing the stages of parallel play, complementary and reciprocal play, and social pretend play.

Total Score ___

Scoring Scheme for Question 2

+2 points each (up to 6 points) for accurate descriptions of the typical activities in each of the three stages.

+2 points for explaining the proper order of the stages—parallel, complementary and reciprocal, and social pretend play.

Total: 8 points

Model Answer for Question 2

Up until about the age of 3, children engage in **parallel play**, in which they play near other children but really don't play with other children. In parallel play they sometimes talk at each other, but their communication is really more like talking to themselves since they don't listen to the other child's messages any more than they expect to be listened to. At about 3 years of age, children enter the stage of **complementary and reciprocal play** where they do begin to interact. Typical games in this stage are "run and chase" and "hide and seek." These games involve some social interaction and also involve taking turns. At about age 3, children begin to engage in social pretend play, first in a simple way where they play make-believe roles they are familiar with, like "doctor-patient" or "mother-baby." As they get older, their social pretend play becomes more complex and they talk and interact together to figure out who is supposed to do and say what. Although children learn more complex forms of play as they get older, they sometimes go back to earlier forms of play as well.

Chapter 10

∎

The Social Context of Early Childhood

Preview of the Chapter

I. **The Family**
   A. Parenting Styles
      1. Authoritarian parents
      2. Permissive parents
      3. Authoritative parents
   B. Why Do Parents Behave as They Do?
      1. Personal traits of parents
      2. The nature of the child
      3. Marriages, social relationships, and work
      4. The broader context of parenting
   C. Child Abuse and Neglect
      1. Enduring effects of abuse
      2. Causes of Abuse
   D. Divorce and Preschoolers
   E. Children in Single-Parent Families
      1. Gender and custody: Issues
   F. Stepfamilies
   G. Sibling Relationships

II. **Children in Poverty**
   A. Homelessness

III. **Day Care and Early Childhood Programs**
   A. Kinds of Programs
   B. Day Care and Development
      1. Health
      2. Cognitive development
      3. Social development
   C. Quality Day Care
   D. Early Academics and the Harried Child
   E. Preschools and Culture
      1. Preschools in Japan, China, the United States, and Russia

IV. **Television and Development**
   A. Television and Social Experience
   B. Television and Cognitive Development
      1. The value of *Sesame Street*
   C. Television and Aggression
   D. Television and Prosocial Behavior

126 The Social Context of Early Childhood

Learning Objectives

1. Identify the relevant dimensions which affect parenting styles and describe the three different styles of parenting.

2. Discuss the factors which influence parents' behavior.

3. Describe the statistics on child abuse, explain the causes that are related to its occurrence, and suggest interventions that may reduce its effects.

4. Describe the incidence of divorce, single parenthood, and remarriage and explain how these situations affect the children involved.

5. Discuss the dynamics of sibling relationships.

6. Describe the incidence of poverty and homelessness and describe how they affect children.

7. Describe the various day care arrangements that are available.

8. Evaluate the effects day care has on child development and discuss the features of day care that are positively related to a child's social, cognitive, and emotional development.

9. Describe the effects that accelerated learning programs have on child development and comment on how culture influences day care programming.

10. Describe the effects that television has on social experience and cognitive development.

11. Discuss the relationship between viewing violence on TV and aggression in children.

12. Discuss the effects of watching prosocial television programs on children's behavior.

Chapter Summary

I. **The Family**
1. Developmentalists think of parenting styles along two continuum: responsive versus nonresponsive and demanding versus nondemanding. Responsive parents are warm and accepting whereas nonresponsive parents are critical, insensitive, and take little pleasure in their children. Demanding parents expect strict obedience whereas nondemanding parents provide little guidance and often give in to their child's demands. Based on these two dimensions, Diana Baumrind has identified three general patterns of parenting: authoritarian, permissive, and authoritative.
2. **Authoritarian parents** are demanding but nonresponsive, value obedience, try to impose absolute standards of behavior, do not explain their demands, and, if the child resists, use punishment to control behavior. They also anger easily, and may punish their child by withdrawing affection which often reinforces the child's already-present sense of rejection. Children of authoritarian parents are often moody, unhappy, fearful, withdrawn, and indifferent to new experiences; and show low self-esteem. They are also likely to be rejected by their preschool peers, and often become less assertive, withdrawn, and ineffectual with their peers.
3. **Permissive parents** are generally uncontrolling and nonthreatening, make few demands, and impose little discipline. While some permissive parents are cool and detached, many are warm.

Children of these parents may feel their parents don't care about them and they have trouble regulating their own behavior. They tend to be impulsive and aggressive, to lack self-reliance and self-control, and are low in social responsibility and independence, but they are more cheerful than children of authoritarian parents.

4. **Authoritative parents** set clear standards and expect cooperation but also are willing to listen to their children, reason with them, and, when appropriate, adjust their expectations. For discipline, they rely on reasoning, called **induction**, which is effective over time. Thus, authoritative parents are both demanding and nurturing, and their children are socially competent, energetic, friendly, curious, self-reliant, self-controlled, and cheerful. They also get along well with other children and have high self-esteem.

5. Parenting styles come from multiple determinants including the parents' personalities and satisfaction with work and marriage, the child's temperament, and the culture. Parents who are irritable, anxious, depressed, or low in self-esteem tend to be authoritarian. Those with positive self-images and who are emotionally expressive are more likely to be authoritative.

6. Easygoing, compliant children usually have the most comfortable relationships with their parents and difficult children place more demands on their parents. The goodness of fit between parents and child influences both the parent's style and the child's behavior.

7. Good marriages tend to produce warm, affectionate mothers and fathers. Also, mothers who are supported by friends and relatives use fewer authoritative punishments and feel more competent and self-assured. Social support is especially important in African-American families due to their minority status. Fathers with satisfying careers and mothers who enjoy their work and have a husband who does not resent their working carry over their positive feelings at home to their children and are more attentive and use severe punishment less. Thus, parenting is shaped by many factors including the parents' histories and personalities, the child's behavior, and the social context.

8. Parents in different cultures rear their preschoolers differently, particularly with regard to the culture's emphasis on conformity versus independence. For example Chinese parents are more restrictive and immigrant parents from Asia and Mexico stress conformity in comparison to the way Anglo children are raised in the United States.

9. Every year nearly 3 million children in the United States are reported as abused. More cases may occur but are unreported, and some differences exist among cultures in what behaviors are considered to be abusive. The effects of abuse are deep and enduring, and can influence every aspect of a young child's social and emotional development. Abused children tend to have insecure attachments to their parents, have trouble forming close ties with others, find new experiences threatening, are less curious, and show signs of poor communication, over-aggressiveness, impulsivity, frequent temper tantrums, self-destructive behavior, and low self-esteem.

10. Abused children may grow up to be abusive parents, probably due to their failure as children to form secure attachments, and their difficulty in dealing with their own fear of failure. A child may, inadvertently, contribute to his own abuse because he needs extra support. Thus premature, ill, or difficult children are most at risk for abuse.

11. Abuse is linked to external stress, and especially to poverty, with its attendant problem of crowded living environments. The rate of maltreatment was 5 times greater in families with incomes under rather than over $15,000. Abuse is also associated with drug and alcohol abuse, low levels of education, teenage parents, and parents who are socially isolated. Finally, the U.S. culture, which stresses the rights of privacy and freedom of parents to discipline their children, may contribute to a high abuse rate. Abuse is best seen as the result of many risk factors, each of which contributes to the tendency to be abusive.

12. Parents at risk for being abusive benefit from educational programs which teach them about child development, provide a link to social service agencies, and enhance their self-esteem. In one study, only 4 percent of mothers in this kind of program engaged in abusive behavior as

compared to 20 percent in a control group. Abuse can also be reduced when parents have others to which they can turn for support.

13. Almost half of children born in the United States in the last decade will see their parents divorce. Preschoolers show the greatest signs of stress since they have few supportive relationship outside the family and they can't grasp the reasons behind a divorce and often blame themselves. Furthermore, they often believe that the parent who moves away no longer loves them, and they fantasize about and exaggerate the possibility of a reconciliation.

14. Little boys usually respond to divorce in one of two ways—by acting out their anger or by becoming more dependent and less masculine. Mothers can help their sons cope by encouraging independent behavior and expressing positive attitudes about her ex-husband and males in general. Preschool girls adjust more quickly, but developmental effects may show up later, in adolescence. Actually, the negative effects associated with divorce may come more from the breakdown in effective parenting that accompanies the separation rather than from the divorce itself, and, if the divorce brings an improved living situation, it may relieve some stresses on the child.

15. After a divorce, nearly 90 percent of children live with their mothers. Single parents head about one-fourth of all families in the United States: one-third of Hispanic families, one-half of black families, and one-fifth of white families. About one-half of all children born in the United States today can expect to spend part of their lives in a single-parent household. This trend is caused not only by divorce but also by an increase in unmarried mothers, and by more gay and lesbian men and women who are choosing to become parents.

16. Among divorced parents, the custodial parent's emotional satisfaction and financial security most strongly affect the child's well-being. In the year following a divorce, the woman's and children's income drops by nearly 75 percent, whereas the man's increases by over 40 percent. Sixty percent of families headed by women have incomes below the poverty line. In all families, what matters most is the extent and quality of their parents' involvement and the quality of their daily lives.

17. Although not always the case, some research suggests that, in divorce, boys may do better living with their fathers and girls with their mothers. In 90 percent of all divorces, the mother is awarded **custody**, the legal right to care for the children. Although early research suggested **joint custody**, in which parents share responsibility for their children, was best for children, newer studies suggest such arrangements are complex and problematic, and may be less advantageous to the child than single-parent custody.

18. Ten percent of children will experience two divorces before they are sixteen. Young children adjust best to a stepparent when the adult tries to develop a warm and non-disciplining relationship.

19. Ambivalence is the typical characteristic of how siblings feel about each other, since they are both rivals and pals. Older children can be cognitively stimulated by teaching a younger child, and they both can benefit by playing together. Communicating about the baby's needs and allowing the child to help in caring for the baby can improve sibling rivalry, which is also less when the older child is temperamentally like the younger, when he can talk about his feelings, and he gets along well with friends. Preschool girls appear to adjust more easily to a new sibling than do boys.

II. Children in Poverty

1. In 1991, one-fourth of children in the United States under six was living in poverty, and the rate has been increasing. Nearly 60 percent of poor children were minorities. Almost 40 percent of poor children live with married parents.

2. Poor children get sick more often, achieve less in school, and have more psychological problems than children who are not poor, and the effects of persistent poverty are worse than those of transient (short-term) poverty. Poor children are also more likely to be exposed to

violence, which further erodes the ability of their parents to provide a nurturing, safe environment.
3. Homeless children experience even more serious consequences, and the majority are developmentally delayed, anxious, depressed, and have learning difficulties. Young girls are the most affected. Few homeless children ever enroll in Head Start or other preschool intervention programs.

III. Day Care and Early Childhood Programs
1. The number of women with preschool children who are employed has risen from 12 percent in the 1960's to 40 percent in 1975, to 60 percent in 1990.
2. Day care is any child-care arrangement parents use when they are away from their children. In 1990, almost half of all preschoolers in day care were supervised by relatives, 25 percent attended a child care center, and 20 percent attended a family day care home. **Family day care**, where care is provided in a private home, can be very good, but can also be unstable, unsatisfying for the child, and unregulated by state agencies. **Center-based day care** programs are licensed and regulated by the government and are located in a central facility. Usually centers are not as flexible in terms of hours and are not "homelike" but offer more stable care. Over the past 20 years, the number of children in centers has surpassed the number in family day care. **Preschools** are similar to day care centers, but focus on the planned development of social and cognitive skills and often operate over more restricted hours. **Compensatory education programs**, like the federally mandated **Head Start** program for 3- and 4-year olds, are designed to serve the intellectual, emotional, and nutritional needs of children from poor families who are at risk for failing in school.
3. Head Start was part of President Johnson's "war on poverty" in the hope that education could remediate the effects of poverty. The Head Start program includes incentives for parents to continue education and job training, provides emotional support for parents, and encourages parents to participate in their children's classes. Those mothers who did attend these classes benefitted in terms of their own psychological health and personal satisfaction.
4. Child developmentalists are concerned that short-term programs like Head Start cannot remediate a life of poverty. Yet, the early Head Start programs produced positive long-term advantages. Children in these programs were less likely to require special education services, to repeat a grade, or to become delinquent, and were more likely as high school students to express pride in their accomplishments. However, children in later years of the program have shown short-term intellectual gains which fall off over the long term. Perhaps this failure to produce long-lasting results is due to the cut-backs in teacher training and pay and classroom materials that have accompanied the more recent years of the program. Perhaps, too, we cannot expect two years of enriched educational experience to fully compensate for a life of poverty. Head Start excels, however, in supporting families, enabling parents to work, providing children with nutritious meals, and ensuring that children have periodic health checks. Unfortunately, the Head Start program is funded to reach only one-fourth of all eligible children.
5. Because children are not randomly assigned to different kinds of day care programs or to stay at home, it is very difficult to tell whether differences in their behavior and development are due to the effects of their day care program or to differences among the families that choose different child care options.
6. Up to age 5, there seems to be little difference in cognitive skills between children with and without day care experience. When cognitive gains do show up, they are probably due to direct cognitive stimulation by teachers and caregivers. Day care children do have more childhood illnesses, but these infections may produce immunities which protect them from illness later on.

7. Early childhood programs of reasonably good quality seem to enhance children's social development, probably because the teachers tend to be less authoritarian than mothers. Day care children tend to be more self-confident, outgoing, independent, and knowledgeable about the world but also less polite and agreeable, louder, more aggressive, and bossier.
8. The quality of day care is influenced by the same things as produce quality parenting: sensitivity, emotional support, and adequate physical and mental stimulation. Group size and the child:caregiver ratio are important: groups should not exceed 15 to 18, and caregiver ratios should not go past 6 to 1 for very young children or 10 to 1 for older preschoolers. Also, caregivers should be well-trained and sensitive to children's needs.
9. During the 1980s, parents put more emphasis on accelerating the development of their children. In preschools, they insisted that the focus shift from process to performance, thereby focusing on achievement, and the "hurried child" was born. Developmentalists reject this early pressure to learn, arguing that it stifles children's normal tendency to explore, play, and learn, and it undermines their confidence and independence. Research shows their concerns to be well-founded for children of different races and social classes.
10. Preschools in different cultures reflect the values of those cultures. In the United States, self-reliance and self-confidence are most valued. In Japan, preschools emphasize group membership. The Chinese value group membership, but even more important is obedience to authority, and preschools are heavily regimented. In Russia, where dramatic social changes have recently occurred, the preschools reflected these changes, moving away from emphasizing conformity and toward more freedom and personal initiative.

IV. Television and Development

1. American 2- to 5-year olds watch an average of 2–3 hours of TV every day, and the number of hours increases with age during these years and levels off during the school-age years. Only sleeping occupies more of a typical preschooler's time.
2. Television reduces the amount of time the family spends together in positive social interactions and it increases the tension in family life. One source of tension comes from commercials, which children don't distinguish from programs, Another danger comes when children spend too much time watching TV and not enough playing with other children. As a group, heavy TV watchers tend to be passive, bashful, and more distractible, but these traits, because they were present at age 3, probably encourage children to watch TV rather than result from too much TV watching. Such children probably would benefit more from playing with peers and learning social skills than watching TV.
3. Generally, preschool children do not make clear distinctions between reality and fantasy on TV, they don't perceive events in the same program as related to each other, and they don't follow a story line until they're about 8 or 9. Children seem to benefit from watching programs designed for them, like **Sesame Street**, especially when adults watch with them and reinforce the concepts presented.
4. The TV shows with the highest levels of violence are cartoons and weekend programming for children. Children who watch television violence become more aggressive and also show a passive acceptance of other people's aggression. Boys watch more TV violence than girls, and lower-class boys watch more than middle-class boys. Thus, those children most predisposed to aggression are most exposed to violence on TV. The relationship between violence and aggression works in two directions: aggressive children watch more violent TV, and TV violence causes children to be more aggressive. Also, it doesn't seem to matter where the TV programs are seen or whether the violence is portrayed realistically or in cartoons: the more the child identifies with the characters he views and believes their episodes reflect reality, the stronger is the link between violence and aggression.
5. Research on the effects of viewing prosocial programs, like **Mister Rogers' Neighborhood**, shows that such programs do encourage greater cooperation, helpfulness, and willingness to

work longer at a difficult task, especially among children from lower-socioeconomic families. Also, children benefit most when other aspects of their environment also encourage prosocial behavior, but the effects of prosocial programming do not seem to be retained over the long-term.

Self Test

A. Matching Questions

___ 1. Where mother drops off baby everyday at a friend's house
___ 2. Usually warm, but uncontrolling
___ 3. Legal care or guardianship of a child
___ 4. Child care in a central facility and which is licensed and regulated
___ 5. Head Start is an example of this
___ 6. Values obedience, has set standards, and does not explain
___ 7. Where both parents share guardianship of their children
___ 8. Day care program for low-income children
___ 9. Sets clear standards, but will explain and compromise
___ 10. Child care that includes planned social and cognitive experiences

a. permissive parent
b. custody
c. authoritarian parent
d. family day care
e. Head Start
f. nursery schools
g. joint custody
h. authoritative parent
i. center-based day care
j. compensatory education programs

___ 11. Percent of black families headed by a single parent
___ 12. Percent of mothers of preschool children who were employed in 1990
___ 13. Number of children in U.S. who are abused every year
___ 14. Percent of children whose parents will divorce
___ 15. Percent of white families headed by a single parent
___ 16. Percent of Hispanic families headed by a single parent
___ 17. Percent of children under the age of six who live in poverty
___ 18. Percent of children who after divorce live with their mothers

a. 20 percent
b. 1 million
c. 25 percent
d. 33 percent
e. 50 percent
f. 3 million
g. 60 percent
h. 90 percent

B. Multiple Choice

Conceptual
Obj. 1
Advanced

1. On the continuum of responsive/nonresponsive and demanding/nondemanding, where would an authoritarian parent fall?
   a. responsive and demanding
   b. nonresponsive and nondemanding
   c. demanding and nonresponsive
   d. accepting and nondemanding

Applied
Obj. 1
Moderate

2. Nick's dad is warm, but very seldom expresses any demands on Nick or control over his behavior. Nick's friends all think his dad is great. Nick's dad most likely has a parenting style called:
   a. permissive
   b. authoritarian
   c. authoritative
   d. modern

Factual Obj. 1 Basic	3.	The kind of discipline that involves the use of reasoning to explain the expectations of parents is called: a. permissiveness b. the method of multiple determinants c. authoritarian control d. induction
Conceptual Obj. 2 Moderate	4.	Which of the following types of parents is least likely to use an authoritative style of parenting? a. Ralph, who is a blue-collar worker in a unionized plant and who has low self-esteem b. Marjorie, who loves her job as a teacher and whose husband supports her decision to work c. George, who is a successful lawyer d. Judy, who is not employed and who has many supportive friends
Conceptual Obj. 3 Moderate	5.	Which of the following is true with respect to the number of reported cases of child abuse in the United States? a. it increased up until about 1980, and has remained about level since then b. it was level until about 1980, but has been decreasing since then c. it has been increasing steadily d. it has always been at about the same level in our society, but is higher in the U.S. than in many other countries
Conceptual Obj. 3 Moderate	6.	Which of the following children is least likely to be abused? a. Mack, who is premature b. Bill, who has an easy-going temperament c. Jeff, who is handicapped d. Jim, who is sick a lot
Factual Obj. 3 Moderate	7.	In terms of cultural influences on child abuse, the U.S. culture probably encourages ___ abuse than that of China and ___ abuse than that of Sweden. a. more; less b. more; more c. less; more d. less; less
Conceptual Obj. 4 Moderate	8.	Generalizing from the text, which of the following children is most likely to be most negatively affected immediately after his or her parents' divorce? a. David, who is 4 years old b. Robert, who is 9 years old c. Linda, who is 4 years old d. Susan, who is 9 years old
Factual Obj. 4, 6 Moderate	9.	After divorce, the income of a woman and her children typically: a. increases by 20 percent b. stays about the same c. drops by 30 percent d. drops by 75 percent

Applied 10. Vernon's parents are getting a divorce. He will live two weeks with his mother, then
Obj. 5   two weeks with his father on an alternating schedule. This situation is best thought of
Basic   as an example of:
            a. a compensatory settlement
            b. authoritative compromise
            c. multiple determinants
            d. joint custody

Factual 11. The typical feeling that a preschooler has for a new brother or sister is most likely:
Obj. 5   a. affection
Basic   b. resentment
             c. interest
             d. both affection and resentment

Factual 12. Which of the following statements about poverty in the United States is false?
Obj. 6   a. Nearly one out of four children under the age of 6 is poor.
Advanced   b. Children under age 6 are the group of people most likely to be poor.
             c. Only about 10 percent of poor children live with married parents.
             d. Poverty hits minority children in greater proportion than white children.

Applied 13. On her way to work each day, Kesha drops off her baby at her church where other
Obj. 7   women take care of him and several other children. Kesha's day care arrangement is
Moderate   best thought of as an example of:
             a. family day care
             b. center-based day care
             c. a preschool
             d. a compensatory education program

Applied 14. Peter is unemployed and poor, and while he is going to school, he takes his daughter to
Obj. 7   a day care program which is subsidized by the government and which is aimed at
Moderate   providing skills necessary to help high-risk children succeed at school. The day care
             arrangement Peter has fits best with which of the following?
             a. compensatory education programs
             b. preschools
             c. family day care
             d. center-based day care

Factual 15. Project Head Start was initiated to counter some of the effects of ___ on child
Obj. 6, 8   development.
Moderate   a. poverty
             b. divorce
             c. television
             d. child abuse

Factual 16. Project Head Start currently reaches about what percent of the children who are eligible
Obj. 8   for it?
Moderate   a. 98 percent
             b. 65 percent
             c. 47 percent
             d. 25 percent

134   The Social Context of Early Childhood

Conceptual
Obj. 9
Moderate

17. Which of the following best states the text's conclusion about the effects of performance-oriented learning programs attempting to accelerate cognitive development in preschools?
    a. The programs work but are very expensive, so they are only available to a small percentage of children who would benefit from them.
    b. The programs do not work: cognitive development in preschoolers cannot be accelerated.
    c. Although some cognitive skills can be developed earlier, the trade-off is often diminished curiosity and later school problems, so the programs should be discouraged.
    d. The programs work and cost much less than people thought, and they are being implemented in most preschools in this country.

Factual
Obj. 9
Moderate

18. Which country focuses most attention on fostering self-reliance and self-confidence in its preschool programs?
    a. the United States
    b. Japan
    c. China
    d. Russia

Conceptual
Obj. 10
Moderate

19. Which of the following statements about children and TV is *false*?
    a. Young children tend not to distinguish between advertising and programming
    b. children generally understand the story line of the shows they watch
    c. children remember very little of what they see on TV
    d. children pay more attention to programs that show lots of action

Conceptual
Obj. 11
Moderate

20. Which of the following statements most accurately reflects the research studying the effects of watching TV violence on aggressive behavior?
    a. watching TV violence causes children to behave more aggressively
    b. aggressive children watch more violent TV programs than nonaggressive children
    c. both a and b are correct
    d. neither a nor b is correct

C. Essay Questions

INSTRUCTIONS

After reading and studying the text, read the question below and write your answer in the space provided. Do not refer to your text or to the Scoring Scheme or Model Answer on the next page.

1. The text discusses several factors as being contributors to the likelihood that child abuse will occur. Identify four different factors which may be linked to abuse and explain how each can contribute to the creation of an abusive situation.

Total Score ___

Scoring Scheme for Question 1

+2 points each (up to 8 points) for defining four factors that contribute to child abuse. These will probably reflect the following ideas: a) parents were abused as children; b) the child's behavior may be difficult; c) poverty or its related problems; d) our culture is violent and values privacy and personal freedom. More than one factor can be drawn from each category, as long as it is clearly different from the other three factors discussed. All four categories need not be described.

+1 point each (up to 4 points) for elaboration and accurate explanation of how each factor contributes to abuse.

Total: 12 points

Model Answer for Question 1

One of the most powerful forces in abusing parents' lives is **having been abused** themselves when they were children. When children grow up in an abusive family, they are likely to form insecure attachments and have fearful relationships with their own parents. As a result, they may never learn to form warm, secure relationships with others, and they also tend to have unreasonably high expectations of their own children. When they encounter personal difficulties, they may take their problems out by abusing their own children.

A second factor that contributes to child abuse is **poverty**. Children from families whose incomes are below $15,000 are much more likely to be abused then those from higher-income families. Being poor imposes many frustrations on parents, and is also linked to living in cramped quarters, having few recreational opportunities, having little education, and to drug and alcohol dependency. All of these factors can increase the probability of child abuse.

The **child's characteristics** also figure into the abuse equation. Children who are premature, sickly, who have behavior problems, or are difficult are more likely to be abused.

Finally, our **society itself** tends to contribute to abuse because we tend to be violent, and we also believe that parents have the right to privacy and to determine how their children will be treated. Thus, our society has been criticized as not doing enough to prevent child abuse.

INSTRUCTIONS
After reading and studying the text, read the question below and write your answer in the space provided. Do not refer to your text, or to the Scoring Scheme or Model Answer on the next page.

2. What effect does viewing violence on television have on preschoolers? What effect does viewing programs depicting prosocial behavior have on preschoolers? Should parents let their preschool children watch TV? Explain your answer.

Total Score ___

Scoring Scheme for Question 2

+2 points that viewing violence causes aggressive behavior

+2 points that viewing violence causes greater acceptability of violent behavior in others

+2 points that viewing prosocial programs leads to greater short-term prosocial behavior

+1 point that the effect of viewing prosocial programs is short-term

+4 points for the idea that TV viewing has both benefits and hazards for preschoolers and that it should be monitored by parents

Total: 11 points

Model Answer for Question 2

Watching violence on television causes children to behave more aggressively and to be more accepting of violent behavior in other people. This seems to be true regardless of whether the show is realistic or is a cartoon. Viewing prosocial programs like **Sesame Street** does lead to short-term increases in cooperation and sharing, but the effects tend to be rather small and do not seem to last over the long term.

The question of whether parents should let their preschool children watch TV is a difficult one. TV can model appropriate behavior and does entertain young children. But it should not be used as a substitute for physical activity and play with other children, which are much more valuable activities. Also, parents should probably limit the total number of hours children spend parked in front of the TV set, should limit the amount of violent programming to which their children are exposed, and should try and watch TV with their kids since their interaction can help make TV watching a more positive experience for their children.

Chapter 11

Physical and Cognitive Development in Middle Childhood

Preview of the Chapter

I. **Physical Growth and Development**
   A. Exercise, Diet, and Health
   B. Poverty and Nutrition
   C. Childhood Obesity

II. **Cognitive Development: Revolutionary Changes**
   A. Piaget's Perspective: Concrete Operations
      1. Classification
      2. Seriation and transitivity
      3. Conservation
   B. The Information-Processing Perspective
      1. Attention
      2. Memory
      3. Metacognition
      4. Problem solving

III. **Cognition in Elementary School**
   A. Reading
   B. Writing
   C. Mathematics

IV. **Individual Differences in Cognitive Development**
   A. Intelligence and Intelligence Testing
   B. Early Tests
   C. How Useful Are Intelligence Tests?
   D. Intelligence and Inheritance

V. **Social Cognition in Middle Childhood**
   A. New Conceptions About Other People
   B. New Conceptions About Relationships
   C. Moral Development

Learning Objectives

1. Describe the pattern of physical growth and development typical in middle childhood and explain how it is influenced by exercise and diet.

2. Discuss the problems of poverty and childhood obesity, and comment on how they are interrelated.

3. Describe in general terms the major changes in cognitive development that occur in middle childhood.

4. Describe the characteristics of Piaget's stage of concrete operations, focusing on the development of classification, seriation and transitivity, and conservation.

5. Explain the information-processing perspective and compare it to Piaget's view of development.

6. Describe development of memory in middle childhood, focusing on the abilities of metacognition and metamemory, and problem solving.

7. Discuss the advances in reading, writing, and mathematics that typically occur in middle childhood.

8. Define the concept of intelligence and describe how it has been measured.

9. Discuss the usefulness of intelligence tests and explain how heredity and environment interact in their influence on intelligence.

10. Describe how children develop new conceptions about other people and about relationships as they enter middle childhood.

11. Discuss Kohlberg's theory of moral development and describe the changes in moral reasoning which occur in the elementary school years.

Chapter Summary

I. Physical Growth and Development

1. Compared to the preschool years, growth during middle childhood is more gradual and physical changes are more subtle. School-age children grow about 2 to 2½ inches and 4½ to 6 pounds per year. Boys and girls weigh the same, are the same height, and can perform athletically at the same level, although some research suggests that African-American first graders were faster and more agile than white students, but white students had an advantage in hand-eye coordination. As in previous periods, both biological and environmental influences affect growth and development.

2. On the average, school-age children spend 16 hours a week watching TV and 5 hours a week in physical activity. Children's diets are generally poor, and one-third may consist of goods high in fat, salt, and sugar, and the children may have high cholesterol which is related to coronary artery disease in adulthood. Only 1 in 3 children participate in daily exercise programs in school, perhaps because schools are overly focused on competitive athletics. New physical education programs that address this need advocate shifting the balance from competition to fun, paying attention to physical differences among children, and helping each child find success at something.

3. Poor diets are due to too much junk food and, in poor families, to the fact that less expensive foods are usually high in carbohydrates and fats. Children who are malnourished do not perform as well on intelligence tests, and are behind their peers in school, perhaps because they may have lower motivation for school tasks. A child's brain needs 2 or 3 times more energy than an adult's brain.

4. At least 5 percent of all school children are **obese**, or weigh at least 20 percent more than their agemates. Obese children are at risk for peer rejection, and, because 50 percent of overweight adults were obese children, are also at risk for diabetes, hypertension (high blood pressure), and heart disease as adults. Obesity is most likely the result of overeating a diet of junk food coupled with inactivity. Dieting and exercise will eliminate obesity, and parents and teachers

need to help obese children feel competent, to praise weight-loss efforts, and to find substitutes for food as a reward.

II. Cognitive Development: Revolutionary Changes

1. The "cognitive revolution" occurs at ages 5–7 and is a time of remarkable changes in children's abilities to think and learn. By age 7, children have grasped conservation, the ability to ignore superficial changes and understand that basic qualities don't change. Second, they reason better about causation and don't assume that events which occur together are causally related. Third, they can classify objects on the basis of several characteristics, and can reason about both natural and arbitrary classes. Fourth, children gain increasing ability to manipulate symbols, which forms the basis of reading and arithmetic.

2. The **5-to-7 transition** is the age span in which these cognitive changes begin, although they continue throughout childhood. Many complex social and intellectual changes occur in the cognitive revolution and it cannot be traced to any particular development. By age 10, children have acquired most of the cognitive abilities needed to cope with ordinary life, which result from major advances in **logic**, referring to the general principles about the relations among objects and people, and **strategy**, the ability to use those principles to solve problems.

3. Piaget believed that children enter the stage of **concrete operations** at about age 7 when the child becomes able to perform mental operations, the ability to mentally represent an action and know that it is reversible. Children now can think logically about concrete objects or events, but still have difficulty reasoning about hypothetical situations until they reach puberty and the stage of formal operations.

4. Until they reach the stage of concrete operations, children cannot classify objects by more than one dimension at a time. In middle childhood children develop a **classification** scheme that allows them to understand how things fit into categories and how categories can be arranged relative to each other. Newer research has shown that when objects are part of a naturally occurring collection, like toy soldiers, children are able to do classifications at younger ages than Piaget suggested. Yet, Piaget was correct in his observations that children's ability to classify and recognize subsets improves dramatically during middle childhood.

5. **Seriation** is the ability to rank objects in a meaningful order. Piaget believed that preoperational children had trouble in understanding the dual role of objects in the middle of a series, that is, that these objects were smaller than some objects but larger than others.

6. Children also acquire the concrete operation called transitivity between the ages of 7 and 11. **Transitivity** is the understanding that if A is larger than B, and B larger than C, then A must be larger than C.

7. **Conservation**, the understanding that quantities don't change just because objects are moved around, is the trademark of the concrete operational period. Children learn conservation of number first, then of liquid and mass, then of weight (at age 9 or 10), and finally, at age 10 or 11, learn conservation of volume. Although some researchers believe that the experimenter's requests make children's responses more confused and that children may acquire concrete abilities earlier than Piaget thought, it is nonetheless true that from age 7 to 11 children acquire a systematic set of rules or operations for reasoning.

8. Whereas Piaget explained cognitive changes in terms of schemes and operations, information-processing theorists explain them by discussing storage space and memory strategies. They focus on the way we perceive information in the brain's sensory register; store it, first in short-term and then long-term memory; and, finally, understand it and respond to it.

9. As children grow older, they begin to understand the consequences of paying attention, and they become better at determining to what to pay attention. When watching TV, young children attend to the visual stimulation before them, but as they get older, they will attend only when the content of the show is engaging.

142 *Physical and Cognitive Development in Middle Childhood*

10. Between ages 5 and 11, memory improves dramatically, primarily because during these years children learn effective strategies with which to organize information. Children may not always use deliberate strategies; however, they do recall things better when they have a network of associations to help them remember. The most basic memory strategy is verbal rehearsal, or repeating information over and over. Also, linking words in order through cumulative rehearsal helps memory. During the school years, children learn to use associations, inferences, and retrieval cues to aid memory. Some researchers believe that improvements in memory with age result more from improvements in retrieval than in encoding.
11. **Metacognition**, the awareness children develop about their own knowledge and memory strategies, is our way of knowing what one does know and what one does not. One aspect of metacognition, metacognitive knowledge, is knowledge the child has about cognition, and it is the skill that aids in deciding how to remember something. Metamemory, or thinking about the process of remembering, is important because what children believe about memory strategies influences whether they use them. The second aspect of metacognition is cognitive monitoring and it includes: self-appraisal, which means you evaluate your knowledge and choose appropriate strategies to improve it, and self-management, which involves selecting appropriate strategies for solving a problem. **Metamemory** is our knowledge about our own memory and what strategies work best for us. Young children have some ideas about how their memories work, but metamemory becomes more efficient throughout childhood.
12. Children get better at problem solving as they get older, in large part because they are able to think about more than one aspect of a situation at a time.

III. Cognition in Elementary School

1. Before they learn to read, children exhibit many activities preliminary to reading, like recognizing letters. These reading-related activities are called **emergent literacy**, and include learning the connection between symbols and sounds, and the conventions of written work. These print conventions are usually mastered by third grade, but metacognition about reading continue to develop for many years, even into adulthood.
2. Unless taught otherwise, elementary school students typically use two strategies when writing: "knowledge telling," which is spilling everything they know in a series of unconnected sentences, and "copy-delete," in which they paraphrase the main ideas from another source. Since these strategies interfere with effective writing, writing is now taught in a process "writing approach" which involves brainstorming, jotting down ideas, writing a first draft, editing, getting peer comments, and making final corrections.
3. As in reading, children have some math skills, like counting and simple addition and subtraction, that precede formal arithmetical learning. As they learn arithmetic, they begin to learn rules. Children sometimes apply rules incorrectly, and they have particular difficulty with word problems until about the age of 10 or 11 when they begin to interpret the problems conceptually rather than look for word clues.
4. Cognitive skills and school work reinforce each other: math requires conservation, science requires classification, social studies requires seriation; and learning facts improves memory skills. Elementary school fosters metacognitive abilities and promotes **cognitive monitoring**, the ability to observe one's own behavior and evaluate it.

IV. Individual Differences in Cognitive Development

1. Differences among children in their cognitive development include the timing of their developmental advances, the speed with which they process information, the size of a child's memory, and the amount of information to which the child has access. Intelligence is a complex ability, composed of many facets.
2. Francis Galton was one of the first people to try to measure intelligence. His test consisted of tests of hearing, vision, and reaction time, but these abilities did not correspond well with each

other or with school success. Alfred Binet, a French psychologist, developed a test in the early 1900s which focused on mental skills like verbal and reasoning ability. Binet's test questions were linked to chronological age, so that average children answered questions appropriate for their age. If a child's mental age, or age of intellectual functioning, exceeded his chronological, or birth, age, the child was considered above average. The **intelligence quotient**, or **IQ**, is calculated by dividing the mental age as measured by the test by the chronological age, and multiplying the quotient by 100.

3. Binet believed that intelligence was complex and varied throughout life. Lewis Terman, however, thought intelligence remained relatively stable, and he revised Binet's test to produce the Stanford-Binet Test, which is still used. David Wechsler also saw intelligence as a composite characteristic and developed tests which yielded IQ scores for several subtests, for two general abilities—verbal and performance—and an overall IQ. Two of his tests are the Wechsler Intelligence Scale for Children (WISC) and the Wechsler Adult Intelligence Scale (WAIS).

4. The intelligence tests given in schools measure the sort of intelligence required to do well in a Western-style educational environment and rely heavily on verbal ability. They are better at predicting who needs special help than who will do well in school, since achievement depends on many factors including motivation. Intelligence tests have been criticized as biased toward white, middle-class culture, but they do a good job in measuring those aspects of mental ability related to school success.

5. Intelligence is affected by both hereditary and environmental influences which interact. Twenty years ago, some scientists, including Arthur Jensen, argued that intelligence was 80 percent genetic, and that the lower average scores of black children were due to genetic differences between the races. Today, most scientists believe that intelligence is quite malleable and efforts to stimulate a child's intellectual development can have a positive impact.

V. Social Cognition in Middle Childhood

1. **Social cognition** refers to thinking about one's self and the other people in one's life. The way children think about others, how they view relations among people, and how they think about moral problems all shift between the ages of 5 to 7.

2. In middle childhood, the child begins to understand the difference between intentional and accidental behavior and begins to recognize that other people have their own feelings, needs, and reasons for their actions. Robert Selman has identified 5 stages in the child's growing ability to understand others. The first shift, from preschool to ages 4 to 9, involves the development of the understanding that different people can view the same situation differently.

3. Before age 5, children usually believe that authority figures are always right. After the 5-to-7 transition, they come to understand that authority can derive from knowledge and experience, and parents don't know everything, a realization that can lead them, usually in about 4th grade, to think of authority as something they can choose to disobey. After age 7, children also come to view friendships as more dependent on shared likes and dislikes and on caring and less on self-interest. By late elementary school, they also perceive that friendship is based on understanding, intimacy, and mutuality.

4. Lawrence Kohlberg believed that moral development is linked to cognitive development and that children pass through distinct stages of **moral development**, the changes in the ability to reason about morality that occur as a child grows up. Kohlberg divided moral development into 3 level—preconventional, conventional, principled (or postconventional)—each having two substages. During most of childhood, children reason at the level of **preconventional thinking**, where decisions about right and wrong are based on the rewards or punishments which follow actions. Elementary school children are also capable of **conventional thinking**, in which decisions of right and wrong are based on how well a person follows the rules of society and play their correct social role.

5. Research has suggested that moral development does seem to progress in the sequence Kohlberg identified, and it is advanced when children are exposed to ethical conflicts and decisions. Research tends not to support the idea that moral reasoning develops in distinct stages. Instead, as in cognitive development, it develops gradually, and children capable of more advanced reasoning sometimes revert to simpler solutions.

Self Test

A. Matching Questions

___ 1. The ability to rank objects in order
___ 2. Period in which children begin to develop a sense of logic and strategy as part of their cognitive skills
___ 3. Understanding that if A is bigger than B, and B bigger than C, then A is bigger than C
___ 4. The understanding and control of one's own thinking skills
___ 5. Period in which children acquire seriation, classification, and conservation
___ 6. General principles about the relations among people and objects
___ 7. The ability to fit things into appropriate categories
___ 8. Overweight by at least 20 percent
___ 9. Depends on the ability to attend to more than one quality of an object at a time.

a. classification
b. 5-to-7 transition
c. conservation
d. metacognition
e. obese
f. seriation
g. concrete operations
h. logic
i. transitivity

___ 10. A measure of the genetic influence in a given trait
___ 11. Repeating information over and over
___ 12. The ability to think about thinking
___ 13. New methods of teaching writing advocate this
___ 14. Thinking about one's self and the other people in one's life, including interpersonal relations and social rules and roles
___ 15. The understanding that letters stand for sounds, and words are read from left to right, for example
___ 16. Where children judge right and wrong according to how well a person follows the rules of society
___ 17. The ability to think about one's own memory
___ 18. Mental age divided by chronological age multiplied by 100
___ 19. The first of Kohlberg's stages

a. metacognition
b. emergent literacy
c. conventional thinking
d. verbal rehearsal
e. intelligence quotient
f. metamemory
g. cumulative rehearsal
h. process approach
i. social cognition
j. preconventional thinking
k. heritability
l. moral development

B. Multiple Choice

Conceptual
Obj. 1
Moderate

1. Which of the following statements about growth during middle childhood is *false*?
   a. Children grow about 2 to 2½ inches per year.
   b. Children gain about 4½ to 6 pounds per year.
   c. By the end of this period boys are significantly taller and heavier than girls.
   d. Boys and girls are about equally matched in athletic ability.

Physical and Cognitive Development in Middle Childhood **145**

Factual
Obj. 1
Moderate

2. About what percentage of elementary-school children participate in a daily program of regular exercise?
   a. less than 5 percent
   b. less than 15 percent
   c. about 33 percent
   d. about 65 percent

Factual
Obj. 2
Basic

3. Poor diet in childhood is related to all of the following *except*:
   a. dental problems
   b. poor performance on intelligence tests
   c. obesity
   d. higher motivation to do well in school

Conceptual
Obj. 3
Moderate

4. According to the text, which of the following children would be in the middle of the "cognitive revolution"?
   a. Fred, age 4, who has just learned the alphabet
   b. Bonnie, age 6, who can do simple addition in her head
   c. Kenny, age 9, who has just learned to say a few words in Spanish
   d. Lorraine, age 11, who is beginning to understand conservation of volume

Applied
Obj. 3
Moderate

5. Jill has just learned to apply the logical rules of screwing and unscrewing bolts to the problem of putting her erector set together. She has just learned what the text calls:
   a. emergent literacy
   b. conventional thinking
   c. metacognition
   d. strategy

Factual
Obj. 4
Basic

6. Piaget's name for the stage that is accompanied by the abilities of seriation, classification, and conservation is:
   a. preconventional thought
   b. concrete operations
   c. conventional thought
   d. metamemory

Applied
Obj. 4
Moderate

7. Kristen now has the ability to group beads by size *and* by color. She has mastered the central skill involved in:
   a. classification
   b. seriation
   c. conservation
   d. transitivity

Applied
Obj. 4
Moderate

8. Luke understand that if Mary is heavier than Linda, and Linda is heavier than Betty, then Mary must be heavier than Betty. Luke has demonstrated the basic principle of:
   a. conservation
   b. transitivity
   c. classification
   d. seriation

146 *Physical and Cognitive Development in Middle Childhood*

Factual
Obj. 4
Moderate

9. Which of the following is the *first* kind of conservation to be mastered?
   a. conservation of volume
   b. conservation of mass
   c. conservation of weight
   d. conservation of number

Applied
Obj. 5
Moderate

10. Dr. Rubinowitz believes that the major changes in thinking that accompany childhood result from the development of better memory strategies and the improved ability to store and retrieve information. The viewpoint which most closely corresponds to Dr. Rubinowitz's view is:
    a. Piaget's theory
    b. Kohlberg's theory
    c. the information-processing view
    d. the psychoanalytic perspective

Applied
Obj. 6
Moderate

11. Barry is trying to remember a list of words. His strategy is to keep repeating all those he knows and gradually adding words, one-at-a-time, to the end of the list, thereby rehearsing the most recent word along with those he already knows. Barry's strategy is an example of:
    a. seriation
    b. transitivity
    c. verbal rehearsal
    d. cumulative rehearsal

Factual
Obj. 6
Moderate

12. Metacognition refers to the ability to think about:
    a. one's memory
    b. hypothetical events
    c. concrete operations
    d. thinking

Conceptual
Obj. 6
Advanced

13. The text reports a study which showed that even kindergartners knew that a delay would interfere with memory but only older children understood that remembering arbitrary word-pairs would be harder than remembering word-opposites. This study demonstrates developmental differences in:
    a. metacognitive knowledge
    b. seriation
    c. conventional thinking
    d. preconventional thinking

Applied
Obj. 7
Moderate

14. Before she is ready to read, Sandy already knows that different letters are associated with different sounds and text is read from the top to the bottom of the page. Sandy's knowledge is an example of:
    a. social cognition
    b. emergent literacy
    c. transitivity
    d. conservation

Physical and Cognitive Development in Middle Childhood 147

Conceptual
Obj. 7
Moderate

15. According to the text, which strategy should first-grade teachers attempt to use as they try to teach their students how to write?
   a. process writing
   b. knowledge telling
   c. copy-delete
   d. preconventional thinking

Applied
Obj. 7
Advanced

16. Gradually, Maureen is getting better at taking timed tests because she is developing the ability to observe her own behavior and evaluate it. Thus, she can tell when she is working too slowly and will have to speed up. Maureen's development is best thought of as an example of:
   a. social cognition
   b. emergent literacy
   c. cognitive monitoring
   d. metamemory

Factual
Obj. 8
Moderate

17. The very first tests of intelligence attempted to measure:
   a. verbal ability
   b. hearing, vision, reaction time, and so forth
   c. reasoning ability
   d. problem solving ability

Conceptual
Obj. 9
Advanced

18. Arthur Jensen and others who accepted his view believed all of the following **except**:
   a. intelligence is largely the result of environmental differences
   b. blacks score lower on the average on intelligence tests than do whites
   c. the reason for the difference in average test scores for different racial groups was that there exist genetic differences between the races
   d. compensatory educations are, for the most part, a waste of time and money

Applied
Obj. 10
Advanced

19. At age 4, Maria gives her father the new hair bow she has been wanting. At age 7, she knows that her father has no use for a hair bow, and she selects a bottle of his favorite aftershave lotion. Maria's development is in the area called:
   a. conservation
   b. metacognition
   c. metamemory
   d. social cognition

Applied
Obj. 11
Moderate

20. When asked if stealing is good or bad, Leonard says it is bad because it is against the law and people should obey the law. Alan says it is bad because people who steal get put in jail. Based on Kohlberg's theory, Leonard's reasoning is most representative of ____ thinking, and Alan's reasoning is most representative of ____ thinking.
   a. preconventional; concrete
   b. conventional; concrete
   c. conventional; preconventional
   d. preconventional; conventional

C. Essay Questions

INSTRUCTIONS

After reading and studying the text, read the question below and write your answer in the space provided. Do not refer to your text or to the Scoring Scheme or Model Answer on the next page.

1. Define classification, seriation, and conservation. Give an example of each which corresponds to the developments that take place as the child moves into the stage of concrete operations.

Total Score ___

Scoring Scheme for Question 1

+2 points each (up to 6 points) for correct definition of classification, seriation, and conservation.

+2 points each (up to 6 points) for correct examples of each advance in thinking:
   a. classification: can now classify on 2 or more variables
   b. seriation: can order an entire series, not just the ends of the continuum
   c. conservation: can understand that quantity doesn't change even though appearance does

Total: 12 points

Model Answer for Question 1

Classification is the cognitive ability to understand how objects fit into categories. For example, a preoperational child can probably classify objects according to one dimension, such as color. In concrete operations, however, the child becomes able to classify according to 2 or more dimensions, for example, by sorting beads by size, shape, and color.

Seriation is the cognitive ability to rank objects in some meaningful order. The preoperational child can usually sort out those objects that are at the ends of the continuum, for example, the longest and shortest sticks, but gets confused in sorting the sticks in the middle. When the child moves into the stage of concrete operations, he can now correctly order the sticks from longest to shortest.

Conservation refers to the ability to focus on more than one dimension of an object at a time and to realize that quantity doesn't change just because an object's appearance might change. In the preoperational stage, a child who watches milk being poured from a short, wide glass into a tall, thin glass might think there is more milk in the second glass, since its level is higher. The concrete operations child understands that the quantity of milk doesn't change, even if its appearance does.

150 *Physical and Cognitive Development in Middle Childhood*

INSTRUCTIONS
After reading and studying the text, read the question below and write your answer in the space provided. Do not refer to your text, or to the Scoring Scheme or Model Answer on the next page.

2. Define the concept of moral development, as the term was used by Laurence Kohlberg. What technique did Kohlberg use to assess one's level of moral development? What change in reasoning marks the difference between preconventional and conventional thinking?

Total Score ___

Scoring Scheme for Question 2

+2 points for a correct definition of moral development which focuses on the reasoning a child uses in determining right and wrong.

+4 points for correctly describing the moral dilemma problem which poses moral questions to which the child responds with an explanation for why he recommended a particular action.

+2 points for the idea that it is the reasons given, not whether the action is judged right or wrong, that determines the level of moral development.

+3 points for the idea that preconventional thinking depends on external, physical events as explanations for moral actions.

+3 points for the idea that conventional thinking is based on how well the person follows the rules and roles of society.

Total: 14 points

Model Answer for Question 2

Kohlberg defined moral development as the changes in the ability to reason about morality that occur as a child grows older.

To measure moral development, Kohlberg related stories in which a character had to make a very difficult choice which called into question the rightness or wrongness of certain courses of action. For example, in one story, a man considered stealing a drug he couldn't afford in order to help his dying wife. After listening to the story, the child needed to decide what the character should do and explain why that action was appropriate. Kohlberg then analyzed the reasons given to determine the level of moral development which characterized the child's thinking.

The main difference between preconventional and conventional thinking is whether the child recommends an action based on the rewards or punishments associated with the action or she justifies the action as being consistent with the rules of society. The preconventional thinker will explain the action she recommends as right because it leads to reward or avoids punishment. For example, she might tell the man to steal the drug because his wife would be very thankful to receive the drug. Conventional thinkers judge an action according to whether it follows the rules of society. Here, the child might tell the man to steal the drug because people who love each other should try to help each other. Thus, it is not the judgment itself that determines the level of moral development, but rather the kind of explanation given that determines the level of a person's moral development.

Chapter 12

Social and Emotional Development in Middle Childhood

Preview of the Chapter

I. **Who Am I?: The Developing Self in Middle Childhood**
   A. Changes in Self-Conception
   B. Self-Esteem and Development
   C. Growth in Self-Regulation
      1. Cognitive growth and self-control
      2. Improving self-regulation

II. **Achievement in Middle Childhood**
   A. How Children Think About Ability
   B. Differences in Achievement Motivation: Goals and Expectations
      1. The influence of goals
      2. The influence of expectations
   C. Parents, Teachers, and Children's Achievement Expectations

III. **Social Relations in Middle Childhood**
   A. Changing Conceptions of Friendship
   B. Middle Childhood Peer Groups
   C. The Growth of Social Skills

IV. **Common Psychosocial Problems of Middle Childhood**
   A. Childhood Phobias
   B. Attention-Deficit Hyperactivity Disorder
      1. Effects of ADHD
      2. Causes of ADHD
      3. Treating ADHD

Learning Objectives

1. Explain the basic themes of development in middle childhood and describe the development of the self-concept during this period of life.

2. Discuss the factors that influence a child's self-esteem and suggest how self-esteem develops during middle childhood.

3. Describe the advances made in self-regulation during middle childhood.

4. Distinguish between achievement motivation and mastery motivation and discuss how children of different ages think about their own levels of ability.

154 *Social and Emotional Development in Middle Childhood*

5. Describe the factors which contribute to individual differences in achievement motivation.

6. Describe the theoretical basis of social relationships according to Sullivan.

7. Discuss how children of different ages understand friendship and how they are influenced by their peer groups.

8. Explain how social skills develop through childhood.

9. Define phobia and discuss the causes and treatments of childhood phobias.

10. Describe attention-deficit hyperactivity disorder and discuss its causes and treatments.

Chapter Summary

I. **Who Am I?: The Developing Self in Middle Childhood**
   1. Two broad themes are stressed in this chapter: middle childhood is a time of developing psychological and social competence in a world that is both expanding and demanding, and middle childhood is a time when psychosocial and cognitive development strongly interact.
   2. When studying the self, researchers consider three interrelated components: the cognitive, the affective, and the behavioral. The cognitive component, or **self-conception**, is the way we think about ourselves. The affective component, or **self-esteem**, is how we feel about ourselves and how we evaluate the traits we associate with ourselves. The behavioral component is **self-regulation**, the extent to which we monitor and control our own behavior.
   3. Preschoolers usually associate their concept of self with the characteristics of their physical bodies. Between ages 6 and 9, however, a more abstract, less physically based view of self gradually emerges. By about age 8, children begin to understand that a person can experience opposite emotions, like joy and sadness, at the same time, although they usually attribute them to different events. By about age 10, children can understand that the same situation can evoke different emotions. This developmental advance is linked to the cognitive ability to consider more than one piece of information at a time.
   4. Elementary-schoolers also begin to understand that the self has many different traits, abilities, and roles. Thus, the self becomes more differentiated in middle childhood, due in part to the growing cognitive ability to integrate diverse pieces of information.
   5. Sex-role identity continue to develop in middle childhood. Even though grade schoolers still prefer same-sex friends and sex-typed behavior, they become more flexible and tolerant of others who might prefer activities that are stereotypically associated with the opposite sex. In general, children's knowledge of sex roles is linked to their cognitive maturity, but their preferences are influenced by the sex-related values they are exposed to at home.
   6. People assess themselves in four basic areas: competence in meeting demands for achievement, success at influencing other people; adherence to ethical standards, and social acceptance by others. Self-assessment in each of these areas adds up to the person's overall level of self-esteem.
   7. Children with high self-esteem have confidence in their abilities, expect to be successful, are more independent and less self-conscious with peers, and are less preoccupied with personal problems. Increasing achievement tends to boost self-esteem, but the reverse does not appear to be true. Parents of children with high self-esteem tend to be warm and accepting toward the child, to be affectionate and involved, strict in setting rules, consistent in enforcing rules, willing to take children's views into consideration, and they use noncoercive discipline (withdrawal of privileges) and explain to the child why certain behaviors are wrong. This is essentially the authoritative style of parenting. When parents don't interact with children in

ways that lead to self-esteem, children suffer. For example, children of depressed mothers have lower self-esteem and African-American children who identify with their minority group have higher self-esteem.
8. Self-regulation improves as children grow older, although individual differences among children do exist. These differences tend to be stable across time, however, and children who can handle frustration, those who are aggressive, and those who are hyperactive tend to retain those traits as they grow older.
9. Cognitive theorists are concerned with what children think as they gain control over their own behavior. Their research shows that "inner speech" is important in understanding self-regulation in children. For example, 4- and 5-year-olds have very little understanding of the thoughts that will help them exert self-control, but 7- to 9-year-olds are much more knowledgeable in how to use their thoughts to control their behavior. For seventh graders, self-regulation proved to be one of the best predictors of academic performance. When children have difficulty with self-control, they can be taught to identify a specific problem they have and counteract the problem by talking to themselves or by using inner speech to think of alternatives which are incompatible with the behavior in question.

II. Achievement in Middle Childhood

1. **Achievement motivation**, the desire to perform well, is developed in middle childhood and differs from **mastery motivation**, the desire to master a challenge in order to acquire a new skill. Erikson saw mastery motivation as the essential task of middle childhood which, if children come to believe they are competent to master things, results in a sense of **industry**. Unfortunately, children who develop a feeling of **inferiority** fail or withdraw from childhood tasks and come to believe they are unable to master new skills and to give up trying.
2. Before age 6, children view ability as the mastery of specific skills, but by age 6 or 7, children begin thinking about ability more as a global, psychological trait. Also, preschoolers equate a good performance with completing a task, but older children are aware of the performance of peers, and for them, doing a good job means doing better than someone else. Finally, preschoolers tend to asses their own ability optimistically and believe they can learn anything: Older children understand the limits of their own abilities more realistically. Because elementary school children value achievement but still have an immature understanding of ability, they are especially vulnerable to the effects of failure, and, if they keep failing, may stop trying.
3. Some children seem to place more importance on **learning goals**, which place value on individual accomplishment for its own sake. Other children emphasize **performance goals**, which place value on achieving in relation to others. Children with learning goals tend to view mistakes as feedback which helps them adjust. Those with performance goals view mistakes as failures that make them look bad in front of their friends and they tend to avoid tasks at which they might fail. Competitive academic environments can increase concerns about performance and thereby interfere with learning.
4. When children believe they have ability in a subject, they perform better, thereby confirming their expectations.
5. Girls generally expect less of themselves than boys even though their past performance is as good or better than boys'. Girls also tend to focus more on negative feedback, rate tasks as being harder, and expect lower achievement for themselves than boys. All these factors may contribute to their lower self-expectations.
6. Children with seriously low achievement expectations usually suffer either from **evaluation anxiety**, in which they feel anxiety in situations where they will be judged, or from **learned helplessness**, the belief that one cannot control the forces in the environment. Children with **evaluation anxiety** do poorly whenever they believe their performance is being monitored.

Children with learned helplessness perform well on tasks they believe are easy, but they quit trying when they think the task is difficult.

7. Differences among children in learned helplessness may arise through parents who tell their children that their effort doesn't matter or they may be somewhat a matter of temperament. Girls are more prone to learned helplessness than boys, perhaps because teachers tend to criticize them for things related to their ability but criticize boys for factors, like effort, not related to ability. Evaluation anxiety, like learned helplessness, may arise from temperament, or may be produced by parents who set unreasonably high standards for performance and react poorly when the child fails. Children with evaluation anxiety or learned helplessness may benefit from encouragement to think that their failure is not due to their lack of ability, but rather a lack of effort.

8. In the United States, Asian-Americans achieve at a higher level in school than do whites, who outperform African-Americans. The superior achievement may be due to their culture's belief that success comes from hard work. While they believe that academic achievement leads to upward mobility in general, African-Americans often believe that this relationship will not hold for themselves. This belief that education will not matter for them may contribute to their poorer academic performance as a group.

III. Social Relations in Middle Childhood

1. Friendships in childhood are critical to the social advances made in middle childhood. Harry Stack Sullivan, like many other psychoanalysts who followed Freud, believed that biological drives and sexual conflicts are not the overriding factors in human development, but rather that interpersonal relationships have a powerful impact on personality. Sullivan believed we are all innately driven to seek security by forming relations with others that make us feel happy and safe. Interacting with others who think well of us fosters a positive self-identity and strong self-esteem.

2. Like Erikson, Sullivan proposed that development proceeds in a series of stages and that the outcome of each stage affects development in subsequent stages. In infancy, babies need physical contact and tenderness from adults; children need adult participation in learning experiences, followed by the need for peer acceptance in early middle childhood. Later in childhood comes the need for a friend of the same sex, and in early adolescence young people have a need for love and sexual contact with an opposite-sex partner. Finally, we feel the need for integration into adult society. Sullivan called friendships in childhood "chumships," and he believed that they are a necessary prerequisite for later intimate relationships and that they can even help compensate for problems earlier in development.

3. At age 5, children make friends spontaneously and define friends as those they play with. By age 8 or 9, friendships deepen to include the idea that friends help each other. At age 11 or 12, friends begin to confide their secrets and are judged according to their ability to understand feelings and keep confidences. This increased capacity for intimacy in middle childhood results from the cognitive advances in understanding intangible emotions and the emotional growth such that children can share their personal secrets and trust another person.

4. In middle childhood, peer groups are nearly always composed of members of the same sex, and boys especially prefer this gender segregation. Also, children at this age are concerned with and able to reason about fairness, and they are extremely norm-conscious, and want to be like everyone else.

5. Elementary school children communicate better than preschoolers in that they can understand what the other person knows, they can direct visual attention to make their points, they are quite good in interpreting nonverbal messages, they are better at sticking to the topic, and they are better at inferring the motives of others. These improved communication skills may result from their increased ability to see themselves in other people's situations. They may also

communicate better than preschoolers because they must do it more effectively and more often, since they spend more time with peers.
6. Children in middle childhood also grow in other social skills. Children whose parents use "reflection enhancing," in which they ask their children to think about how their behavior affects others, have children who were less likely to be rejected by peers and more often chosen to be companions. Children who are slower to develop may have parents who are harsh or autocratic, or they may lack models for appropriate behavior. Special programs can help these children.

IV. Common Psychosocial Problems of Middle Childhood

1. Problems which were given less attention in younger children are usually treated more seriously in middle childhood because adults become concerned about potential long-term effects, because some problems are not noticed until middle childhood, and because problems which persist into middle childhood may signal more serious deficiencies.
2. Intense, irrational fears directed toward specific objects or situations are called **phobias**, and they are often accompanied by physical symptoms. Childhood phobias usually fall into 3 categories: phobias about physical injury, about natural events (like fear of the dark), or about social situations (like fear of crowds).
3. Psychoanalytic theory suggests phobias result from unconscious conflicts. Therapy consists of trying to identify and understand the conflicts. A social learning therapist would view phobias as responses learned either through direct experience or observation. In this view, what is learned can be unlearned, and therapy is directed at relearning not to be afraid. A cognitive-behavioral therapist looks for stimuli that are controlling the fear response. Through the process called **desensitization**, the therapist teaches the child to remain calm when the feared circumstances are gradually invoked. All these methods have been successful, especially when used together.
4. **Attention-deficit hyperactivity disorder (ADHD)** is a disorder in which children can neither pay attention nor remain still. It affects 2 to 5 percent of elementary school children, most of them boys. Not all children with attention-deficit disorder are hyperactive, but many suffer from both problems. Children with ADHD are more likely to experience academic problems, behavioral problems, conduct disorders, and delinquency, with effects carrying through adolescence.
5. Most researchers believe ADHD has some biological basis resulting from prenatal or perinatal (just after birth) conditions, problems with metabolizing glucose in the brain, or inherited factors. Twenty percent of hyperactive children have a parent who was hyperactive. However, other researchers believe that both heredity and environment play a role. The drug Ritalin has been used to treat this disorder, although it works better for children that have both attention-deficit disorder and hyperactivity than for those who are not hyperactive. Since Ritalin is a stimulant, it does increase the ability to concentrate, but it is effective for only about 4 to 6 weeks. Therefore, it should be used initially while a behavior management program in which children earn tokens for good behavior is put in place, and then discontinued. Dietary restrictions, including the elimination of food additives, do not reduce hyperactivity and is not a general treatment for the disorder.

Self Test

A. Matching Questions

___ 1. The desire to perform well
___ 2. The various attributes people see themselves possessing
___ 3. The desire to learn something in order to acquire a new skill
___ 4. The extent to which we monitor and control our own behavior
___ 5. One's feelings about oneself
___ 6. Develops from continual failure

a. self-esteem
b. mastery motivation
c. industry
d. inferiority
e. self-conceptions
f. achievement motivation
g. self-regulation

___ 7. The belief that you can't control your environment
___ 8. Term associated with the work of Harry Stack Sullivan
___ 9. The crisis of middle childhood over the sense of accomplishment
___ 10. Treatment for a phobia
___ 11. Involves wanting to do better than other people
___ 11. Affects more boys than girls
___ 12. Nervousness associated with being judged
___ 13. An intense, irrational fear
___ 14. Involve the placement of value on accomplishment for its own sake

a. evaluation anxiety
b. phobia
c. learning goals
d. desensitization
e. learned helplessness
f. attention-deficit hyperactivity disorder
g. industry versus inferiority
h. chumship
i. performance goals

B. Multiple Choice

Factual
Obj. 1
Basic

1. Self-conceptions are most closely related to which of the following components of the self?
   a. the behavioral
   b. the affective
   c. the Oedipal
   d. the cognitive

Applied
Obj. 2
Moderate

2. Lucy tells her counselor that she feels like she is an untalented, unattractive person. These feelings form the basis of her:
   a. self-esteem
   b. self-conceptions
   c. ability for self-regulation
   d. self-control

Applied
Obj. 2
Advanced

3. Candace doesn't think it is possible to feel two opposite emotions at the same time, but her brother Ricky believes that opposite feelings can coexist, as long as they each apply to a different event or situation. Based on research reported in the text, you would guess that Candace is about ___ years old and Ricky is about ___ years old.
   a. 8; 10
   b. 5; 10
   c. 5; 8
   d. 10; 5

Social and Emotional Development in Middle Childhood 159

Conceptual
Obj. 2
Moderate

4. Self-esteem is assessed as the sum of peoples' assessments in all of the following areas *except*:
   a. competence in achievement
   b. how well they regulate their behavior
   c. moral worth
   d. success at influencing others

Factual
Obj. 2
Moderate

5. Which of the following parental behaviors has *not* been shown to be related to high self-esteem in children?
   a. loose in setting rules land limits, allowing children to in large part determine their own behavior
   b. willingness to listen to and consider the child's viewpoint on matters of rules and discipline
   c. warmth and acceptance
   d. use of noncoercive discipline rather than physical punishment

Applied
Obj. 3
Moderate

6. As Jackie grows up, she develops ways of keeping her impulses under control. For example, she learns that instead of yelling "I'm hungry" in church, she quietly asks her father if she can have something to eat as soon as the service is over. Her behavior is being influenced by her gradually improving:
   a. performance goals
   b. self-regulation
   c. learning goals
   d. desensitization

Conceptual
Obj. 3
Moderate

7. Sometimes children who have trouble controlling their impulses can be helped by teaching them to identify those situations that trigger their impulsive behavior and then talking to themselves and telling themselves to behave more appropriately. This technique is most closely related to the function called:
   a. inner speech
   b. time out
   c. desensitization
   d. mastery motivation

Factual
Obj. 3
Moderate

8. According to the text, a child's ability to successfully self-regulate her behavior has been shown to be a good predictor of:
   a. achievement motivation
   b. developing phobias in middle to later childhood
   c. desensitization
   d. academic performance

Applied
Obj. 4
Moderate

9. Randy wants to practice his video game so he can go to the arcade and beat the scores of all of his friends. The concept which best describes Randy's behavior is:
   a. achievement motivation
   b. learning goals
   c. evaluation anxiety
   d. mastery motivation

Social and Emotional Development in Middle Childhood

Conceptual
Obj. 5
Advanced

10. Lynn believes that doing a good job means doing something better than someone else. Pat believes that ability means mastering specific skills which he believes can be done with little or no difficulty, no matter how hard they are. Lynn is probably ___ whereas Pat is probably ___.
    a. a boy; a girl
    b. a girl; a boy
    c. a preschooler; in middle childhood
    d. in middle childhood; a preschooler

Applied
Obj. 5
Moderate

11. Juan is not too much concerned with the grades he gets in school but is very concerned with mastering the content he studies. The term which best describes his attitude is:
    a. achievement motivation
    b. performance goals
    c. learning goals
    d. evaluation anxiety

Conceptual
Obj. 5
Moderate

12. Which of the following is more true of boys than girls?
    a. Boys expect less of themselves in achievement situations.
    b. Boys tend to view their errors as not indicative of their true ability.
    c. Boys perform better than girls in achievement situations.
    d. Boys are more prone to learned helplessness.

Applied
Obj. 5
Moderate

13. Larry has given up trying in school because he feels that no matter what he does, other children will always do better. Larry's attitude is best thought of as an example of:
    a. a phobia
    b. time out
    c. evaluation anxiety
    d. learned helplessness

Factual
Obj. 6
Basic

14. According to the text, Harry Stack Sullivan believed that all humans are motivated to seek:
    a. pleasure
    b. self-actualization
    c. security
    d. achievement

Conceptual
Obj. 7
Moderate

15. Michael defines friendship as the relationship in which one person helps the other. Generalizing from the text, Michael is about how old?
    a. 4 or 5
    b. 6 or 7
    c. 8 or 9
    d. 11 or 12

Applied
Obj. 9
Basic

16. Bobby was playing outside when he was stung by a bee. Now he is terribly afraid of bees, spiders, all flying insects, and of playing in the grass. Bobby's behavior is best thought of as an example of:
    a. a phobia
    b. evaluation anxiety
    c. learned helplessness
    d. desensitization

Social and Emotional Development in Middle Childhood **161**

Applied
Obj. 9
Moderate

17. According to the text, which would be the least common phobia for a child to have?
    a. fear of oneself and what one might do to oneself
    b. fear of falling from a high place
    c. fear of storms
    d. fear of going to school

Applied
Obj. 9
Advanced

18. Dr. Smith believes that phobias can usually be traced back to some earlier developmental period in which the child had "bad," or socially unacceptable, thoughts. Dr. Smith's view fits most clearly with which of the following perspectives?
    a. biological perspective
    b. cognitive perspective
    c. social learning perspective
    d. psychoanalytic perspective

Applied
Obj. 10
Basic

19. Jeff has a problem in paying attention to an activity for more than just a few minutes at a time. Although he sits quietly in class, he does not seem to be learning because his mind wanders from one thing to the next. Jeff's problem is most likely:
    a. high evaluation anxiety
    b. an attention-deficit problem
    c. hyperactivity
    d. low achievement motivation

Factual
Obj. 10
Moderate

20. Which of the following is not a characteristic associated with attention-deficit hyperactivity disorder?
    a. It can sometimes be treated effectively with Ritalin.
    b. It can sometimes be treated with a diet low in sugar and artificial additives.
    c. It affects 3 to 4 times as many boys as girls.
    d. It is linked to delinquency later in childhood.

C. Essay Questions

INSTRUCTIONS

After reading and studying the text, read the question below and write your answer in the space provided. Do not refer to your text or to the Scoring Scheme or Model Answer on the next page.

1. What kind of parental behaviors tend to produce children with high self-esteem? How is self-esteem related to achievement in school?

Total Score ___

Scoring Scheme for Question 1

+2 points each (up to 6 points) for three separate types of parental behavior linked to high self-esteem. These will probably fall into the following categories:
  a. warmth and acceptance
  b. clear rules with consistent enforcement
  c. willingness to consider children's views
  d. discipline by withdrawal of privileges and reasoning rather than physical punishment

+3 points for the idea that achievement influences self-esteem but self-esteem does not seem to influence achievement.

Total: 9 points

Model Answer for Question 1

Parents of children with high self-esteem tend to have four things in common. First, they are warm and accepting of the child. Second, they are strict in setting rules and limits and are consistent in enforcing them. Third, they are willing to listen to their children and take their views and ideas under consideration when setting standards. Finally, they tend not to use physical punishment but rather to use the withdrawal of privileges. Also, they explain to their children why certain behaviors are wrong.

Self-esteem seems to be influenced by achievement. When a child performs well, his self-esteem is usually enhanced. The relationship does not usually work in the other direction, however. Raising a child's self-esteem does not usually lead to an increase in achievement.

164 *Social and Emotional Development in Middle Childhood*

INSTRUCTIONS

After reading and studying the text, read the question below and write your answer in the space provided. Do not refer to your text, or to the Scoring Scheme or Model Answer on the next page.

2. How are the concepts of achievement motivation and mastery motivation related to the concepts of learning goals and performance goals? Which of these sets of concepts would seem to apply more to girls than to boys?

Total Score ___

Scoring Scheme for Question 2

+2 points for making the connection between achievement motivation and performance goals.

+2 points for stating that both achievement motivation and performance goals emphasize the desire to perform well on a task in order to demonstrate competence.

+2 points for making the connection between mastery motivation and learning goals.

+2 points for stating that both mastery motivation and learning goals emphasize learning for its own sake rather than to do better than others.

+2 points for identifying some research that suggests girls are more concerned with achievement than boys. This could include the idea that they are more prone to learned helplessness.

+2 points for suggesting that girls seem more concerned with achievement motivation and performance goals than boys.

Total: 12 points

Model Answer for Question 2

Achievement motivation, which is the desire to perform well, is closely tied to performance goals, which also emphasize the value of doing better than others. On the other hand, mastery motivation, which is the desire to accomplish something because one wishes to learn the skill involved, is much like the concept behind learning goals, which focus on those goals that place value on doing something for its own sake and not because there is some extrinsic reward attached.

Research on the differences between what boys and girls expect suggests that girls are more concerned about achievement than boys and they expect less of themselves, even though their real achievements are at least as good or better. Thus, girls seem to pay more attention to achievement motivation and performance goals than do boys.

Chapter 13

The Social Context of Middle Childhood

Preview of the Chapter

I. **Children in Families**
   A. The Family Mosaic
   B. Parenting Styles: Effects on School Success and Behavior
   C. Parents' Employment and Unemployment
      1. Unemployment and poverty
   D. Latchkey Children
   E. The Effects of Divorce
      1. The effects of father absence

II. **The Child in the Peer Group**
   A. The Structure and Functioning of Children's Groups
      1. Group characteristics
      2. Group functioning
   B. The Peer Group as a Context for Development
   C. Social Acceptance: The Effects of Personality and Culture
      1. Peer acceptance and culture
      2. Emotional buffers for rejected children
      3. Intervention strategies

III. **Schools and Development**
   A. Schools and Achievement: Expectations, Biases, and Culture
      1. The power of expectations
      2. Race and class biases
      3. Different messages for different genders
      4. What makes good teachers?

IV. **Living with Danger**

Learning Objectives

1. Discuss the effect that parenting styles have on children in middle childhood.

2. Summarize the statistics regarding the number of women with children who are employed and discuss the effect of that employment on these children.

3. Discuss the effects that divorce has on the children in the family.

4. Explain why different children in the same family are different from each other.

5. Describe the structure and functioning of children's peer groups.

168   *The Social Context of Middle Childhood*

6. Discuss the importance of the peer group on a child's development.

7. Identify the characteristics that are associated with popularity in middle childhood and suggest how unpopular children can be helped toward better social adjustment.

8. Describe the educational conditions that best foster development.

9. Describe how teachers and students interact and suggest how the self-fulfilling prophecy can influence achievement.

10. Explain how race, culture, and sex are related to educational performance and achievement.

11. Describe how our society has viewed the education of special needs children and explain the advantages and disadvantages of mainstreaming versus segregated classrooms.

12. Discuss how family life interacts with educational achievement.

13. Describe how a culture of violence affects children and discuss what can be done to prevent the negative consequences of such violence.

Chapter Summary

I. The Child in the Family

1. In middle childhood, the pressures to perform, to compete, and to be popular all begin to grow. Parenting styles continue to affect development in middle childhood and parenting patterns—authoritarian, permissive, or authoritative—tend to remain the same as the child grows up.

2. The authoritarian style of parenting, with its perfectionism, rigidity, and harsh discipline, affects children negatively, especially boys. Authoritarian parenting is linking with children who are lower in social responsibility, higher levels of aggressiveness, and, in boys, inappropriate social assertiveness and lower cognitive ability, competence, and self-esteem. Permissive parents, who set few limits and rarely punish, also have children who are overly aggressive, and who tend to be more impulsive, less self-reliant, and less responsible. Authoritative parents set clear standards, exert firm discipline, but are warm, listen to their children, and respond to their children's reasonable demands. Children of authoritative parents are socially competent, responsible, and have high self-esteem.

3. Parenting style and the child's temperament interact, each influencing the other. Research has shown that aggressive children seek instant gratification, ignore the possible consequences of their actions, are underresponsive to many kinds of social stimulation, and increase their aggressiveness in response to punishment. These characteristics all influence how parents must deal with these children.

4. Some new research suggests that the way parents think about, or attribute, their children's behavior influences the way they discipline them. Authoritarian mothers attribute bad behavior to the child's negative qualities; nonauthoritarian mothers view the causes of misbehavior as being outside of their child, being in the environment. Also, younger-looking children are treated more leniently than are children who look more mature.

5. Of all women, mothers with children are more likely to work than women without children: 70 percent of women with children aged 6 to 17 were employed in 1986, and 63 percent of all women with children were working. By 1995, about 2 out of 3 children will have mothers who work. Research indicates that the mother's satisfaction with her role, whether she is working

or not, is a more important influence than whether she works or not. Children of parents who feel good about their lives tend to be better adjusted than children of dissatisfied parents.

6. Daughters of working mothers tend to be positively adjusted, perform well in school, have less sex-stereotyped attitudes about employment, and have higher self-esteem and career aspirations than do girls whose mothers stay at home. For boys, those raised in middle-class homes are less likely to develop sexist attitudes, but don't do as well in school. For working-class boys, the differences between those whose mothers work and those whose don't is minimal, perhaps because traditional sex roles are held more firmly in these families.

7. Family life should be viewed as a process that is influenced by many factors.

8. How unemployed fathers feel about their joblessness influences the responses of their children. Men who feel threatened and pessimistic tend to become more irritable, less nurturant, and more arbitrary. Consequently, their children are at greater risk for social and emotional problems, deviant behavior, and lower expectations. Children in these circumstances benefit from strong support from their mothers. Children who grow up in poverty are at risk for depression, poor peer relations, antisocial behavior, low self-esteem, and school difficulties.

9. About 75 percent of mothers of school age children work and about 25 percent of school-age children are **latchkey children** who stay home by themselves while parents work. Overall, research shows that latchkey children and children cared for by a parent or grandparent were very similar on measures of emotional adjustment. But children of authoritative parents or those who go straight home after school and stay there are less susceptible to peer pressure to get in trouble than are those who "hang around" with friends after school. However, a study of eighth graders showed that those who took care of themselves were at risk for using alcohol, tobacco, and marijuana. Also, children of authoritative parents are less susceptible to peer influence than are those who are raised permissively.

10. Latchkey children in urban areas express more fear at being alone than their rural or suburban counterparts. To help children feel secure, parents can specify a regular place where they are expected and provide activities for them, leave instructions about how to handle an emergency, ask the child to "check-in" when he arrives home, identify neighbors who can help in an emergency, encourage children to call if they are worried, give instructions about how to deal with strangers, and parent in an authoritative way.

11. Until recently, younger children were thought to be most adversely affected by their parents' divorce. More recent work, however, suggests that children in elementary school also may experience academic and behavioral problems after divorce. Although boys appear to be more affected than girls at about age 6 or 7, this difference seems to be temporary and no persistent sex differences in adjustment seems to occur. Some research also suggests that divorce may produce a "sleeper" effect, with children who appeared to make a good adjustment to an earlier divorce experiencing adjustment problems years later.

12. There is a great deal of variability in how children are affected by divorce. Children adapt best if family conflict is low, if there is emotional support, and when the pre-divorce life-style can be maintained. Much of the damage thought to result from divorce may instead be traced to stress and conflict both before and after the divorce rather than to the divorce itself.

13. Siblings raised in the same family may have very different impressions of family life. These differences result from the interaction of each child's unique temperament and abilities, the particular circumstances into which each child is born, and the match between the personality of the child and those of the parents.

14. Later-born children are usually more popular with peers than first-borns, perhaps because they spend less time alone with parents and more with peers. Birth order effects are complex and depend on spacing, number, and gender of their siblings. Some children intentionally develop interests different from their siblings, a process called **sibling deidentification**. By choosing to be different, children determine their own personalities and develop traits which may continue throughout adulthood.

II. The Child in the Peer Group

1. The development of a peer group is one of the most important transitions of early childhood. These peer groups are characterized by sameness: same age, same sex, same race. Boy's play is rougher, more competitive, and less racially segregated, and takes place in larger groups than does girl's play, which takes place in more intimate, exclusive groups and centers more on friendships than activities.

2. In the classic Robbers Cave experiment boys at camp who were divided into two groups formed loyalties to their own group and directed aggression against the other group. Simply getting the groups together for shared activities did not diminish the rivalry, but having them work together cooperatively on a joint project did reduce competitiveness and increase cohesiveness. Thus, cooperative interaction can foster harmony within and between groups. Also, leaders who have an authoritative style, rather than an authoritarian or permissive, encourage group contentment with cohesion.

3. The quality of children's peer relationships is associated with both delinquency and mental health. Delinquents differed from nondelinquents in that they were more aggressive and were less well-liked by other children. Peer ratings in third grade was a better predictor of mental health 11 years later than were IQ, school performance, school attendance, or teacher ratings.

4. Popularity among school children comes to those who are socially skilled, have above average intelligence and strong academic skills, and are physically attractive; and popular children tend to be later-borns, come from happy families, and have high self-esteem. In middle childhood, a non-supportive relationship with the father or an authoritarian mother was linked to rejection by peers, especially if the child is aggressive. At this age, race is not an influence on peer acceptance.

5. **Sociometry** is a method for studying relationships within a group. Use of this technique reveals that children can be categorized into four groups with respect to popularity: **stars**, who are smart, attractive, have good social skills, and act as leaders; **amiables**, who are smart and attractive, but have lower social skills and are less likely to be leaders; **isolates**, who are ignored and who have poor social skills but don't behave in bizarre ways that cause rejection; and **rejects**, who are actively disliked and engage in inappropriate and unwelcome behavior.

6. Social isolates can become more popular by learning to ask if they can join a group and by learning to avoid making inappropriate remarks and getting involved in disagreements. Rejects need to learn to control their disruptive behavior and to perceive social cues in a less aggressive way. Rejects can be aggressive and bullying (more common for boys) or depressed and timid (more common for girls), but both groups are not well skilled at sharing, cooperating, and empathizing. Some research suggests that both isolated and rejects may be suffering from depression.

7. Although aggression is linked to peer rejection in both Canada and China, shyness led to rejection for Canadian children, and positive social relationships in China, probably due to the emphasis in Chinese culture on inhibition and self restraint. Thus, cultural differences in the basis of peer relationships do exist.

8. Children who are rejected by peers fare better if they have a warm relationship with their mother or a close relationship with a sibling. Psychologists who work with rejected children sometimes encourage them to *think* others will like them. Isolates can be encouraged to join groups and taught how to initiate membership. For rejects, the most important remedy is to control aggression. In fact, childhood aggression is the best predictor of adjustment problems later in life, including drug addiction and criminality. Intervention programs for aggressive children usually teach children to get control over their aggressive outburst and channel aggressive energy into non-harmful behavior.

III. Schools and Development

1. The level of achievement in American schools is lower than in other countries. Teachers' expectations influence and determine students' performance, a situation called the self-fulfilling prophecy. In a classic study, teachers were led to believe low-achieving students were really high achievers. At the end of the year, these students had made greater gains in achievement than previous high-achievers the teachers believed were low-achievers, thus demonstrating the power of the self-fulfilling prophecy.
2. Research shows that teachers tend to like black children less than white, and low-income children less than children from middle-income homes. Thus, racial and socioeconomic prejudices can, according to the self-fulfilling prophecy, influence student achievement. Teachers also prefer children with good work habits, and judge children according to work habits even more than by their grades or actual skills.
3. Culture shapes our expectations and, hence, performance as well. Asian children outperform white Americans, perhaps because their culture stresses that academic success is the result of effort and hard work. Also, American children spend fewer hours in school, less time on homework, and dislike homework more. American parents and children expressed greater satisfaction with school and schoolwork. Perhaps American parents set lower performance standards and provide less support for excellence. American teachers differ from Asians in that they emphasize ability rather than effort and are less likely to encourage students to work harder to gain success.
4. Teachers also treat boys differently from girls. Boys get more attention and less criticism than girls. Also, criticism directed at boys is often for not following rules or trying hard enough to succeed. Teachers are more likely to criticize the intellectual aspects of girls' work, giving the message that they needn't work harder because they don't have the necessary ability. Where boys are encouraged to persevere through hard tasks, girls are taught to give up. This kind of differential criticism may be related to the fact that girls do better than boys in elementary school, but boys begin to do better than girls in high school, especially in science and math.
5. Good teachers in middle childhood are warm, set clear learning goals, and provide appropriate rewards and punishments. They are authoritative and respond differently to the needs of difficult children.
6. Until 1950, most special needs children (who comprise about 10 percent of all school children), such as those who were mentally retarded, emotionally disturbed, or with speech impediments, learning disabilities, or visual or hearing impairments, were placed in regular classrooms with the nonhandicapped. This policy, called **mainstreaming**, was reversed in the 1960s and 1970s as special classrooms were created for these special needs children. In the late 1970s, opinions shifted again, and mainstreaming was mandated by federal law wherever possible.
7. Mainstreaming has advantages which include the reduction of prejudice about handicapped people, the opportunity to develop relationships with a broad range of peers, the reduction of the stigma associated with being handicapped, and the prevention of misdiagnosed children being erroneously placed in a special educational setting. Its disadvantages center on the problem of providing successful instruction to a large groups of children without leaving behind or making unpopular those who might require special help. A reasonable solution is to mainstream special needs children most of the day, and provide special support and individualized instruction in addition.
8. Children do better in school when parents are actively interested in their homework, when they create an atmosphere conducive to studying, and when they provide sources of intellectual stimulation. Children of parents who provide learning opportunities for their children during the summer show improvements in learning here as well as during the school year. Also, schools can provide support for a child when the family life is difficult, for example, during a divorce. Children whose lives are stressful don't do as well in school, are less motivated, and

172   The Social Context of Middle Childhood

are more disruptive. Parents should inform schools when there are problems at home, and schools need to keep both parents informed of the child's progress.

IV. Living with Danger

1. Abroad, wars or other armed conflicts cause most deaths, with 9 times more civilians than soldiers being killed. In Chicago, 25 percent of children witness a homicide before age 17. Many children cope with violence by either behaving aggressively or withdrawing emotionally, even developing posttraumatic stress disorder. Children growing up with violence can experience numbing detachment, which interferes with the development of empathy and moral reasoning.
2. Children can benefit from discussion of moral issues, as long as the adults in the children's life are coping well enough. When adults can no longer cope, however, infant mortality rates soar and care-giving breaks down. Children will be minimally effected if parents can maintain a strong parent-child attachment, retain their own self-esteem and identity, and establish routine and stable care-giving arrangements. Accordingly, programs that help parents cope are also good for children.

Self Test

A. Matching Questions

___ 1. Children who are simply ignored
___ 2. Linked to high levels of aggression, and lower ability, competence, and self-esteem
___ 3. Related to not wanting to be like one's brother or sister
___ 4. Placement of special needs children in classrooms with nonhandicapped children
___ 5. Children who stay home alone while parents work
___ 6. A method of measuring relationships among a group of people
___ 7. Linked to aggressiveness, impulsiveness, and lack of self-reliance and responsibility
___ 8. Children who are liked by others, but who have lower social skills and leadership abilities

a. latchkey children
b. isolates
c. permissive parents
d. amiables
e. authoritarian parents
f. mainstreaming
g. authoritarian parents
h. sociometry
i. authoritative parents
j. rejects
k. stars

___ 9. Teachers are concerned about their children
___ 10. Teachers reject these children
___ 11. Teachers become attached to these children
___ 12. Teachers are indifferent to these children

a. rejects
b. isolates
c. amiables
d. stars

B. Multiple Choice

Applied
Obj. 1
Moderate

1. Diane is an aggressive child, and is also impulsive and not very self-reliant or responsible. Her parents don't seem concerned with her behavior, though, because they believe that children should be allowed to behave however they wish. This situation is best thought of as the result of:
   a. mainstreaming
   b. permissive parenting
   c. sibling deidentification
   d. authoritarian parenting

Factual
Obj. 2
Moderate

2. By 1995, about what percent of women in the United States who have children between the ages of 6 and 13 will be employed?
   a. 45 percent
   b. 50 percent
   c. 66 percent
   d. 87 percent

Conceptual
Obj. 2
Moderate

3. Generalizing from information presented in the text, which of the following women is most likely to have happy, well-adjusted children?
   a. Ruth, who works full time, loves her job, and feels that her children are being well cared for.
   b. Jane, who works full time, but feels guilty she is not spending more time at home.
   c. Andrea, who works full time, but dislikes her job and would prefer not to work.
   d. Margaret, who stays at home with her children, but really wishes she were back at work.

Conceptual
Obj. 2
Advanced

4. Which of the following statements about latchkey children is *true*?
   a. They are generally less well-adjusted than children who have a caregiver present after school.
   b. They are generally better-adjusted than children who have a caregiver present after school.
   c. Those who have authoritarian parents do better than those with authoritative or permissive parents.
   d. Those with authoritative parents do better than those with permissive parents.

Conceptual
Obj. 3
Moderate

5. Which of the following statements about children of divorce is *false*?
   a. Boys adjust better to divorce than girls.
   b. Children do better if the family was not dysfunctional before the divorce.
   c. Children benefit from contact with the father only if he is well-adjusted and isn't in a conflict situation with the mother, who has custody.
   d. Children who adjust well at the time of the divorce often feel bitter and troubled later in life.

Conceptual
Obj. 4
Advanced

6. According to the text, which of the following children is most likely to be popular with peers?
   a. Fred, who has two younger sisters.
   b. Mary, who has two younger brothers.
   c. Jason, who is an only child.
   d. Linda, who has an older brother and an older sister.

Applied
Obj. 4
Moderate

7. Justin's younger brother is a successful athlete: He made the all-city wrestling team when he was in eighth grade, and was voted the outstanding athlete in his school. Justin's response is to devalue athletics and concentrate his time and energy on school work. Justin's behavior is best thought of as an example of:
   a. a sociometric reaction
   b. reaction formation
   c. sibling deidentification
   d. birth-order-biases

Conceptual
Obj. 5
Moderate

8. If you divided a group of children into two groups and had the groups compete against each other in a series of contests, you would expect the aggression directed at members of one's own group should ___ as a result of these competitions and aggression directed at members of the other group would ___.
   a. increase; increase
   b. decrease; decrease
   c. decrease; increase
   d. increase; decrease

Factual
Obj. 6
Moderate

9. Which of the following has been shown to be the strongest predictor of male delinquency?
   a. racial or ethnic group
   b. social class
   c. intelligence
   d. how well they get along with their peers

Applied
Obj. 7
Moderate

10. Dr. Robinson is interested in studying popularity so he interviews each member of a peer group and asks who each child would and wouldn't want to invite to a party. The technique he is using is called:
    a. sociometry
    b. the correlational approach
    c. the cross-sectional method
    d. the longitudinal method

Applied
Obj. 7
Basic

11. Tommy is actively disliked by his peers because his behavior is disruptive and inappropriate. Tommy would fit best into which of the following groups?
    a. isolates
    b. amiables
    c. stars
    d. rejects

Conceptual
Obj. 7
Advanced

12. According to research presented in the text, the problem which may very well underlie inappropriate aggressive behavior in children is that they:
    a. had a parent who was alcoholic
    b. have trouble processing information accurately
    c. have undergone too much sibling deidentification
    d. are less intelligent than their peers

Applied
Obj. 9
Moderate

13. Darwin goes to school expecting it will be a successful experience. Darwin's teacher, however, expects Darwin will have trouble learning and be a discipline problem. In fact, Darwin's success in school is poor and he develops behavior problems which have not been present before. This example is best thought of as an example of:
   a. open education
   b. traditional education
   c. deidentification
   d. the self-fulfilling prophecy

Factual
Obj. 10
Moderate

14. In comparison to American children, which of the following is an accurate description of Asian children?
   a. Asian children spend less time actually in school than American children but spend more time doing homework.
   b. American children dislike homework more than Asian children do.
   c. Asian children get less help with their homework than American children do.
   d. American teachers focus more attention on how hard a child works whereas Asian teachers focus on how much ability the child has.

Conceptual
Obj. 10
Advanced

15. Which of the following statements about differences between girls and boys is *accurate*?
   a. Girls get more attention from teachers.
   b. Girls do better than boys in high school.
   c. Boys get more criticisms than girls.
   d. Boys are usually criticized for not having enough ability.

Factual
Obj. 11
Moderate

16. Mainstreaming refers to:
   a. the use of open education techniques in the classroom
   b. the placement of special needs children in classrooms with nonhandicapped children
   c. the expectation that younger siblings will develop in the same general ways as their older brothers or sisters
   d. a technique used to evaluate social relationships present in groups of people

Factual
Obj. 12
Moderate

17. According to the text, children learn best in all of the following situations *except*:
   a. when their parents do not expect them to be "in school" all the time and encourage them to take a vacation from school work during the summer
   b. when parents are interested in the child's homework
   c. when parents augment school learning by providing an intellectually stimulating atmosphere at home
   d. when parents create an atmosphere where studying is expected and appropriate

Factual
Obj. 12
Moderate

18. When children are exposed to a stressful family event, like a divorce, the best advice to give parents about informing the school is to:
   a. inform the child's teachers and school officials of the situation
   b. inform the child's teachers, but ask that they ignore the information when dealing with the student
   c. inform school officials, but ask that they not inform the child's teachers
   d. inform no one so the child will not be treated differently or stigmatized

176 The Social Context of Middle Childhood

Factual
Obj. 13
Moderate

19. A study of children in the southside of Chicago found that what percent of them had witnessed a homicide by the age of 17?
   a. 5 percent
   b. 12 percent
   c. 25 percent
   d. 60 percent

Factual
Obj. 13
Moderate

20. The effects of violence on children is minimized if parents do all of the following *except*:
   a. maintain a strong parent-child attachment
   b. refuse to acknowledge the violence as a means of teaching the child that it doesn't affect the family
   c. retain their own self-esteem and identity
   d. establish a regular and stable care-giving arrangement

C. Essay Questions

INSTRUCTIONS
After reading and studying the text, read the question below and write your answer in the space provided. Do not refer to your text or to the Scoring Scheme or Model Answer on the next page.

1. Describe three different advantages associated with being popular in middle childhood.

Total Score ___

178 *The Social Context of Middle Childhood*

Scoring Scheme for Question 1

+3 points each (up to 9 points) for any reasonable argument as to how popularity can contribute to positive adjustment. Examples include:
   a. because they have good peer relations, popular children are at lower risk for delinquency or mental health problems
   b. popular children are liked more by teachers and teachers' expectations may positively affect their educational achievement
   c. popular children are more likely to be leaders, giving them experience that can translate positively in later development
   d. popular children tend to come from happy homes, and happy families foster many positive abilities and attitudes
   e. popular children tend to be smart and attractive, and these are positive characteristics that will carry over into later development
   f. popular children act appropriately and so are included in many learning situations where less well-adjusted children might be excluded

Total: 9 points

Model Answer for Question 1

Popular children are liked more by their peers than unpopular children, and they have better social skills and are more likely to act as leaders. Thus, they are in a position where they influence others, make judgments, and develop other skills that will be important later in life.

Popular children are also treated more favorably by their teachers. Because these children are favored by teachers, they will probably perform better as well, since teachers' expectations exert a powerful influence on their students' performances.

Finally, children who have poor peer relations are at risk for delinquency and for mental health problems. Because popular children have very positive relations with their peers, they develop positive self-concepts and may be happier and healthier throughout their lives.

INSTRUCTIONS

After reading and studying the text, read the question below and write your answer in the space provided. Do not refer to your text, or to the Scoring Scheme or Model Answer on the next page.

2. Describe three different advantages associated with being popular in middle childhood.

Total Score ___

Scoring Scheme for Question 2

+2 points each (up to 8 points) for mention of at least four advantages or disadvantages.

Advantages of mainstreaming can include such things as:
    a. allows them to interact with a wide variety of peers
    b. reduces stigma associated with segregation
    c. aids social development
    d. helps dispel prejudices about the handicapped
    e. prevents the ill effects of misdiagnosis

Advantages of special education can include such things as:
    a. teachers in a large regular class must gear lessons for the nonhandicapped
    b. special needs students may benefit from individualized instruction
    c. special needs students may need more attention than is available in regular classrooms
    d. special-needs children may be socially rejected by other students

+4 points for the idea that a combination of some time in regular classrooms and some in special education classrooms may be the best solution.

Total: 12 points

Model Answer for Question 2

Mainstreaming special needs children means that special needs children are placed in regular classrooms along with their nonhandicapped peers. The advantages of mainstreaming include that it allows handicapped children to benefit from interactions with a wide range of children, especially if the mainstreamed child is successful in making friends. Mainstreaming also reduces some prejudices against the handicapped and encourages people to treat handicapped people the same as those who are not handicapped. The major disadvantage of mainstreaming is that the child, because of her handicap, may not be able to keep up with children in a regular classroom. When the teacher is responsible for the education of twenty or more other students, the special needs child may not get as much help as she needs.

Special education classrooms do provide the individualized instruction and attention a handicapped child may need, but children in special education classrooms may be stigmatized as "different." Also, if a child is misdiagnosed and placed by mistake in a special education classroom, he may be held back by lowered expectations.

The text suggests a compromise approach where special needs children are mainstreamed for part of the school day, but are also included in special education classrooms either during or outside school which can help them with special problems or skills they need to acquire.

Chapter 14

The Transition into Adolescence

Preview of the Chapter

I. **The Biological Transition into Adolescence**
   A. The Physical Changes of Puberty
      1. The growth spurt
      2. Becoming a sexual being
      3. Variations in the timing of puberty
   B. Adjusting to Puberty
   C. Early Versus Late Maturation

II. **The Cognitive Transition into Adolescence**
   A. How Does Thinking Change in Early Adolescence?
      1. Thinking about possibilities
      2. Thinking about abstract concepts
      3. Thinking about thinking
      4. Thinking in multiple dimensions
      5. Adolescent relativism
   B. Why Does Thinking Advance in Adolescence?
      1. The Piagetian view of adolescent thinking
      2. The information-processing view of adolescent thinking

III. **Emotional Transition into Adolescence**
   A. Changes in Self Conception
   B. Changes in Self-Esteem
   C. The Adolescent Identity Crisis
   D. Feeling Independent
   E. Acting Independently

IV. **The Social Transition into Adolescence**
   A. The Generation Gap: Fact or Fiction?
   B. Changes in Family Relationships
   C. Changes in Peer Group
      1. Cliques and crowds
   D. Intimacy and Friendship
   E. Dating and Sex
      1. Adolescent intercourse
      2. Homosexuality

182   The Transition into Adolescence

Learning Objectives

1. Describe the physical changes that occur during puberty.

2. Explain the adjustments that accompany puberty and comment on the advantages and disadvantages associated with early and late maturation.

3. Describe the changes in thinking that characterize the transition from childhood to adolescence.

4. Discuss the Piagetian and information-processing perspective as they relate to the development of adolescent cognition.

5. Discuss how the person's self-conception and self-esteem develop during the transition from childhood to adolescence.

6. Describe the process at work as the adolescent develops a sense of identity.

7. Define the concept of autonomy and discuss how the family situation can influence its development.

8. Discuss the ways in which adolescents and their parents typically interact.

9. Describe how peer groups change in the development from childhood to adolescence.

10. Define the concept of intimacy and discuss how it develops.

11. Describe the emergence of relationships with opposite-sex peers, and comment on the development of sexual behavior.

12. Report on the frequency with which adolescents use contraceptives, describe why contraceptives are not used more, and comment on what adults can do to increase contraceptive use by adolescents.

Chapter Summary

I. The Biological Transition into Adolescence

1. The physical changes that accompany sexual maturation are called **puberty**. They include: rapid growth and weight gain, further development of the gonads (sex glands), development of secondary sex characteristics, changes in body composition especially for fat and muscle, and changes in the circulatory and respiratory systems leading to strength and stamina.

2. Increases in the levels of certain chemicals called **hormones** (**testosterone** for boys, **estrogen** for girls) lead to the **adolescent growth spurt** which marks the first half of puberty and in which children can grow at the same rate as toddlers (about 4 inches per year for boys and 3½ inches for girls). The growth spurt occurs about 2 years earlier in girls than in boys.

3. **Primary sex characteristics** involve those developments linked directly to sexual reproduction. **Secondary sex characteristics** include those changes related to physical appearance.

4. In boys, the changes in physical development occur in the following order: rapid growth of testes and scrotum and appearance of pubic hair; the beginning of the growth spurt, enlargement of the penis and thickening of pubic hair; growth of facial and body hair and lowering of the voice. The first ejaculation usually occurs about a year after the beginning of the accelerated growth of the penis.

5. Girls' development is in a less regular sequence, but usually begins with the development of breast buds or growth of pubic hair. Later, breasts develop nipples and areola (the area around

the nipple) and enlarge, and pubic hair thickens. **Menarche**, the first menstrual period, occurs later in puberty, and ovulation and the ability to carry a baby to full term usually follow menarche by several years, although it is possible for a girl to become pregnant at any time following her first period.
6. The age at which puberty begins and the speed at which it occurs varies widely among individuals and differs among various cultures. For example, in the United States, girls reach menarche at an average age of 12, but in New Guinea, the average age is 18. Both genetic and environmental factors play a part in determining the onset and duration of puberty.
7. For girls, maturation appears to be more difficult if it occurs at a time associated with other emotional conflicts, such as entering junior high school. Although some studies suggest that hormone levels are related to mood in puberty, most research shows this connection is weak at best.
8. For boys, early maturation is linked to increased popularity, more positive self-conception, and greater self-assurance, but also to more delinquency, conformity and humorlessness. Because girls mature about 2 years earlier than boys, early maturing girls are out of sync with classmates. Although they may be popular, they are usually less self-assured and poised, they receive more attention, especially from older boys, which may cause anxiety, and they may be drawn into delinquent behaviors. Early-maturing girls, like boys, may be drawn into deviant activities by older adolescents and have lower educational aspirations.

II. The Cognitive Transition into Adolescence
1. Psychologists group the advances in thinking that come with adolescence into five categories: thinking about possibilities, about abstractions, about the process of thinking, about several issues at once, and seeing things as relative rather than absolute.
2. Whereas children's thinking is oriented to concrete events that they can directly observe, adolescents have the ability to think about what might be. Related to this new ability to think about possibilities is the adolescent's development of **hypothetical thinking**, or thinking that involves "if-then" thinking.
3. A second notable characteristic of adolescent thinking is the ability to understand abstract, conceptually-based relationships and concepts. This ability underlies the adolescent's interest in topics such as interpersonal relationships, politics, religion, morality, friendship, democracy, fairness, and honesty.
4. The ability to think about thinking, called metacognition, permits teenagers to think about the strategies they use to solve problems and to think about their own thoughts and feelings. A byproduct of metacognition is a kind of egocentrism characterized by an intense preoccupation with the self. Adolescents develop **personal fables**, or beliefs that they are so unique that what happens to others will not happen to them. These personal fables can cause the teen to feel invulnerable and lead to risky behavior based on the belief that bad things only happen to others. Also, adolescents sometimes experience the effect called the **imaginary audience**, which is an extreme self-consciousness and belief that others are constantly watching and evaluating one's actions. These effects diminish as the adolescent gets nearer to adulthood.
5. Whereas children tend to think about things one aspect at a time, adolescents can consider several dimensions of a situation at once. This makes possible more sophisticated and complicated relationships with other people.
6. Children tend to see things in absolute terms, as either one thing or another. Adolescent thinking, though, is characterized by relativism, the ability to see that situations are not just good or bad but rather can be interpreted in many different ways.
7. According to Piaget, adolescence is the time when the child moves from concrete thinking to the **formal operational stage**. Piaget believed that this movement occurs when biological changes allow more complex thinking and when the environment calls for it. This disequilibrium produces a shift to formal thinking, which is based on abstract principles of

logic. Although Piaget thought formal operations developed in stage-like fashion, more recent research suggests that these skills develop more gradually and continuously.
8. **Information-processing theorists** believe that the advanced thinking that comes with adolescence is the result of better strategies for the input, storage, manipulation, and use of information. Changes that information-processing theorists observe in adolescents include an increased short-term and long-term ability to pay attention, improvement in both memory ability, improvement in organizational strategies, and improvement in knowledge about their own thinking processes (metacognition).
9. **Behavioral decision theory** suggests that all behaviors can be analyzed in a process that involves: identifying alternative choices, identifying the consequences of each choice, evaluating the desirability of each consequence, assessing the likelihood of each consequence, and combining all this information according to some decision rule. Most studies show that adolescents use the same basic cognitive processes as adults, but may reach different decisions because they evaluate consequences differently.

III. **The Emotional Transition into Adolescence**
1. Although conventional wisdom suggests that adolescence is a period characterized by low self-esteem, research shows that self-esteem remains fairly stable from age 13 on, and may increase in middle and later adolescence. Research also shows, however, that self-esteem is lowest among young adolescents (12–14) than in the periods just before or after, and this is especially true for white females, who seem especially sensitive to their perceived conflict between school achievement and popularity with boys.
2. **Barometric self-esteem** fluctuates with changes in a person's situation or personal climate. **Baseline self-esteem** is a more stable, general feeling about oneself. The lowered self-esteem sometimes seen in young adolescents appears to be due more to fluctuation in barometric self-esteem. Adolescents vary in the development of self-esteem. Research shows that about one-third of adolescents have consistently high self-esteem, and one-sixth have chronically low self-esteem. Also, one-half showed steeply declining self-esteem, but one-third showed a small increase in self-esteem during adolescence. Self-esteem today is usually viewed as multidimensional, and an individual may have high self-esteem about one part of her life and low self-esteem about another part.
3. Adolescents who belong to a minority group are more likely to have self-esteem problems than those in the majority. This is especially true for those who attend school or live in a community in which there are few others like them.
4. For Erik Erikson, establishing a sense of identity is the major task of adolescence, called the crisis of **identity versus identity diffusion**. How one resolves this crisis depends on one's resolution of the previous developmental crises, and it will similarly affect how one resolves subsequent crises in adulthood.
5. Erikson argues that establishing an identity is so demanding that we should create a time for adolescents free from excessive obligations so they can focus on their search for who they are. This **psychosocial moratorium** in our society corresponds to the years in school when adolescents are largely free from economic and family obligations and they can experiment with a variety of roles and identities.
6. Erikson contends that the key to resolving the identity crisis lies in the adolescent's interactions with others, and is aided when others are supportive and react positively to his interests and aspirations. Erikson also believed that a sense of identity begins to develop at puberty but continues on into adulthood. Through our interactions with others, we learn about ourselves. When the identity crisis is successfully resolved, it culminates in a series of basic life commitments.
7. Because identity formation depends so heavily on with whom the adolescent interacts, culture exerts a strong influence. Sometimes adolescents immerse themselves in their minority or

ethnic culture, rejecting the white majority culture, as they move through the identity formation process. Having a strong ethnic identity is associated with higher self-esteem for minority children, especially among African-American and Hispanic youth.

8. Minority youth have four possibilities open to them in dealing with their ethnicity: assimilation (adopting the majority culture and rejecting the ethnic culture), alienation (living within the majority culture but feeling outcast), separation (adopting the minority culture and rejecting the majority culture), and biculturalism (maintaining ties to both the majority and minority culture.) In the past, minority youth have been encouraged to assimilate the white culture, but assimilation is difficult due to prejudices by whites and rejection by their minority friends. Some suggest that biculturalism will be a more viable alternative, but more research is needed to help us understand identity formation among adolescents who belong to minority ethnic groups.

9. **Emotional autonomy** relates to the individual's growing ability to separate and become independent from others in terms of their close relationships with other people, especially the parents. **Behavioral autonomy** is the capacity to make independent decisions and follow through with them. Both kinds of autonomy develop during adolescence.

10. Emotional autonomy from parents is achieved as the adolescent no longer needs to turn to parents when upset, no longer sees the parents as all-knowing or all-powerful, begins to see their parents as people, and becomes more involved in relationships with peers.

11. The process of **individuation** involves becoming a separate person who acts independently and accepts responsibility for choices made. Individuation does not necessarily involve stress and turmoil, but rather involves a growing ability that develops from childhood into adulthood. Individuation is related to how much adolescents de-idolize their parents, see their parents as people, and depend on themselves, and all three characteristics increase during adolescence.

12. The cognitive changes that occur during adolescence contribute to the adolescent's ability to behave independently. Adolescents are more likely to conform to peers' opinions rather than parents on day-to-day social matters such as choice of dress and music, but are primarily influenced by parents on questions of values, religious beliefs, or ethics. During early adolescence, conformity to parents decreases and to peers increases. Later in adolescence, conformity to peers declines as well, as the individual becomes more independent.

IV. The Social Transition into Adolescence

1. Generally, most adolescents get along well with and respect their parents. Of the 25 percent of teenagers who have problems, 80 percent also had problems with parents during childhood. Thus, only 5 percent of families who enjoyed positive relationships in childhood develop serious problems in adolescence. Adolescents usually have basic values similar to those of their parents, although may disagree about matters of personal taste such as dress, music, and pattern of leisure activities.

2. Although for most families adolescence is not a time of storm and stress, early adolescence, especially around the time of puberty, does often involve an escalation of conflict, especially between teens and their mother. Later in adolescence, relationships become less conflicted and adolescents become more objectively aware of their families' shortcomings.

3. Peer groups become more important in adolescence, with high school students spending twice as much time with peers as with parents. Adolescent peer groups also function more often without adult supervision, compared to children's peer groups, and in adolescence peer groups increasingly include opposite-sex friends. Also, in adolescence peer groups become larger, and beginning in early adolescence, teens begin to be able to distinguish the members of different crowds and identify the stereotypes that characterize the different groups.

4. Whereas **cliques** are small groups of 2 to 12 members, usually of the same sex, who share common activities or are friends, **crowds** are large groups that are organized on the basis of shared activities rather than close friendships. Crowds, thus, serve to locate the adolescent with

regard to the social structure of the school and define the norms and standards for acceptable behavior.

5. The need for intimacy with friends emerges at age 11 or 12. It begins in early childhood on the basis of play or association ("he calls me.") and prosocial behavior ("She helps me."), and later in childhood enlarges to include intimacy and trust ("I can tell him secrets.") and loyal support ("She'll stick up for me.").

6. During adolescence, the need for intimacy intensifies and centers on self-disclosure. It increases because adolescents now have the cognitive abilities to understand another's view and also want information with which to understand their awakening sexuality. Although teenagers develop increasingly closer ties with their friends, their ties with their parents also remain strong.

7. Dating can mean interactions involving members of the opposite sex from group dates to steady involvement with one other person. Group dating usually has a positive impact on the psychological health of young adolescent girls, but serious couples dating may have a more negative effect, especially if there is pressure to engage in sex. Because boys tend to begin dating later and date younger girls, they may not be similarly affected.

8. About three-fourths of all teenagers report having sexual fantasies, mainly about TV and movie stars, and one-half of adolescent boys and one-fourth of adolescent girls masturbate, with girls beginning at about age 12 and boys at age 14.

9. Most studies suggest that the developmental progression of sexual behavior has not changed much over the past 30 years, and that this sequence is much the same for males and females, although boys begin earlier. Necking and petting are more common and occur earlier than genital contact and intercourse, which occurs before oral sex.

10. About 12 percent of boys and 6 percent of girls report having intercourse before age 13, although African-American boys and girls percentages are 42 percent and 10 percent, and Hispanic boys and girls are 19 percent and 4 percent, respectively. Sexual activity occurs earlier in rural and inner-city communities than in suburbs. Thus, there are large cultural variations. Sexual activity in adolescence does not appear to be associated with psychological disturbance, self-esteem, or life satisfaction.

11. Although 20 percent of boys have engaged in homosexual activity to the point of orgasm by age 16, over 90 percent of young people develop an exclusive preference for heterosexual relationships by the end of adolescence. The incidence of homosexuality has remained unchanged since studies began in the 1940s, and evidence suggests that homosexuality is the result of the complex interplay of biological (hormone and genetic) and social factors. Homosexuality is not considered to be a form of psychopathology.

12. Although older adolescents are more likely to use contraceptives than those who are younger, only one-third of sexually active adolescents always use birth control, and one-sixth of sexually active 15- to 19-year-olds report that they never use contraceptives. The reasons that adolescents don't use contraceptives include: contraceptives are not readily available; adolescents do not have sufficient knowledge about sex, contraception, and pregnancy; they may not recognize the seriousness of pregnancy, perhaps because their cognitive development does not yet include hypothetical thinking and does involve the personal fable that pregnancy won't happen to them; and they don't want to acknowledge that they are planfully and willingly sexually active.

13. Adults may be able to improve the contraceptive behavior of adolescents by: making contraceptives accessible, providing sex education before adolescents become sexually active, making adolescents feel free to talk about issues concerning sexuality, and encourage the mass media to portray safe sex more realistically.

14. **AIDS** (Acquired Immune Deficiency Syndrome) is an as yet incurable and fatal disease that results from contracting the HIV virus through contact with infected semen, vaginal secretions, or blood. Because teenagers tend not to use condoms and yet be sexually active, they are at

risk for developing AIDS. Although the risk of contracting AIDS is substantial and information campaigns have attempted to inform teenagers of this risk, many young people, especially minority teens, remain confused and misinformed about AIDS. Sex education programs that combine AIDS information with the distribution of condoms holds the most promise for reducing AIDS occurrences among adolescents, and these programs do not increase the likelihood that teenagers will become sexually active.

Self Test

A. Matching Questions

___ 1. Hormone associated with males
___ 2. Involves identifying and evaluating the consequences of choices
___ 3. The physical transformation to adolescence
___ 4. The first menstrual period
___ 5. Occurs in the first half of adolescence
___ 6. Chemical substances involved in puberty
___ 7. Associated with the development of the reproductive organs
___ 8. Facial hair, a deeper voice, and enlargement of the penis, for example
___ 9. Related to our ability to introspect and understand how we solve problems
___ 10. Based on the belief that one is unique
___ 11. Related to extreme self-consciousness
___ 12. Piaget's label for adolescent thought

a. puberty
b. adolescent growth spurt
c. primary sex characteristics
d. menarche
e. hormones
f. secondary sex characteristics
g. formal operational thought
h. personal fables
i. imaginary audience
j. metacognition
k. testosterone
l. estrogen
m. behavioral decision theory

___ 13. A group of 2-12 friends
___ 14. The capacity to make decisions and follow them through
___ 15. Centers on the question "Do I like myself?"
___ 16. Concept which centers on the idea of fluctuation in different situations
___ 17. Erikson's major concept pertaining to adolescence
___ 18. A period free from other obligations
___ 19. The relatively stable feeling about one's self
___ 20. Concerned with the question "Who am I?"
___ 21. The process of becoming a separate person

a. barometric self-esteem
b. identity
c. self-esteem
d. psychosocial moratorium
e. identity versus identity diffusion
f. autonomy
g. baseline self-esteem
h. AIDS
i. cliques
j. crowds
k. individuation
l. emotional autonomy
m. behavioral autonomy

B. Multiple Choice

Conceptual
Obj. 1
Moderate

1. Which of the following is a male primary sex characteristic?
   a. deepening of the voice
   b. growth of the penis
   c. manufacture of sperm
   d. increased sweat gland development

188 *The Transition into Adolescence*

Applied
Obj. 1
Basic

2. Maureen has just had her first menstrual period. This event is referred to as:
   a. menarche
   b. the female adolescent growth spurt
   c. a secondary sex characteristic
   d. puberty

Applied
Obj. 2
Advanced

3. According to research presented in the text, which of the following adolescents is most likely to have difficulty in coping with the physical changes of puberty?
   a. Richard, who reaches sexual maturity as he enters junior high.
   b. Robert, who reaches sexual maturity midway through junior high.
   c. Linda, who reaches sexual maturity as she enters junior high.
   d. Susan, who reaches sexual maturity midway through junior high.

Conceptual
Obj. 2
Advanced

4. According to the text, which of the following groups is at higher risk than their peers for developing delinquent behaviors and having difficulty in school?
   a. early maturing boys and girls
   b. late maturing boys and girls
   c. early maturing boys and late maturing girls
   d. early maturing girls and late maturing boys

Conceptual
Obj. 3
Moderate

5. Metacognition thinking bears the greatest similarity to thinking:
   a. about thoughts
   b. through hypotheses
   c. about possibilities
   d. about abstract concepts

Applied
Obj. 3
Moderate

6. Jim doesn't worry about birth control because he perceives himself to be invulnerable to serious problems and therefore believes that he would never make a girl pregnant unless he wanted to. Jim's behavior is best thought of as an example of:
   a. the imaginary audience
   b. a personal fable
   c. metacognition
   d. postconventional moral reasoning

Applied
Obj. 3
Advanced

7. Ralph has become preoccupied with his ears, which he thinks are too large and stick out too much. He feels that everyone who looks at him is staring at his ears and that when he is not around people talk about how large they are. Ralph's behavior is best thought of as an example of:
   a. the imaginary audience
   b. a personal fable
   c. postconventional moral reasoning
   d. adolescent relativism

Factual
Obj. 4
Moderate

8. Disequilibrium caused by the interaction of biological maturation and environmental demands is the basis for which of the following perspectives?
   a. the metacognitive view
   b. the information-processing perspective
   c. Piaget's theory
   d. behavioral decision theory

Factual
Obj. 4
Moderate

9. The theory which views development as the gradual accumulation of more and more knowledge is:
   a. Piaget's theory
   b. the information-processing approach
   c. metacognitive theory
   d. behavioral decision theory

Factual
Obj. 5
Moderate

10. People in which of the following age groups generally have the lowest self-esteem?
    a. 8-11 years old
    b. 12-14 years old
    c. 15-17 years old
    d. 18-22 years old

Applied
Obj. 5
Moderate

11. Jane's mother is concerned about Jane because her feelings about her self-worth seem to fluctuate widely from one day to the next. Jane's mother is describing:
    a. barometric self-esteem
    b. baseline self-esteem
    c. the psychosocial moratorium
    d. the personal fable

Factual
Obj. 6
Moderate

12. According to Erikson, the central conflict to be resolved in adolescence centers around the concept of:
    a. establishing autonomy
    b. improving self-esteem
    c. developing an identity
    d. intimacy

Factual
Obj. 6
Basic

13. According to most writers, when is the development of one's identity essentially complete?
    a. by the end of middle adolescence (about age 15)
    b. by the end of late adolescence (about age 20)
    c. by the middle of early adulthood (about age 28)
    d. it is never complete

Applied
Obj. 6
Advanced

14. Dr. Cook believes that one major value of a high school education is that it keeps teens in a fairly safe, non-threatening environment so they can concentrate on their personal development rather than on job or family responsibilities. Dr. Cook's view is best seen as consistent with the concept of:
    a. baseline self-esteem
    b. psychological moratorium
    c. barometric self-esteem
    d. baseline self-esteem

Factual
Obj. 7
Moderate

15. Being able to watch out for yourself and make your own decisions lies at the center of the concept of:
    a. intimacy
    b. autonomy
    c. identity
    d. psychological moratorium

190 / The Transition into Adolescence

Factual
Obj. 7
Basic

16. In the period from early through middle adolescence, conformity to parents ___ and conformity to peers ___.
    a. remains the same; increases
    b. increases; increases
    c. decreases; increases
    d. decreases; remains the same

Applied
Obj. 8
Advanced

17. Mr. and Mrs. Jones are worried that their nine-year-old, with whom they presently have a very good relationship, will become a very troublesome, disruptive adolescent. Their fear can be put in a realistic context by telling them that research shows that about ___ percent of children such as theirs experience serious problems during adolescence.
    a. 50
    b. 33
    c. 10
    d. 5

Applied
Obj. 9
Moderate

18. Yvette spends a lot of time with six or seven friends who like to do and talk about the same things. These friends are best thought of as:
    a. a clique
    b. a personal fable
    c. a crowd
    d. an imaginary audience

Applied
Obj. 11
Moderate

19. Which of the following children is most likely to experience psychological problems as the result of serious dating that includes pressure to engage in sexual intercourse?
    a. Heather, who is 12
    b. Beth, who is 16
    c. Bob, who is 12
    d. Mark, who is 16

Conceptual
Obj. 11
Advanced

20. According to the text, by the end of adolescence about what percent of people in America show an exclusive preference for heterosexual relationships?
    a. 50 percent
    b. 75 percent
    c. 90 percent
    d. 99 percent

C. Essay Questions

INSTRUCTIONS
After reading and studying the text, read the question below and write your answer in the space provided. Do not refer to your text or to the Scoring Scheme or Model Answer on the next page.

1. Is it an advantage or a disadvantage to be an early maturer? Be sure to answer this question from the perspective of both boys and girls.

Total Score ___

Scoring Scheme for Question 1

+2 points for the general theme that early maturation is both an advantage and a disadvantage. This does not need to be stated explicitly, but can be inferred from the answer given.

For the boy:
+2 points for any of the positive characteristics associated with early maturation.

+2 points for any of the negative characteristics associated with early maturation.

For the girl:
+2 points for any of the positive characteristics associated with early maturation.

+2 points for any of the negative characteristics associated with early maturation.

Total: 10 points

Model Answer for Question 1

The effects of being an early maturer are both positive and negative, and are different for boys than they are for girls.

For boys, maturing early places the boy in a position of admiration of peers and encourages him to associate with other boys. This early attention is positive in that it tends to push the boy into leadership roles among his peers and lead him to be more popular, to feel more positive about himself, and to be more self-assured than boys who mature later. Yet, early maturation is also accompanied by difficulties. Associating with older boys may lead to delinquency and trouble at school. Also, being pushed into leadership roles too soon can lead early maturers to have limited creativity and willingness to take risks.

Since girls mature about 2 years earlier than boys, the early maturer is noticeably different than her classmates, and she may feel awkward and self-conscious and may be less self-assured than her peers. She may be popular, however, especially with older boys, and their attention can cause her distress. Like her male counterparts, if she associates with older teens, she may be drawn into delinquent activities and achieve less in school. The positive side of maturing early for a girl, as for a boy, is that she must learn to cope with being different from her peers and these coping skills may translate into creativity and independence which are valuable traits throughout life.

INSTRUCTIONS

After reading and studying the text, read the question below and write your answer in the space provided. Do not refer to your text, or to the Scoring Scheme or Model Answer on the next page.

2. Suggest three reasons why so few sexually active adolescents use contraception regularly and cite three things that parents can do to improve the contraceptive behavior of adolescents.

Total Score ___

Scoring Scheme for Question 2

For reasons why adolescents don't use contraception:

+2 points for stating that contraceptives may not be available.

+2 points for suggesting that adolescents are insufficiently educated about sex, contraception, or pregnancy.

+2 points for suggesting that, due to immature cognitive abilities, adolescents do not recognize the seriousness of pregnancy or feel immune to it.

+2 points for recognizing that adolescents may be unwilling to acknowledge that they are planfully and willingly sexually active.

For things parents can do:

+1 point for making contraceptives available.

+1 point for providing sex education.

+1 point for encouraging adolescents to talk with adults about their questions and concerns.

+1 point for advocating more responsible portrayal of safe sexual practices in the media?

Total: 9 points (up to 6 on part 1 and 3 on part 2)

Model Answer for Question 2

There are several reasons why not all adolescents use contraceptives when they are engaging in sex. First, many adolescents do not like to think of themselves as planning to engage in sex. Instead, they prefer to think that they will not have sex, but that sometimes they just got swept away by passion. Bringing a contraceptive means that they are planning to have sex, so they forget the contraceptive to protect their self-image. Second, they may have trouble getting contraceptives, either because they don't know how to get them, because they are not available when they are needed, or because they are embarrassed to ask for them. Finally, some teenagers may not know how to use contraceptives or may be mistaken about when they should be used.

To encourage adolescents to use contraceptives, adults should make sure they are available, make sure teenagers know how and when to use them, and encourage teens to talk to them when they have concerns or need information about sex.

ANSWER KEY

ANSWER KEY

Chapter 1

A. Matching

1.	f	11.	b	21.	k	31.	f
2.	b	12.	g	22.	j	32.	a
3.	g	13.	a	23.	a	33.	e
4.	d	14.	i	24.	e	34.	c
5.	e	15.	j	25.	b	35.	l
6.	c	16.	g	26.	d	36.	i
7.	d	17.	l	27.	k	37.	g
8.	h	18.	d	28.	m		
9.	e	19.	h	29.	h		
10.	f	20.	f	30.	b		

B. Multiple Choice

1.	d, 6	6.	b, 12	11.	d, 15–16	16.	d, 22
2.	a, 8	7.	a, 13	12.	c, 17	17.	a, 23
3.	b, 10	8.	b, 13	13.	b, 18	18.	c, 25–26
4.	d, 12	9.	b, 13	14.	a, 21	19.	b, 30
5.	c, 12	10.	c, 15	15.	a, 21	20.	b, 32–33

Chapter 2

A. Matching

1.	a	14.	a	27.	i	40.	c
2.	i	15.	f	28.	h	41.	d
3.	e	16.	i	29.	c	42.	b
4.	g	17.	f	30.	b	43.	a
5.	j	18.	d	31.	j	44.	b
6.	c	19.	c	32.	k	45.	j
7.	b	20.	a	33.	i	46.	f
8.	f	21.	b	34.	g	47.	i
9.	b	22.	f	35.	h	48.	g
10.	h	23.	d	36.	f	49.	h
11.	k	24.	g	37.	a	50.	e
12.	e	25.	k	38.	e	51.	d
13.	d	26.	e	39.	j		

B. Multiple Choice

1.	b, 41	6.	a, 47	11.	a, 58	16.	a, 68–69
2.	d, 42	7.	c, 48	12.	c, 58	17.	d, 70
3.	c, 43	8.	d, 51–52	13.	c, 60	18.	b, 72
4.	b, 44–45	9.	a, 55	14.	a, 61	19.	b, 73
5.	c, 46	10.	d, 56	15.	c, 63	20.	b, 75

Chapter 3

A. Matching

1.	n	8.	j	15.	g	22.	g
2.	e	9.	a	16.	e	23.	h
3.	m	10.	c	17.	d	24.	i
4.	h	11.	b	18.	b	25.	c
5.	d	12.	f	19.	f	26.	f
6.	i	13.	l	20.	a	27.	a
7.	k	14.	c	21.	i	28.	d
						29.	b

B. Multiple Choice

1.	b, 80	6.	c, 87	11.	c, 92	16.	b, 99
2.	a, 83–84	7.	d, 88	12.	c, 93	17.	c, 103
3.	b, 84	8.	a, 90	13.	b, 95	18.	b, 104
4.	d, 85–86	9.	d, 91, 88	14.	a, 96	19.	a, 104
5.	a, 87	10.	c, 92	15.	b, 98	20.	d, 105

Chapter 4

A. Matching

1. e
2. b,
3. g
4. f
5. a
6.
7. d
8. f
9. g
10. b
11. d
12. e
13. c
14. a

B. Multiple Choice

1. a, 116
2. c, 116
3. a, 117
4. b, 118
5. c, 118
6. d, 118–120
7. c, 121
8. c, 121
9. d, 123
10. d, 125
11. a, 126
12. a, 126
13. b, 126
14. b, 129
15. c, 130
16. c, 131
17. d, 132
18. d, 132
19. b, 135
20. a, 135

Chapter 5

A. Matching

1. d
2. e
3. c
4. f
5. b
6. a
7. c
8. b
9. g
10. a
11. d
12. e
13. h
14. j
15. f
16. g
17. h
18. m
19. n
20. a
21. i
22. b
23. l
24. k
25. d
26. g
27. e
28. j

B. Multiple Choice

1. c, 141
2. a, 143
3. a, 143
4. d, 145
5. b, 146
6. a, 149
7. d, 149
8. b, 151
9. c, 151
10. a, 152
11. b, 155
12. a, 155
13. c, 156
14. c, 158
15. b, 160
16. d, 160
17. a, 163
18. d, 165
19. d, 167
20. a, 168–169

Chapter 6

A. Matching

1. f
2. a
3. e
4. b
5. c
6. d
7. c
8. d
9. a
10. e
11. h
12. b
13. g
14. c
15. f
16. h
17. d
18. e
19. f
20. c
21. i
22. a
23. b

B. Multiple Choice

1. d, 174
2. a, 175
3. b, 175
4. d, 179
5. b, 180
6. c, 181
7. d, 181–182
8. b, 183
9. c, 184–185
10. a, 187
11. c, 187–188
12. c, 189
13. b, 189
14. a, 191
15. c, 192
16. a, 193
17. b, 196
18. b, 197
19. d, 199
20. a, 199–200

Chapter 7

A. Matching

1. e
2. d
3. g
4. a
5. b
6. c
7. c
8. d
9. a
10. b

B. Multiple Choice

1. b, 208
2. a, 209
3. d, 209–210
4. c, 210
5. b, 211
6. a, 211
7. d, 212
8. a, 212–213
9. b, 214
10. d, 214
11. a, 215
12. b, 216
13. d, 216–217
14. b, 217
15. c, 218
16. d, 220
17. c, 222
18. c, 223–225
19. c, 226
20. d, 227

Chapter 8

A. Matching

1. g
2. a
3. j
4. d
5. i
6. e
7. f
8. c
9. h
10. d
11. i
12. b
13. h
14. g
15. f
16. a
17. c
18. d
19. a
20. c
21. g
22. h
23. f
24. e
25. b

B. Multiple Choice

1. c, 234
2. a, 235–236
3. d, 236
4. b, 237
5. a, 237
6. d, 239
7. d, 241
8. a, 242
9. b, 242
10. c, 243–244
11. b, 244
12. c, 246
13. b, 247
14. d, 248
15. a, 251
16. c, 252
17. c, 254
18. b, 256
19. d, 260–261
20. b, 262

Chapter 9

A. Matching

1. g
2. f
3. c
4. i
5. a
6. h
7. b
8. h
9. f
10. a
11. c
12. b
13. e
14. d
15. g
16. i
17. e
18. f
19. c
20. b
21. a
22. d
23. i
24. h

B. Multiple Choice

1. a, 269
2. c, 270
3. d, 270
4. b, 270
5. c, 272
6. d, 273
7. a, 273–274
8. a, 276–277
9. b, 277
10. b, 278
11. d, 279
12. d, 279
13. a, 280
14. d, 281
15. b, 282
16. c, 285
17. c, 286
18. c, 290
19. a, 293–294
20. b, 294

202 *Answer Key*

Chapter 10

A. Matching

1. d
2. a
3. b
4. i
5. j
6. c
7. g
8. e
9. h
10. f
11. e
12. g
13. f
14. e
15. a
16. d
17. c
18. h

B. Multiple Choice

1. c, 303–304
2. a, 304–305
3. d, 306
4. a, 307–309
5. c, 311
6. b, 313
7. b, 313
8. a, 314–315
9. d, 317
10. d, 318
11. d, 318–319
12. c, 320
13. b, 326
14. a, 327
15. a, 326
16. d, 327
17. c, 329
18. a, 330
19. b, 333–334
20. c, 334–335

Chapter 11

A. Matching

1. f
2. b
3. i
4. d
5. g
6. h
7. a
8. e
9. c
10. k
11. d
12. a
13. h
14. i
15. b
16. c
17. f
18. e
19. j

B. Multiple Choice

1. c, 342
2. c, 344
3. d, 345–346
4. b, 347
5. d, 349
6. b, 350
7. a, 350
8. b, 353
9. d, 353
10. c, 354
11. d, 356
12. d, 357
13. a, 357
14. b, 358
15. a, 360
16. c, 362
17. b, 363
18. a, 365
19. d, 365
20. c, 370–371

Chapter 12

A. Matching

1. f
2. e
3. b
4. g
5. a
6. d
7. e
8. h
9. g
10. d
11. i
12. f
13. a
14. b
15. c

B. Multiple Choice

1. d, 377
2. a, 377
3. c, 379
4. b, 380
5. a, 381
6. b, 382
7. a, 382–384
8. d, 383
9. a, 384
10. d, 385
11. c, 386
12. b, 387
13. d, 389
14. c, 391
15. c, 392
16. a, 397
17. a, 397
18. d, 397–398
19. b, 399
20. b, 399–400

Chapter 13

A. Matching

1. b
2. g
3. e
4. f
5. a
6. h
7. c
8. d
9. c
10. a
11. d
12. b

B. Multiple Choice

1. b, 408
2. c, 410
3. a, 410–411
4. d, 412
5. a, 414–415
6. d, 416
7. c, 417
8. c, 419
9. d, 420
10. a, 421
11. d, 421–422
12. b, 425
13. d, 427
14. b, 428
15. c, 429–430
16. b, 431
17. a, 433
18. a, 433
19. c, 435
20. b, 436

Chapter 14

A. Matching

1. k
2. m
3. a
4. d
5. b
6. e
7. c
8. f
9. j
10. h
11. i
12. g
13. i
14. m
15. c
16. a
17. e
18. d
19. g
20. b
21. k

B. Multiple Choice

1. c, 443
2. a, 444
3. c, 446
4. a, 447
5. a, 449
6. b, 449
7. a, 449
8. b, 451
9. b, 453
10. b, 454
11. a, 455
12. c, 456–457
13. c, 459
14. b, 458
15. b, 460
16. c, 463
17. d, 464
18. a, 467
19. a, 470
20. c, 472